A CARRIER

AT

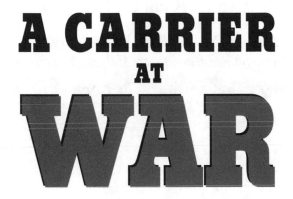

Also by Richard F. Miller

Harvard's Civil War: The History of the
Twentieth Massachusetts Volunteer Infantry

Co-author, *The Civil War: The Nantucket Experience*

A CARRIER AT WAR

On Board the USS *Kitty Hawk* in the Iraq War

RICHARD F. MILLER

Potomac Books, Inc.
Washington, D.C.

Library of Congress Cataloging-in-Publication Data

Miller, Richard F., 1951–
    A carrier at war : on board the USS Kitty Hawk in the Iraq War / Richard F. Miller.—1st ed.
        p.   cm.
    Includes bibliographical references and index.
    ISBN 1-57488-960-5 (hardcover : alk. paper)
    1. Iraq War, 2003—Naval operations, American.   2. Kitty Hawk (Aircraft carrier)   3. Miller, Richard F., 1951–   I. Title.
DS79.76.M55   2005
956.7044′345—dc22   2005009213

Printed in Canada on acid-free paper that meets the American National Standards Institute Z39-48 Standard.

Potomac Books, Inc.
22841 Quicksilver Drive
Dulles, Virginia 20166

First Edition

10 9 8 7 6 5 4 3 2 1

This book is dedicated to 1st Lt. Samuel H. Miller (ret.).
He sailed in a different war but an indivisible cause.

Contents

Preface

IN his preface to *Two Years Before the Mast*, Richard Henry Dana Jr. reflected on his years at sea spent as a sailor on a merchantman. One observation still resonates for reporters who were embedded with the troops during the Iraq War, whether they traveled in Humvees or berthed in racks on Navy warships:

> [I]t must still be plain to every one . . . who goes to sea as a gentleman, "with his gloves on," (as the phrase is), and who associates only with his fellow-officers, and hardly speaks to a sailor except through a boatswain's mate, must take a very different view of the whole matter from that which would be taken by a common sailor.

Although reporters who were embedded with the Navy were given officers' privileges, they were also given almost unlimited freedom to roam the ship and speak with whomever they pleased. Unburdened by the social rigidities of Dana's day and freed from the hierarchy of rank, reporters were free to dine in mess halls and wardrooms, shower in the enlisted as well as officers' heads, walk the officers' blue p-ways, and smoke on the enlisted persons' sponson. For myself, I can say that most of the things I learned about today's Navy came from dozens of conversations with those whom Dana defined as "common sailors" (and proudly included himself in their number).

I accepted this assignment not because I am a journalist (I am not) but because I am a historian who specializes in Civil War soldiers and the influence of class, race, local community, ethnicity, and religion on combat morale and unit cohesion. No matter how anachronistic it may appear to weave Civil War anecdotes into a narrative of today's surface ship warfare, I remain convinced that all wars share certain characteristics and that, if nothing else, the brain chemistry of war—the adrenaline, sleeplessness, aggression, guilt, and war's strange seductiveness—transcends time. Perhaps most military historians are warriors manqué, and at 51 years old, the embed program was the only way I would ever be able to approach the experience.

Yet keeping a journal did not originate with me. Fortunately, it did occur to William Fowler, friend and director of the Massachusetts Historical Society. On the eve of my departure, he gently admonished me "to remember the debt you owe to those Civil Warriors upon whose diaries, letters, journals and memoirs you have feasted for all of these years! Try keeping some kind of a journal yourself." I will always be grateful to Dr. Fowler for his suggestion.

There was another aspect to this venture, one more personal and not connected with academic interests. When Dana shipped on the *Pilgrim* in 1834, he had been forced to withdraw from Harvard College because of an eye disease (probably severe conjunctivitis) and, like many contemporaries, believed there was medicinal value in a sea voyage. From a wealthy and distinguished Massachusetts Brahmin family, Dana could have traveled as a passenger on any ship he chose. Instead, by going as a common seaman, he wanted to be tested, as many of his social class were to be in the Civil War that awaited them a generation later. Early in his voyage, he was asked to "send down the royal yard" from the mast, which he did with much trepidation. Dana recalled, "I got through without any word from the officer, and heard the 'well done' of the mate, when the yard reached the deck, with as much satisfaction as I ever felt at Cambridge on seeing a '*bene*' at the foot of a Latin exercise." For me, going on a warship in a time of war was a way of awarding myself a *bene*, for simply having gone.

Cousin Ellen Ratner, Bureau Chief of Talk Radio News Service, pushed me into this trip and paid for the airfare to Bahrain by using her own frequent flyer miles. ("This proves that it must be for love and not money," she declared.) It's a love she has shown me for almost every day of our 51 years (we were born 29 hours apart), even when I've been cranky and didn't deserve it. I am similarly grateful to Talk Radio News correspondent Cholene Espinoza, Air Force Academy graduate, U-2 pilot, and now captain of commercial heavies. A voice of sanity in the midst of war, she watched my back in Bahrain before going to Kuwait, where she was embedded with the First Marines, First Tank Battalion as they fought their way to Baghdad. Traveling the "river of steel," she proved as strong as any.

I'm also grateful to the Coalition Press Information Center (CPIC) in

Bahrain, especially Capt. Roxie Merritt and Lt. Cdr. Dave Werner. Watching them watch the media was reminiscent of the scene in *Close Encounters of the Third Kind* where alien first meets *Homo sapiens*, separated by a few feet of space but light years in perspective. In the case of CPIC, perspectives were aligned not by a Schoenberg melody but by humor and grace.

As a taxpayer and American citizen, I wish to express my profound gratitude to Capt. Thomas A. Parker and the entire crew of the USS *Kitty Hawk*. Without a single exception, I was shown courtesy and kindness by every sailor, officer and enlisted alike, with whom I spoke. They certainly had more compelling things to do—and rarely enough time in which to do them— than talk with me. The two weeks I spent on the *Kitty Hawk* was probably the longest consecutive period in the last thirty years in which I wasn't insulted or treated rudely by anyone.

I wish to express my thanks to the hardworking and conscientious people of the ship's Public Affairs Office (PAO). Led by Lt. Brook De Walt and Lt. j.g. Nicole Kirscher, both ably assisted by Chief Petty Officer Maria Mercado, the PAO was tasked with the impossible: to invent by the hour the rules of the brand-new embed program. The Department of Defense (DoD) gave local commanders wide discretion for rule-making and news disclosure decisions, and being on a warship at sea adds new meaning to the word *local*. Like mothers fretting over their young, the PAO watched, worried, and assisted the media where possible but, like a wise parent, also knew when to let go. They were joined by Lt. Cdr. Michael Brown of Adm. Moffit's staff, who also spared little and did much to make certain that the media got their interviews and knew the rules, all the while lending a quiet dignity and thorough professionalism to the process.

Of the media, I wish to thank Mark Faram, Paul Hanna, Hu Xiaoming, Uichiro Oshima, Hiroshi Tanabe, Jim Wolf, Ted Ishihara, Jim Furlong, Kendra Helmer, Leila Gorchev, and William Reilly from C-SPAN. Something like a sea-going version of *The Front Page*, the experience was also as humorous and occasionally as poignant as the original Hecht-MacArthur play.

I am also grateful to my agent, Deborah Grosvenor, as well as to Richard Russell, my editor at Potomac Books. Getting a book into print involves the harshest criticism of them all, the hard work of literary industry professionals who stake not just money but also their reputations on the finished product. So much of what is valuable in this work I owe to them, and any shortcomings and errors remain mine alone.

Thanks are also due to Jihad, Murad, and Ibrahim Haddad. While I was away, they kept an eye on my family and house. They thought nothing of doing it; I thought of little else, and I am deeply grateful for their concern.

And finally, not just in the beginning but always and forever, I acknowledge the support of my wife, Alyson, so proud of being risk-averse yet willing to let me go to the Persian Gulf in a time of war, and my astonished children, Eli, Caroline, and Pesha, who have become so used to seeing their father haunt libraries that they probably remain, to this very day, unsure whether I really sailed on the *Kitty Hawk* or whether the whole thing was just another of their father's silly jokes.

The Offer

*We talked of war. Johnson: "Every man thinks
meanly of himself for not having been a soldier,
or not having been at sea."*

Boswell, *The Life of Samuel Johnson*
APRIL 10, 1778

IN LATE FEBRUARY 2003, I received an astonishing proposal from
Ellen Ratner, my cousin, radio personality, member of the White House
press corps, Fox News contributor, and bureau chief of the Washington-
based Talk Radio News Service: "Would you like to embed with the military
in the Persian Gulf?

"Do what?"

"Embed."

"I thought only tumors or thunderstorms could be 'embedded.'"

She explained that the Defense Department was creating slots for reporters to live with, share air, and witness the operations of military units as they
fought the maybe war with Iraq. Although the buzzword *embed* was new to
me, I did have some familiarity with the program. I had seen television clips
of reporters in their twenties and thirties with full packs humping along trails
with military instructors at a special camp set up for the purpose of teaching
civilians how not to get killed if, as, and when the shooting started.

"No. I'm not going. You're crazy."

"But you're perfect. You're a military historian. You could report live
from the field and offer a whole new perspective."

"C'mon, Elzee, I'm a Civil War historian. What the hell do I know about J-DAMs?"

"What's a J-DAM?" she asked.

After twenty years as a licensed therapist in Boston, Ellen had moved to Washington, D.C., in 1990 to create the Talk Radio News Service from nothing. She knew psychology and she also knew me.

"Joint direct attack munitions," I replied.

"See. I never heard of that bomb. You're perfect!"

"How did you know it was a bomb?"

It turned out that Cousin Ellen had somehow wangled three embed slots from the Department of Defense but had only two reporters prepared to go. She needed a third but couldn't go herself—too many live radio appearances, too many White House press conferences, an office to run, and, I suspect, a preference for sleeping in her own bed. Along with taking up a scholar's life three years earlier, I had also become a consultant to Talk Radio News Service. When Ellen needed a conservative foil to replace a no-show guest, I would every once in a while get the call. But I also edited her weekly column for World Net Daily and had a sense for her "requirements."

"I'm not going to tout your left-wing bullshit. You know I support this war."

"Of course, Cousin Richard. You just report it as you see it."

"Not until I talk to Alyson. . . . What am I saying? No! I'm not going!"

In truth, I was ambivalent. I wanted to go, wanted the experience, but was unsure exactly what part of me was doing the wishing. The stakes were high enough to justify hard questions. I have been happily married for twenty-seven years. Together Alyson and I have raised three wonderful children; our family is close and oddly enough, as the years pass, seems to be getting closer. My life as an independent scholar, while sedentary, is nevertheless one that I've been lucky enough to choose. In my dotage, I have become a creature of habit. In thinking about entering a war zone, the words of my grandfather, of blessed memory, come to me still: "What do you need it for?"

I certainly had a few respectable motives for seriously considering this adventure. Much of my published work as a Civil War historian relates to social factors during the nineteenth century that influenced combat psychology: class, ethnicity, regionalism, and more recently, religion. Some of these, at least in their Victorian-era permutations, were no longer relevant in today's world. But some of them might be. Civil War regiments were often motley mixtures of foreign-born and natives, laborers and what used to be called "gentlemen," Catholics and Protestants, English, German, and Irish, Black and White. Managing what we moderns term "diversity" was as much an issue then as now. And certainly the emotions experienced by combatants haven't changed—the fear, anxiety, boredom, concern for loved ones at home, and a less discussed emotion, the appeal of war. It isn't something that men admit very often, but many actually *like* it—the adrenaline, the risk of death, the escape from bourgeois banality, and a peculiar consummation of masculine achievement that, in spite of more recent efforts to socially reconstruct men along feminist lines, has, for some, always demanded vindication in battle.

Neurochemistry may have a hand in this. Professor Gerald Linderman, in *Embattled Courage*, observes that many Civil War soldiers "experienced in combat a swelling exhilaration, an elevation of feeling," and he goes on to quote World War II historian J. Glenn Gray's phrase, the "delight in destruction." John Keegan in *The Face of Battle* is perhaps more incisive. In describing the peculiar ferocity (even by World War I standards) with which German machine-gun fire was poured into the advancing British lines at the Somme, he states that "easy killing does seem to generate in human beings symptoms of pleasure, which the zoologist Hans Kruuk has tried to relate to the compulsive behavior of certain predatory animals when they come upon groups of prey which are unable to escape from them." Civil War soldiers often grumbled in camp, but on leave, some wanted only to return.

I was curious. How did these seeming universals play out in modern combat?

But I am a creature of neurochemistry, too. Now I was being given the choice of going to a war, albeit as a noncombatant. And the risks were already beginning to excite me. I had to face a question perhaps universal to passionate scholars of anything: Given the chance to observe what I study, was I going to study, or had I all along actually been studying to go?

I had been to the altar once before. In 1971, during my sophomore year in college, I was reclassified from II-S (student deferment) to I-A (good to go). At first I panicked. Through some paperwork screwup, the college registrar had failed to submit the proper forms to my draft board. Rectifying matters would have been easy. But, in gambling parlance, I let it ride. Fetching the mail became an exciting event. Had I been called, I would have gone. However, the troop drawdown from Vietnam was well under way, and the Nixon administration, understanding that the draft was a serious political liability (arguably providing the foot soldiers for many an anti-war protest), decided to abandon the effort. Sometime later that year, the government announced that anyone who had been classified I-A for the prior six months would now be reclassified I-H—called only in the event of a national emergency. When my new Selective Service card arrived, I breathed less a sigh of relief than felt a secret disappointment. At 19 years old, I hadn't the presence of mind to enlist. I thought that if I trusted to events, I might get there; it would at the very least allow me to plead compulsion to my parents. But it was not to be.

And so the test was not taken. Now, in a very small way, the test had returned. Of course, as a journalist I'd be a defined noncombatant and protected under the Geneva Convention. Nevertheless, as any good military historian knows, combat isn't usually what kills—it's disease or, in today's military, accidents: plane crashes, friendly fire, slips and falls, accidental discharges, getting hit by a vehicle, or any of the myriad ways to die that result from cramping hundreds of thousands of very young men (and now women) and incredibly powerful weapons systems into small spaces. The point was that this venture was fraught with higher risks than spending a day in the Reading Room at the Massachusetts Historical Society.

I prepared for a serious sit-down with Alyson. Twenty-seven years of marriage isn't just a romance; it's a complex, deeply nuanced understanding between two people that embodies entire worlds. Staying power is partly attributable to having one's partner act as a circuit breaker for bad ideas. And all of the mistakes I've made in life were but a fraction of the errors that might have been without Alyson's counsel. "Men," she often reminded me, "are really little boys with long pants."

And so for twenty-seven years my comings and goings had been as predictable as an airline and, later, library schedules. I thought about how to ask my spouse, "Do you mind if I traipse off to the Persian Gulf to cover a war? Yes, I'll either be with the Marines dodging bullets behind sand dunes or on an aircraft carrier, maybe incommunicado for an indefinite period of time. No, I don't know how long I'll be. That's right, I'm not a journalist, have never worn a uniform or been anywhere near combat." This was not a promising opener.

"Do it," Alyson said. "It's the chance of a lifetime."

"Are you sure?"

"Yes. Remember, Richard, that when you're on your deathbed, the one thing you won't regret is the trip you *did* take to Paris. And by the way—do get a haircut."

Offer Accepted

Blue, navy blue, I'm as blue as I can be
'Cause my steady boy said "Ship ahoy"
And joined the Nay-ee-ay-vee

——*"Navy Blue"*
DIANE RENAY, 1964

February 23–March 2
Concord, Massachusetts

I STRIKE THE DEAL with Ellen: I'll go to sea until the conclusion of Shock and Awe, then home. There is a reason for this. We both agree that shortly after the war starts, the story will move to the ground troops. If there'll be a war, that is.

My E-mail inbox is at high tide. Messages from Ellen, the DoD, CPIC in Bahrain, other reporters, and incredulous acquaintances. This trip intervenes like a heart attack. When my life stopped, I was organizing research notes on martyrdom and the Civil War (first the article and later the book) and trying to arrange a speaking engagement for one of my professors, an Emerson scholar with something to say in this year marking the 200th anniversary of the Sage of Concord's birth. I was also gathering material for an article about Civil War hero William Francis Bartlett, a young Harvardian who might have lived and died in affluent obscurity, were it not for the Civil War. He left the service a major general.

But all of this is now consigned to the long train of yesterdays. Today I call my older brother Aaron, who just last month left the U.S. State Department after twenty-six long years spent mostly trying to resolve the Israeli-Palestinian dispute. He knows the reality of today's Middle East as well as anyone.

"Well, Dick," he said, "I must say that it's a *bold* move." (I find the word *bold* unsettling.)

"Anything special I should pack?" I asked.

"Let's start with what you shouldn't pack," he replied. "What's your itinerary?"

"Boston to Washington to Amsterdam to Bahrain. A few days in Bahrain, then to one of the carrier battle groups in the Persian Gulf. Coming back, I'll just reverse the order."

"Bahrainian customs both ways, then?"

"Yes."

"Don't bring your siddur. Are you still laying tefillin?" he asked.

"As often as I can."

"Well, don't bring them either. Bahrain is about as liberal a Gulf state as there is, but under these circumstances, I wouldn't take any chances. Remember the line from the Jimmy Buffet song."

"What's that?"

"Changes in latitude, changes in attitude."

Ellen has obtained three embed slots. Two are with Marine units now in Camp Doha in Kuwait. The third is with the Navy. Sending me in with the Marines is out of the question. For starters, I'm fifty-one years old and have finally won the grand prize of a lifetime of bad eating and lack of exercise— type 2 diabetes and hypertension. Both are now under control so long as I eat rabbit food and take my pills. Still, MREs aren't diabetes-friendly. With the ground forces, Ellen is sending in two good reporters. Garreth Schweitzer has worked with Ellen for several years and knows the talk radio business inside out. He's also twenty-four years old and in excellent physical shape. The second ground force slot is being filled by one of the more unusual journalists likely to cover this war. At thirty-eight years old, Choline Espinoza is arguably long in the tooth for this kind of assignment, save for three things: she is an Air Force Academy graduate, a former U-2 pilot, and in better physical condition than most twenty-year-olds. I am to go with the Navy.

Lots of things will have to come together quickly. I need my passport renewed, Ellen has to make a substitution with the Navy (the embed slot is in her name), and I have to make many personal preparations. Passport Express is a State Department program that provides passports as fast as twenty-four hours; however, to avoid long lines of procrastinators, they require some evidence of need and urgency. Ellen happily supplies proof of both with a sponsorship letter on Talk Radio News stationery.

Next is Ellen's request to substitute me for her. On February 25, the Pentagon's Maj. Timothy Blair approves the change. Then I must complete the "Sub-Coalition Press Center Bahrain Embark Request & Media Contact Information Form." It asks for a list of the equipment I'll bring, my Social Security number, a name to notify in case of emergency, and, in case of a dire emergency, my blood type.

Of course, there isn't a soul in the Department of Defense who could identify me on a police lineup. I pay my taxes and do my bit to keep the Uncle Sam show open, but for all they know, I'm a spy, or mentally unbalanced, or an Al Qaeda terrorist, or perhaps all three. Presumably, the requirement that embeds be sponsored by a credentialed media organization screens for some of these things; presumably, too, my Social Security number will be matched against those of known bad actors. I'm going to be admitted onto a warship in a time of war, and frankly, I want them to screen the living daylights out of me.

They don't. But there is one thing that does interest them, and it is the one thing that seems to trump all other considerations—protection from lawsuits (the Department of Self-Defense?). A transcript of a Q&A about the embed program between Pentagon brass and journalists that is E-mailed to all embeds contains the following exchange:

Q: Clark Hoyt, Knight-Ridder.
  Could you just summarize for us exactly what each correspondent heading for an embed should have in their possession in the way of identification, releases and so forth?

A: Bryan Whitman.
  There is only one document that your embedded reporter has to show up with when he comes to his unit and that is the hold harmless agreement. He must present a hold harmless agreement signed by himself and by your news organization in order to be accepted into that unit.

Hail lawyers, Caesars of warfare!

But the most important feature of the embed program is that its important features are being invented as the program rolls out. Nothing like this has ever been done before. The military, like courts of common law, has been around for a long time and, like the law, has a vast paper memory of laws, rules, and customs for guidance in contingencies. However, there is little to help out with this program. To bring me current, Ellen forwards her previous E-mail correspondence with the Pentagon. One catches my eye. It was sent on February 12 from Cdr. Randy Sandoz, who works for Bryan Whitman, the deputy assistant secretary for media operations. "I would be remiss if I didn't begin by reminding everyone," Cdr. Sandoz begins, "that the President has not made a decision to use military force with respect to Iraq." (This becomes a trope in almost all subsequent E-mails to embeds from the Pentagon.) The feature of no fixed features is apparent in the same E-mail, where, amid a blizzard of acronyms, abbreviations, alphabet titles, and other forms of mil-speak, the construction-in-progress reality of the program is very clear. For example, in the same memo:

> I know you have been giving a great deal of thought to whom you might assign to these difficult and dangerous assignments. I appreciate the planning you have done to date and remind you that our planning continues. I anticipate that as additional units receive deployment orders I will have more embed opportunities to offer. I must also emphasize that not every country hosting U.S. forces has agreed yet to accept journalists into their country. Therefore, some of these embed opportunities may require additional time to be approved and some may not be able to be executed at all. . . . This effort to embed news media in these kinds of numbers with our combat forces is very ambitious. As questions, problems or issues arise, let's discuss and resolve them early.

Here is the translation: There may be no war; if there is a war, you may not receive an embed slot; if you do, there's a possibility that countries through which you must travel or stay may not want you; furthermore, what we're doing has never been done before, and things will go wrong, so let's everyone be flexible.

On February 28, final instructions are E-mailed from Cdr. David E. Werner with CPIC in Bahrain. I count 86 reporter-recipients next to the "To" heading. Included are many major news organizations, such as CBS, the *New York Times*, the *Los Angeles Times*, Reuters, Associated Press, Time magazine, and the *Washington Post*, as well as some smaller ones such as the *Navy Times*, C-SPAN, the *San Francisco Chronicle*, and the *Seattle Post-Intelligencer*. Also included are foreign news services, especially from Japan: Kyodo News and *Asahi Shimbun*. (Two reporters from Al-Jazeera are also recipients. I hope the Navy has done background checks.)

More important, this memo represents something like final instructions. It recommends that we not arrive in Bahrain earlier than March 4th (which suggests the date before which the war cannot possibly start); once there, we should expect to remain for several days, awaiting assignment to a carrier battle group. Immediately after arriving, we should check in with the CPIC office located in Room 610 in the Diplomat Hotel (on reading this, I make reservations there); at that time, we'll be registered and briefed. We must bring both a passport and one other photo identification. We must be on the approved list to embed: in short, no walk-ins will be permitted. Nightly briefings are held in the hotel's Skylight Lounge, and the first night's meeting is mandatory.

One question is answered right off: We will be transported to the aircraft carrier by plane, not boat.

Into the Maw

March 3
1200
Boston

OFF! ON THE WAY to the airport, I stopped at my lawyer's office and signed my will. Bills paid and will signed—the dear ones at home are "good" for at least a month. Now it's the air shuttle from Boston to Washington. Tonight, I sleep at Ellen's; tomorrow, I go to Walter Reed Army Hospital for smallpox and anthrax shots. Then at 1745 it's KLM Royal Dutch from Dulles to Amsterdam, a seven-hour layover, and then on to Bahrain. Into the maw!

Weekend developments are a mixed bag. Turkey nixes U.S. troops on its soil and perhaps the northern front against Iraq as well: unhappy Americans, happy Kurds. But it is reported that Khalid Sheik Mohammed has been captured, and that's a big score—a very big score—for the good guys. In the meantime, cable news television is crowded with ex-military and neo-con talking heads assuring the rest of us that all invasion preparations are in place, and the phrase du jour is "good to go." Confidence is high. Of course, as a Civil War historian, I cannot but think of First Bull Run— confidence was high there as well. Yet neither General Franks nor Secretary Rumsfeld strikes me as latter-day Irwin McDowells. Still, it is always prudent to remember, as my *zede* would say in Yiddish, "*Menschen tracten und Gott'er laughten*" (man plans, God laughs). For those less favorably disposed to theological possibilities, there is Napoleon's reply when he was

— 11 —

urged to promote an especially brainy officer to his general staff: "Smart, yes," Boney supposedly answered, "but is he lucky?"

The sky is clear and blue, as the aviators say, CAVU (clear air visibility unlimited). Soon Manhattan appears outside my window, and even from that altitude I can see ground zero. During my twenty-five years as an investment banker, the hours I spent in the World Trade Center probably added up to a full month. Unnumbered meetings with lawyers, other investment bankers, commercial bankers, municipal officials, bond insurers, financial printers, and closings for several huge bond issues—in those towers I had learned a good chunk of what I knew about structuring tax-exempt bonds: floating interest rates, puts and calls, remarketing agreements, and a hundred other tools of the public finance trade. Although my honeyed recollections of Wall Street in the 1980s remain, now the towers are gone and with them, the peculiar wheel-and-deal culture that seemed diminished when the towers collapsed. Those bastards from Al Qaeda knew exactly what they were doing when they hit us there. So as the jet flew over New York City, I could only think, "It's time for payback."

It is fitting that this journey begins with a flyover of the first battleground of this war.

1430
Ellen's Office
Georgetown

Arrived. First stop is Ellen's pied-à-terre in Georgetown. To be embedded, I must have press credentials. Unlike a license to read law, dispense pills, sell stock, or embalm bodies, obtaining a press credential requires no training, just sponsorship. So Ellen escorts me to the Senate Sergeant-at-Arms office (which credentials reporters to cover the U.S. Senate). Watching Ellen worm her way through the bureaucracy is a treat. She pretends to smile, pretends to laugh, and feigns an interest in whatever she's being told while at the same time she has a genuine recollection of the names of everybody's grandchildren, the health of their spouses, and the status of the grievances—their tiresome commutes or their podiatric complaints. It seems as if influence peddling in Washington is as much about charming secretaries and staffers as it is about buying votes on the Senate floor. Normally, the wait for this kind of credential is thirty days, but Ellen, employing a highly gendered version of "hail fellow well met" glad-hands her way into an immediate issuance.

I've been given a green plastic card bearing my picture and titled "United States Senate and House of Representatives News Galleries 107th Congress 2nd Session." It has a little horizontal notch at the top to allow for a metal clip, and many reporters seem to wear their credentials around their necks. It reminds me of the brutal military credentialing of old, when soldiers would string around their necks the severed ears of their enemies or Indians their enemies' scalps. It says, "Watch out for me! I'm a killer!" But now in press land, the only thing slain is rival media and ideologically disagreeable politicians.

On our way out of the Dirksen Office Building, Ellen suddenly realizes that she's late for a radio show. She darts to a nearby pay phone. Meanwhile, I take a self-guided tour down the hall and pause before a building directory. I see that none of the senators who were defeated in the last election have had their names removed.

It is trillions for defense but not one penny for a new sign.

2030
Ellen's Office
Georgetown

It's now time to learn the tools of my trade, of which there are two: a satellite telephone and a digital voice recorder. "Sat phones" have a ring of romance about them, a high-tech version of Stanley-meets-Livingstone-type news dispatches from the heart of a soaking rain forest, empty desert, or impossibly high summit. The sat phones' chief claim is that once charged— and they come equipped with a solar panel in case an electric outlet's not handy—one can theoretically broadcast from anywhere. The effects on combat reporting, which often occurs in places where wall outlets aren't handy, have been dramatic. As was proved during the Afghan War, when the number of working electrical outlets in the whole country could probably be counted on one hand, journalists could give live feed while under fire, from behind rocks, in bomb craters, or from twelfth century rural villages somewhere in the mountains. All that was required was that the sat phone be stationary long enough to be able to get a fix on a satellite. But with the introduction of video sat phones, voice-only broadcasting has already become passé and is resorted to only when the video phone can't be used. Since I'm broadcasting for talk radio, which requires only voice, I won't need a video phone. And it's a good thing, too. Talk radio and print journalism are the only two places left where one can be both plug-ugly and successful.

The satellite telephone is the size and shape of a laptop computer. There are three critical pieces: the phone, its antenna, and a thin copper wire that connects the two. This last item is important, because the antenna panel— it's not a thin metal rod but a flat panel—bears these words: "WARNING Microwave Radiation Minimum Safe Operation Distance 1 Meter." Especially scary is the fact that the phone comes helpfully equipped with a connecting wire only about six inches long. "I think the warning is overrated," says Jay, Ellen's intern assigned to teach me how to use the phone. "But some people are sensitive about it, so I brought you this." He gives me a new copper wire that stretches about ten feet.

But it augurs badly that Jay, the office expert on all matters involving electrons, cannot connect with a satellite even from the wilderness of Georgetown.

0800
March 4
Walter Reed Army Hospital

This morning I received my smallpox and anthrax vaccinations at Walter Reed Army Hospital. Finding the hospital was easy enough; but getting to the entrance was more difficult. Concrete Jersey barriers were erected in the driveway to slow vehicles to a crawl before forcing them to turn right, then left, then right again, and so forth. The shadow of the 1983 suicide car bombing of the Marine Corps barracks in Lebanon grows longer—and darker—with each passing year.

At the end of this obstacle course are uniformed military. Polite, they stop the taxi and look inside before quickly waving us through. I don't mind it a bit. The Lefties don't like it, but to paraphrase Oliver Wendell Holmes Jr.'s famous remark about taxes, "Security is what we pay for civilized society."

But getting here also required surmounting another kind of obstacle—the lawyers. "The Department of Defense has agreed to administer anthrax and smallpox vaccine to your media employees who will be participating in the DoD's embedding program," wrote Bryan G. Whitman, deputy assistant secretary of defense, to Ellen Ratner in February. The word *agreed* will always alert the wise reader to the probability that if Uncle Sam is "agreeing" to something, then you, the signatory, must also agree to something. Just a few sentences later, Whitman specified my end of the bargain:

> These vaccines carry risks along with benefits. . . . Vaccine recipients must read and consider the educational material we are forwarding with this message and agree to indemnify and hold the United States Government harmless against any adverse reactions or other negative effects from the vaccine.

Of course, the government wasn't going to take my word that if I died from the shot my estate wouldn't sue. As a young child, I was vaccinated against smallpox, and I'll bet the family doctor never asked my mother what Whitman now asked of me:

> . . . news media organizations and media employees must sign a similar agreement which will cover . . . any adverse reactions or negative effects from the vaccinations. A copy of this signed "Release, Indemnification, and Hold Harmless Agreement and Agreement Not To Sue" must be provided to the medical treatment facility prior to receiving any of the vaccinations.

Also, we had to pay for the shots. But smallpox, with mortality in excess of 30 percent, was a screaming bargain at $5.80 per dose; anthrax required six doses over an 18-month period and, at $94.96 per shot, was priced the same as a cabinet of good Havanas. Still, I considered it a bargain; it included at no additional charge the clubhouse bragging rights that came with getting the shot. These shots were offered at eight inconvenient (for a Boston boy) locations, including Camp Doha Clinic in Kuwait; Sayliyah Clinic in Doha, Qatar; and Landstuhl Regional Medical Center in Landstuhl, Germany. In this country, they were available at army hospitals in Georgia, Texas, Hawaii, and thankfully, Washington, D.C., at Walter Reed.

The DoD also wasn't just going to take my word that I had "read and considered" the educational material disclosing the risk factors. Getting the shots would take three minutes; sitting through the mandatory briefings—

during which all would be disclosed—would take about two hours. I was joined by a 32-year-old reporter from the *Washington Post* who was also embedding. We were taken to a doctors' conference room by Col. Moore, a bespectacled but ruddy-faced and robust-looking Army physician who was garbed in woodland camo. He would also conduct the briefing, supplemented by handouts and slides.

The briefing was graphic. There were color slides of smallpox victims, showing the course of the disease, with their faces shown becoming progressively more scrofulous until finally disappearing beneath an epidermal terrain of welts and pustules. The anthrax slides were worse. They were mostly pictures taken during autopsies, depicting the human brain and chest cavity in normal subjects and then in those who had died of inhalational anthrax, the deadliest form of the disease and the one most worrisome to the Army. The autopsy slides of normal tissue were bright pink and glistened like good food photography on laminated menus; they almost convinced me that it is possible to die healthy. But the images of brains, lungs, and hearts from patients who had died from inhalational anthrax were sickening. Black, necrotic, and shrunken, these might have been postmortems of whoever had modeled for Albrecht Dürer's engraving *Knight, Death, and the Devil.*

Dr. Moore provided a live sound track for the slide show. His comments were all about risk, downsides, and dark possibilities—but I'll bet these were not the same set of risks that the Army lawyers were worried about. He spent minimal time on the risks of *taking* the shots and the rest of the time describing the perils of *not* taking the shots. He observed that whoever had mailed powdered anthrax spores to the Senate Office Building and the post office was still at large, and, given that we were on the brink of war, who could say what that perp was planning next? Perhaps he was lurking near a Navy ship or an Army base, Dr. Moore speculated. Moreover, given the probability that Saddam Hussein had biological weapons, anyone bound for the Persian Gulf would have to think seriously before refusing to take the shots. Having the vaccines was to our advantage, because as far as Dr. Moore knew, the Iraqis had none. "Most Iraqis have no protection against these weapons," he said, "and if Saddam is dumb enough to use them, on our way to Baghdad we'll be stepping over the bodies of his soldiers and any Iraqi civilians unlucky enough to have been downwind." Better them than us, I thought.

After 90 minutes of this, it was time, as we used to say in the investment business, for the doctor to ask for the order.

"If you're willing to sign the indemnity agreements," Dr. Moore said, "then we can go ahead with the vaccinations." He paused to allow us to scan the two documents before leading us through their contents.

Two separate but virtually identical agreements were presented for our signatures (each called "Release, Indemnification, and Hold Harmless Agreement and Agreement Not to Sue"). One mentioned smallpox and the other anthrax. Like most professionally drawn agreements, these created a semifictional world of preambles in which (usually) the signatory concedes all kinds of facts that serve as the premises for what the agreement is about. In this case, the agreements were about not suing the government if the vaccine should kill or maim us. Any good lawyer knows that it takes only one ex-smoking, about-to-be ex-living plaintiff in front of the right Mississippi jury to threaten the average multinational tobacco company with a downside earnings surprise.

The agreements provided that "I understood" the benefits and risks of the vaccines, that the upsides and downsides had been disclosed to me, that I had been instructed in how to care for the vaccination sites, and that therefore "I agree to voluntarily, willingly, and knowingly assume any and all risks, known and unknown, in any way associated with the [smallpox/anthrax] vaccine." As additional protection for Uncle Sam, I also "understood" that "I am not required to receive the [vaccine]" and that each shot is "entirely voluntary and is based on my personal assessment of the benefits and risks for me." Further, the shots were not required for embedding, and if I decline them, I would still be permitted to embed.

Then the money clause:

> I agree to release, indemnify and hold harmless the U.S. Government and any of its agencies or instrumentalities, including but not limited to the officers, employees, and contractors of the Department of Defense, from and against any claims, demands, actions, liens, rights, subrogated or contribution interests, debts, liabilities, judgments, costs, or attorneys' fees arising out of, claimed on account of, or in any manner predicated upon my receipt of the [vaccine], including my illness, infirmity, or death or the illness, infirmity or death of any person, in any manner, caused or contributed to by the Government, whether by negligence or otherwise.

Was any base not covered by the army's legal eagles? Actually, one did occur to me. What if my wife "caught" something as a result of my vaccination and died from it? Couldn't I then sue, claiming wrongful death? Perhaps I could, but my right to do so was short-lived, because the next paragraph provided: "I agree that I will never institute, prosecute, or in any way aid in the institution or prosecution of any demand, claim, or suit against the U.S. Government," etc. In short, according to this language, I couldn't even support a wrongful death action by her estate. And just to make certain that should I die, no one else could bring an action for my wrongful death, I also "agreed" that "the provisions of this agreement shall be binding upon my guardians, administrators, executors, heirs, and assigns." I don't know if excorporate CEO and now Secretary of Defense Donald Rumsfeld had had a hand in this, but bully for him if he did. The best private-sector lawyers I knew couldn't have drafted it any better.

I immediately signed and was escorted to a seat along a wall of seats. Sitting with me are soldiers, men and women, who are also awaiting their vaccinations. But for the most part, these "men and women" are actually boys and girls, about the same ages as my son and daughter. Some of these kids still have teenage acne; some of the boys' faces still betray the hand of an inexperienced shaver.

These small things level me in a big way. This business suddenly assumes a sober aspect. The abstractions, maps, and talking heads of television news now give way to the realization that these young people are the children of my contemporaries—fathers and mothers aged somewhere between 45 and 55 years of age. I can't pretend to know what it's like to have a child facing combat. But like every parent, I've had children at risk, and it frightens me to think what the parents of these kids may have to go through.

Another aspect of this looming war appears more clearly now. The war is like a giant twister whose puckered vortex sucks up everyone and everything. The White House, Pentagon, State Department, media, and all their respective myrmidons are obsessed with it; foreign relations fracture, some are newly cemented, and the United Nations teeters; soldiers, journalists, terrorists, spies, voyeurs, opportunists, diplomats, technicians, aid workers, doctors, and countless others are streaming toward the Persian Gulf, a vast river of polymath entrepreneurs and clanging ambitions. Has not every war produced promotions, book deals, medals, reputations made and lost, national interests vindicated, riches piled high, shifts in social and political paradigms, and politicians made and ruined? War can blight humanity, but it can also represent a kind of controlled instability that may never end as it began but nevertheless spells opportunity for the moribund career and the restless ambition. It's not why wars start or are fought, but it is an unavoidable and parasitic consequence.

That the Civil War "made" Ulysses S. Grant, William Tecumseh Sherman, and Philip Sheridan is by now a trope. During my own lifetime, World War II made President and Supreme Allied Cdr. Gen. Dwight D. Eisenhower, President and PT-109 commander John F. Kennedy, Senator "Tailgunner" Joe McCarthy and B-24 pilot Senator George McGovern, actor Audie Murphy, journalist Edward R. Murrow, and so many others, down the line to my own father. I could not imagine any of these men even aspiring to the heights they eventually reached without, as Civil War veteranhero Oliver Wendell Holmes Jr. put it, "the incommunicable experience of war."

I believe in the necessity of this looming war, but now I look around and feel guilty. I am also a drop in that river bound for the Persian Gulf. My well-wishers all said that this trip, this "adventure" would be the experience of a lifetime. And it probably will be. But as I look at these soldier boys and girls, the "experience of a lifetime" is now bordered with sadness. The bill for this adventure will be paid by them. All of the lofty ambitions and unseemly calculations—many worthwhile, many not, and many whose value is presently unknowable—rest on the shoulders of these children, the national children, our children.

The world now seems to define itself in relation to this conflict. Who or what you are depends on how you view the prospective war. Pro, con, or ambivalent (and there seem to be damned few of the latter), the war has become a vast inkblot of self-revelation. War solves nothing, the peaceniks insist. Not so. War, this war at least, solves the problem of who you are and how you see the world.

And all before the first shot has been fired!

1100
Examination Room
Walter Reed Army Hospital

Shirtless and cold, I sit in an examining room awaiting my smallpox shot. *Shot* is actually an inaccurate term for what is about to happen. Unlike an injection, where some liquid is propelled into the skin through a hollow needle, the smallpox vaccine is administered by a solid needle with a forked tip. This tip is contaminated with the *vaccinia* virus, which cannot cause smallpox but will provide immunity that works against the smallpox virus. Dr. Moore's stats were compelling: 95 percent of those vaccinated have full immunity within ten days; full protection lasts between three and five years, and partial protection continues for years afterward, although boosters are required after ten years.

The odds of any side effects are mathematically remote. According to the literature, for every one million recipients, about one thousand experience some side effect. Of these, between fourteen and fifty-two people have life-threatening side effects. Yet mortality was only between one and two people per million. Moreover, Dr. Moore explained that by eliminating certain high-risk categories—people with weakened immune systems or active cases of eczema, chickenpox, impetigo, shingles, or uncontrolled acne; pregnant women; and people who have a known allergy to the vaccine—the risk of side effects is reduced even further. And for geezers like me, who have already had the vaccine without any side effects, the odds of having an adverse reaction now are probably zero.

The truth is that there isn't much recent history with biological warfare. Chemical warfare is a different matter. The last century's war-wearied world practically inaugurated its grand cycle of violence through the use of chemical weapons during World War I. Gas-masked British troops, rifles at the ready, advancing across no-man's-land are among the defining images of that war. More recently, there have been only episodes, such as Saddam's use of nerve gas against the Kurds or allegations that the Soviets deployed so-called yellow rain in Asia during the 1970s and other chemicals in Afghanistan during the 1980s.

But as the country learned during the anthrax mailings, biological agents are deadly but difficult to deploy on a large scale. The technology required for aerosolizing microbes, the problems in dispersing them, and the high risks of blowback—for example, if Saddam unleashes smallpox on Israel, he is also likely to kill large numbers of Palestinians—have made intentional biological warfare a historically rare thing.

Yet the few examples of deliberate germ warfare are notorious. It wasn't until the 1870s that Koch advanced the germ theory of disease; nevertheless, for centuries primitive observation was enough to infer that diseased bodies or textiles that once covered sick bodies could spread disease. Leaving decaying human or animal carcasses in wells of drinking water dates back to antiquity. During the Middle Ages, plague-infected corpses were catapulted into besieged cities; indeed, the Black Plague itself, which devastated Europe in the 1340s, probably originated in the Crimea, when in 1346 the Tartars flung such corpses into the Genoese camp; infected Genoese then returned to Italy and are thought to have introduced the epidemic that quickly killed one in three people.

In U.S. history, while Lefties love to talk about how it was the White man who distributed infected blankets to the Indians—for example, in 1763 British Gen. Jeffrey Amherst was neither the first nor the last White man who did precisely that to the Indian tribes along the western frontier—in truth, disease as a weapon was used by both White invaders and Indian defenders. Indians newly enslaved by the conquistadors reportedly dumped carcasses into wells and seasoned their masters' baked goods with the blood of infected people; the Iroquois also dumped rotting carcasses into the water supplies of British soldiers. Nor were strategies of this sort limited to clashes of civilizations. In *Disease in the Civil War*, Paul E. Steiner reports that Confederate surgeon Gen. Samuel P. Moore accused Union forces of deliberately sending a smallpox-infected Negro across the Rappahannock River into the rebel camp to spread the disease. Despite a few other alleged incidents, regarding smallpox, Steiner concludes, "Because of the general availability of vaccine, it is unlikely that smallpox would have been selected [by Union or Confederate armies], or that it would have been very effective in any of these situations."[1]

But *unintended* or natural biological warfare was a very different matter. Here, the concept of blowback—unintended consequences—becomes more important. In describing its effects on Civil War armies, Steiner is probably expressing the same concern that most worries men like Moore today: "Military history usually concentrates its attention on the clash of arms, although at the time of the Civil War, this might represent less than half the paper strength of one or both sides. The rest was beneath the sod, in hospitals, on medical leave or sick in camp." The important thing to remember isn't the number of people who died—terrible as that was—but the number who

---

1. Paul E. Steiner, *Disease in the Civil War: Natural Biological Warfare in 1861–1865* (Springfield, Illinois: 1968), 43.

became disabled from disease and unable to wage the war. The biggest single biological killer in the U.S. Army between 1861 and 1866 was "diarrhea and dysentery, acute and chronic," which resulted in 44,558 deaths. But this was out of 1,739,135 cases, and soldiers' letters of the day were replete with descriptions of this debilitating experience that was politely known as "the Quick Step." The fourth largest killer was malaria, with 10,063 deaths, but this was from 1,315,955 cases, most of which represented badly weakened, hospitalized, or discharged men. Smallpox was rarer, although percentage-wise far deadlier—7,058 deaths from 18,952 cases.[2]

In short, what worried Moore and his colleagues wasn't that an unvaccinated Army would die if exposed to Saddam's biological weapons—there were follow-up vaccines and antibiotics available to deal with that contingency—rather, it was that the Army's ability to wage war would be sapped by sick soldiers needing treatment. They would overwhelm a system of military hospitals designed to treat battle casualties, not mass epidemics. And to illustrate exactly how bad this could be, Steiner reports that, from a total Federal soldier population of 2,772,408, 6,029,560 cases of disease (this excludes wounds, accidents, and injuries) were recorded in the army between 1861 and 1866. In other words, the average Union soldier showed up at sick call almost 2.2 times during his service. So the issue wasn't so much death as disability, which, from the necessarily cold calculations of combat efficiency, was actually worse than death. After all, the dead require few resources beyond mortuary units, while those disabled by disease are not only (from the standpoint of frontline strength) as useless as the dead but also sinkholes of resources and personnel.

Being Navy bound, I could easily imagine what could happen if a warship somehow sailed into a microbial cloud of anthrax or smallpox. A captive population, all breathing the same air through the same HVAC system, could reach a 100 percent infection rate within a few minutes. At least the Army had the advantage of wind, humidity, and terrain. The experience of World War I taught that poison moved in clouds with the wind, was dissipated by humidity or its own weight, or eventually was obstructed by terrain; achieving toxic concentrations was easier to theorize in a laboratory than to reproduce on a battlefield. But on a ship, things were different. A ship had mobility of its own, and a captain who knew that a poison cloud

2. Steiner, *Disease in the Civil War*, 3, 10.

lay ahead could steer around it. But what if a motorboat 10 miles away or an Iraqi naval vessel disguised as a merchantman (like the old Q boats of World War I fame) fired a Silkworm or some other bad-news projectile at a ship?

My growing dread was interrupted by the arrival of the corpsman. He was a young man attempting a mustache.

"How are you today, Sir?" he politely inquired.

"I'm always doing great before I get stuck!" I replied.

"We'll do the smallpox on your upper left arm. You'll be going to another room for your anthrax shot."

I smiled and glanced at his preparation table. Neatly arranged on it were needles, a blue marker, a vaccine bottle, plastic gloves, some sterilized goop, and a clear plastic bandage about the size of a Post-It™. The corpsman offered careful instruction on how to care for the vaccination, and as I listened, despite the two-hour briefing, it only now occurred to me exactly what a smallpox vaccination really was—an intentional infection that converted the living body into a vast petri dish to culture the disease before spreading it within, followed by the body's shift into drug company mode to produce the antibodies against real smallpox. But what the hell was the blue marker for?

"According to your records, Sir, you've had smallpox vaccine before. So I'm going to make twelve scratches on your arm, but in a pretty tight circle. You may feel a little prick each time, but it's not too bad."

It might not be too bad or it might be very bad, but I'd be damned if I was going to acknowledge pain in a U.S. Army hospital. So I fixed my lips into a rigid smile and determined to keep it there come what may. The blue marker, it turned out, was to mark the sites for the needle.

The first scratch was barely a prick and I was a twelfth of the way home. But then I felt a sharp sting, and a rasped "Damn!" from the corpsman told me that the problem wasn't just in my head but was indeed in my arm.

"Sir, I'm really sorry," he said apologetically, as he wiped a tiny stream of blood trickling down my biceps. "I put the needle in too far. I don't understand how that happened, but I'm going to get Dr. Moore, so just hang on here."

In a moment, he returned with Dr. Moore. After a few well-practiced "Huh-huhs" and "I sees," Moore said to the corpsman, "As they get older, you have to allow for the possibility that the skin becomes thinner. You should adjust the pressure on the needle accordingly."

What a relief! Together with crumbling teeth, thinning air, aching joints, and afternoon naps, I can now add a thin skin to the list of infirmities of old age.

Amsterdam, the Kingdom of Bahrain, and Other Hotels

The best part of the invasion is that I have the feeling that friends are approaching. We have been oppressed by those terrible Germans for so long, they have had their knives so at our throats, that the thought of friends and delivery fills us with confidence!

> —Diary of Anne Frank, Entry after learning the news of the Allied invasion in Normandy

March 5
0720 (local)
Amsterdam

*E*LLEN AND I ARRIVED in Amsterdam after a long flight made bearable by a new feature on the airplane: a video map that depicts the flight's progress in real time, showing location, direction, airspeed, local time, and ETA. This gave me something on which to hyperfocus rather than the possible terrorist connections of the guy sitting across the aisle. In Amsterdam, we have a seven-hour layover. What can I hyperfocus on now?

We decide to take the train into the central city, an easy thing to do because cheap public transportation connects the airport with downtown. I visited Amsterdam 34 years earlier during a coming-of-age trip after my high school graduation. Lured by its forbidden pleasures, I didn't recall much other than sleeping on Dam Square by night and having the Dutch police turn the water hoses on us in the morning. But it wasn't a hostile shower, only a shower intended as a public sanitation measure. That struck me then as something uniquely Dutch: accommodate what you can't control and make the best of it. Amsterdam—then and now—is clean without being Teutonic, a compact, slightly disordered but not distempered town. Not much had changed. People are kind to strangers; unlike Paris, there were few outstretched palms with fingers beckoning for a tip. I haven't a clue whether the Dutch like Americans, but I do believe that they like people generally, with few questions asked.

Ellen must have her Dutch cocoa. It's something she's heard about from friends, and it becomes our mission. My blood sugar won't permit cocoa, but I must have my coffee. So we wander about looking for a Dutch coffee house, picking our way through streets lined with souvenir and sex shops. Then we chance upon The Grasshopper. Inside are several red-eyed, fashionably unshaven, smirking twenty-somethings who hop to our service. In a moment, Ellen is sipping her cocoa topped with a hillock of whipped cream. I work my coffee.

"Would you like to see *the* menu, Sir?" the Dutch boy-surrogate-proprietor asks.

"Certainly," I reply, a little confused. I had already seen the menu and already was sipping my coffee. But there is something odd here. Instead of bringing the menu to me, the Dutch boy walks across the room and pushes a large red ball (the size of a grapefruit) embedded into the wall. Suddenly a lighted display appears. While he grinned, I walked over and stood by his side and blinked uncomprehendingly at the entrées inscribed on metal plaques riveted to the wall.

"Sir," he said politely, "I can offer any of these already rolled, or mixed with tobacco, or loose-leafed, if you prefer."

The entrées included such old standbys as Acapulco Gold and Marrakech, as well as a list of colors and cities I've never heard of. This was a dope bar that sold a little coffee and cocoa on the side!

Ellen and I declined but stayed to chat. So the Dutch had finally done it.

Besides legalized prostitution, soft drugs, and gambling aplenty (we're told that the casinos are owned by the royal family), Amsterdam had remade itself into a European Las Vegas. Unlike the American version, however, they didn't have to fake culture for the tourists. They had the real thing in abundance. The barkeep explained to me that Amsterdam is now a popular weekend destination for all the Eurotrash (his word) who couldn't legally get stoned, laid, or impoverished by the slots in their own countries.

Zoning law looked to be Amsterdam's greatest failure. Shop windows featuring leather and dildos share street space with more conventional stores; attractively designed packets of marijuana seeds are available at the same place you buy your tulip bulbs.

"Could you imagine raising your kids in a place like this?" Ellen asked me.

Before I could reply, "What, are you nuts?" I remembered that we were not the first sojourners to feel discomfited by Dutch liberality and, oddly enough, for similar reasons. In 1609 a small community of Puritan Separatists had left England, for Holland, attracted by its reputation for religious toleration. But within ten years, they decided that Holland was too tolerant. Their leader, William Bradford, kept a journal in which he declared that, among other things, Dutch society was ruining the Puritans' children, who "were drawn away by evil examples into extravagant and dangerous courses, getting the reigns [sic] off their necks, and departing from their parents." The parents, fearing that "their posterity would be in danger to degenerate and be corrupted," left Holland in 1620 and returned to England. A month later, 40 of them were on the *Mayflower*, bound for Plymouth Rock.

1040
The Anne Frank House and Museum

How fitting that we should visit this place. The sad events it chronicles may be sixty years old, but it jolts me into the present. The Amsterdam of happy hippies, medically managed brothels, and sex toys now gives way to something else, the recognition, almost a smell, from the rot concealed deep within Europe's soul; not even a multimillion-casualty world war was enough to excise it. As I stand in front of the house at 263 Prinsengracht Street, where a Dutch-Jewish family by the name of Frank hid from the

Nazis for almost three years, this distinctly European odor is suddenly every-where. But it doesn't come from the Frank house. It comes from every other building on this street. It comes from every street in Amsterdam.

Inside, we walk the tortuous path from room to room. The tiny living quarters are connected by narrow halls, back stairways, and false doors. Between 1942 and 1945, eight Jews used this place to hide and try to save themselves, not just from the German invader but from their neighbors; four of these Jews belonged to the Frank family. The Dutch have preserved this house and made it into a unique walk-through museum, a national version of the Stations of the Cross. For this, they deserve credit from the living, as well as from their God. In a sense, they need it, because prominently dis-played on the walls are copies of arrest and deportation orders signed by the local Gestapo and police authorities, and for the most part, the signatories aren't German—they're Dutch. In fact, it was probably locals who informed on the Franks, who were then arrested and deported to the camps. Young diarist Anne ended her days in one of Germany's greatest contributions to the unmaking of Western civilization, the concentration camp at Bergen-Belsen. The only family member who returned alive was her father, Otto Frank. After the war, he returned to the hideout and found his daughter's now famous diary scattered on the floor.

"You look upset," Ellen said, squeezing my arm. Indeed, I was shaking.

"I don't understand," I finally said to her, while I looked at some arrest order on the wall, "how you can be so critical of Israel in the face of things like *this*. It makes me feel so sad and so angry." She paused a moment to look at the arrest order.

"That's because," she finally said, "I can feel the sadness without the rage."

1530
Business Class Cabin, KLM Airlines
Somewhere over Turkey

As our Bahrain-bound jet flies over Germany, southeastern Europe, and the Balkans, I think about the world's current fix. I start with this morning's visit to the Anne Frank house. Dying in 1945, Anne Frank numbered among the last victims of 1930s appeasement. The Munich Agreement of 1938, in

which British Prime Minister Neville Chamberlain and French Premier Édou-
ard Daladier appeased Hitler by selling out Czechoslovakia, has been dominating the national op-ed pages lately. Does the Munich analogy, so often
invoked as an argument against appeasing tyrants in exchange for peace,
work to explain today's crisis with Saddam?

One must be very careful here. Somebody once said that, while the past
does not repeat, it does rhyme. So one must listen to the meter closely—and
Munich in 1938 and Saddam in 2003 do share one abstract perplexity.
Given that the future is unknowable, is it possible to conduct a *moral* foreign
policy—one that seeks to protect the greatest number of innocent lives by
stymieing tyrants—that is not inherently preemptive? Believing the sultry
lies and prevarications of tyrants will always be preferable to war. It will
always be argued that the tyrant is not what he seems, that his evil is less
than it appears, or that his contribution to regional stability is indispensable—or, at any rate, the certainty has more value than the risk of a vacuum.
Thus did the 1930s appeasers believe that Hitler was less fervent an anti-
Semite than the case proved, that his obsession with *lebensraum* was for
domestic political consumption only, and that a rightist Germany was an
indispensable bulwark against a Comintern belonging to that other serial
killer in statesman's clothing, Joseph Stalin. The same arguments are played
out today in the *New York Times* and the *Weekly Standard*. Where the Germans needed order, the Iraqis are ungovernable without a strongman; where
Hitler kept the NKVD at bay, Saddam is a counterweight to Iran's Islamo-
fascist clerics. Hitler was bad, but a Red Berlin was unthinkable; Saddam,
too, is appalling, but who can say with any certainty that his replacement
wouldn't be worse?

Confronting tyrants requires waging a certain war against mere possibilities with even less certain outcomes. Who, the lefties argue, would want to
die for that? Saddam may have the rudiments of a nuclear weapon—but it's
unlikely he has a completed fission device today. He probably does have
stockpiles of chemical and biological weapons—but he's never deployed
them against Paris, London, or Washington and seems unlikely to do so
anytime soon. Perhaps there are Iraqi links to Al Qaeda, but they are difficult
to see through the thick mud of terror-state secrecy. The tragedy of Munich
in 1938 became clear only after German troops crossed into Poland on September 1, 1939, clearer still if one were standing next to the stacks of bodies

at the newly liberated Auschwitz in 1945. But in 1936, when Stanley Baldwin refused to take German rearmament seriously, was he, in that year and to his best lights, wrong? When do the lessons of history acquire enough gravity to risk unbalancing the international order?

This is a knot tighter than Gordius's. How to cut it? I am brought full circle to the Anne Frank house. The consequence is not a political issue; it is moral. It says, as the Talmud does, "He, who has saved one life, is the same as if he had saved the entire world." But there is a corollary: "He, who refuses to save one life, is the same as if he has destroyed the entire world." Because in the end, that is what will result from appeasement, only on the scale of nations. And millions die. No matter how powerful the rationalizations are, there is no moral good that can result from leaving a killer in power. In the end, all of the realpolitik arguments will be sunk.

The image of Anne Frank dying of typhus in Bergen-Belsen, of the bloated bodies of Kurdish women and children lying in the streets of Halabja, of the mountains of skulls gathering dust in Phnom Penh, and of the unrecognizable forms of still-clothed bodies stacked in pits outside Srebenica make clear the disconnect between politics and morals. That the world is a hypocritical place is something that all of us will have to answer for, but it is not an excuse for inaction. In Iraq, we have an opportunity to right a wrong we were complicit in during the decade before the 1991 Gulf War. And to make matters worse, we screwed the Shiites of southern Iraq after that war by encouraging them to revolt against Saddam and then failing to support them. We will have to answer for that, too.

Anyone who fails to understand these things isn't immoral; they are morally disabled. They have no moral imagination.

In the midst of all this cogitation, I notice that the plane is half empty, and the half that is filled looks to be mostly American military. Of course, nobody wears a uniform—where we're going, the lower the profile, the better—but the haircuts and the bearing are clues. This is later confirmed during some chit-chat with a man from Georgia who is also a chief petty officer in the Navy. He is a reservist who specializes in communications and is headed for the naval base in Bahrain. He has a son who is the same age as mine, and we trade anecdotes, quips, and pieces of hard-earned parental wisdom.

Thus do children unite the parents of the world.

Manama Airport, Kingdom of Bahrain
2220 (local)

We land in Bahrain, reputedly the most liberal of the Gulf sheikdoms. People here seem disconnected from the buildings they inhabit. The airport is bright, new, modern, and at this hour half-empty, but the custom agents and guards look bored, perform their jobs laxly, and wear dark green uniforms that fit poorly. The floors are clean and shiny, but the people walking on them—the women in black, head-to-toe abayas and the men in white robes, red-checked kaffiyehs, and sandals—don't quite fit in with the modern architecture. However, there are some who fit in quite well. They are Indian and Pakistani guest workers imported by the kingdom to do the work that the Arabs won't or can't do. Whether they wear suits or slacks and a shirt, they're dressed for this century's business, both white- and blue-collar.

My brother Aaron's caution about customs was wise but inapplicable to the late shift at this airport. No one asks me to open my bags or questions me about anything. A sleepy-eyed government man with thick gold rings on his fingers and too much pomade in his hair glances at my passport, barely looks at me, and then gives me a visa. The Coalition of the Willing may be on the brink of war, but nobody in the kingdom appears to be. That's probably because the dog they're betting on in this looming fight with Saddam belongs to the United States—which is probably how the kingdom prefers matters.

But these musings are largely abstractions about "the other," differences between peoples—some real, some imagined, and many amplified by a media accustomed to portraying as representative the most extreme elements of any group. Christian evangelicals become hatchet-wielding Carrie Nations, Jews become Palestinian-whipping Simon Legrees, and, of course, Arabs become crazed terrorists eagerly awaiting the summons to don explosive vests in exchange for the promise of dark-eyed virgins in Paradise.

Yet there is a catalyst that can dissolve many differences, at least the imagined ones, an experience that melts walls and merges one's own experience with that of "the other"—a single human contact. In my case, the human being arrived with our taxi to the Diplomat Hotel.

"This first time for you in Bahrain?" the driver asks, as he hoists our bags into his taxi. He is garbed in the long white gown, kaffiyeh, and sandals of the locals. And wrapped around his fingers is a string of prayer beads.

"Yes," I answered curtly.

The instant he had finished loading our bags, he approached Ellen and me and made a very polite bow.

"Welcome, welcome, welcome to my country!" he said enthusiastically. He smiled and opened the passenger door.

His name is Ibrahim and, like the patriarch he's named for, he embodies the commandment of hospitality. "Love ye therefore the stranger," God instructs Israel in Deuteronomy 10:19, in words affirmed by the Prophet Muhammad, "for ye were strangers in the land of Egypt." I reckon Ibrahim to be about my age.

"This is beautiful country," he gushed. "I hope you spend much time here."

At first I thought he must think that we're with the secret police, but no. One look at us would convince him otherwise. Perhaps he's angling for a tip.

"How much is the fare from the airport to the hotel?" I asked.

"As you wish, my friend," he replied. "As you wish."

"Come again?"

"As you wish, as you wish. You will pay me what you will."

I looked and noticed that there was no fare meter. But Ibrahim did have a taxi drivers' license.

"Mr. Ibrahim," I said, "there's got to be a fare from the airport. I mean, what if somebody decided that they didn't wish to pay you anything?"

He turned toward Ellen and me and smiled.

"I have driven taxi in Manama for over twenty years," he replied. "Nobody ever wished to pay me nothing."

"You're lucky," I replied.

"No, no, no, my friend," he said, shaking his head. "You must trust. People much better than that."

The bare bones of Ibrahim's story was not unlike that of most people I knew. He had three children, the oldest of whom was approaching college age. His first born was a boy who likes soccer, wants to attend school in the United States, and has a special yen for all things mechanical. Ibrahim's been married to the same woman for more than twenty years, and he proudly displays various gifts she's made for him that are in the taxi—little rugs, beaded things, colored strings, and whatnot. He likes his job, has too many bills, and is unhappy that the prospect of war has hurt the Manama tourist trade.

And he loves to go hawking.

"You mean with a real bird?" I asked in my dumbbell way.

"Oh, yes," he replied. "Every year I take family, we meet friends, and make a camp out there," he said, motioning somewhere into the Bahrainian night. But as he talked on, it was clear that hawking was only a small part of this experience. The larger part was that to "make a camp" was simply a vacation, a chance for him to play with his guy pals while his wife spent time with her girlfriends and everyone's kids played together. They ate and slept outdoors, hawked (whatever that consisted of), and sometimes went fishing and hiking. Except for the hawking, it could have been Vermont or Nantucket.

We asked him to give us an evening tour of Manama, but that was just to keep him talking. There was something very sincere about this man, something beyond a merchant's love. As we approached the Diplomat Hotel, Ellen finally asked him if he was interested in being our driver for a few days.

"Very good, oh yes, very good," he said happily. He wrote down his cell phone number and handed it to me.

"Now what do I owe you?" I asked when we arrived at the hotel.

"As you wish, as you wish," he repeated.

Hell if I knew what the angle was, but angle or no angle, it worked, because I handed him every Bahrainian dinar in my pocket.

March 6
1830
Conference Room, Diplomat Hotel

About thirty reporters have gathered in this hotel conference room. If I didn't know I was in Bahrain, I could just as easily be in Cleveland. The Diplomat is a Radisson, a franchise, and it delivers on the franchise's universal promise, a type of divine corporate covenant involving the unity of the name: If it bears our name, it shall be alike, everywhere in the universe. And that's mostly true here, too, as long as you don't leave the hotel and can ignore the people in twelfth-century garb strolling through the lobby.

To be sure, there are no twelfth-century people in the Conference Room.

A racially and ethnically diverse crowd, but entirely "Western" looking, with a tilt toward Ralph Lauren, Tommy Hilfiger, and L.L. Bean. Just then, there's a friendly tap on my shoulder. It's Lt. Hanley from Public Affairs, and he hands me a brand-new Zippo® lighter as thanks for the cigar I had given him. It bears the colorful logo of the Fighter Weapons School of the U.S. Navy. Ah, how I miss smokers' etiquette!

The purpose of tonight's briefing is to review the ground rules for ship-bound reporters. Lt. Cdr. David Werner explains these while various agreements are circulated for our signature. I may be the only person present who has a law degree, but the spirits of my fellow members of the bar haunt the room. Werner explains that no one goes anywhere without signing these agreements, which are the essence of contracts of adhesion and are about as negotiable as the rental contract one signs at a Hertz counter. The first to be signed is the release, wittily named "Indemnification, and Hold Harmless Agreement and Agreement Not to Sue."

It's a good thing that this agreement wasn't first presented to the families of reporters considering embedding. The reappearing buzz phrase is "expose media employees to the same risks and hazards as those to which the military members of military units are exposed, including the extreme and unpredictable risks of war, combat operations and combat support operations, as well as common and uncommon hazards of military living." Typical of all well-lawyered agreements, a variety of "understandings" are imputed to the signatory; however, while most signatories in this room, including me, probably knew what the words *said*, few of us had any experience as to what they *meant*. First up is our declaration that we "fully understand and appreciate" the fact that "the military environment is inherently dangerous and may result in death or personal injury" and also, just in case any plaintiffs' lawyers try to get wise, the agreement makes clear that these risks extend to "damage to personal property."

Of course, these broad, self-protective generalizations weren't enough. As the agreement descends into a litany of risk factors, matters are specified; even matters that don't yet or may never exist are specified: "strenuous and inherently dangerous activities" include "transportation in, and close proximity to, military tactical vehicles, aircraft, watercraft, and other Government (and Government contracted) vehicles and may involve substantial serious injury or death as the result of the media employee's own actions or inactions, the actions or inactions of others including agents, contractors, officers, service members, and employees of the Government," and so forth. Especially terrifying for geezers like myself was this paragraph:

> The embedding process requires media employees to be in overall good physical health and condition. Persons who are not in overall good physical health and condition should not participate in the embedding process. . . . Persons with a history of heart or lung disease or conditions, like coronary disease, or other chronic or pervasive diseases or conditions should not partici-pate. Likewise, those women currently pregnant may not participate.

Topping this was the next sentence of this paragraph, the reading of which caused me to visualize the lawyers' drafting session, during which somebody piped up that the foregoing "wasn't enough." So in accordance with the time-tested legal drafting principle of belt and suspenders, the following was added: "Anyone suffering from any injuries, conditions, ailments or preex-isting conditions that could be affected by the embedding process may not participate." It all boiled down to the same principle as the surgeon gener-al's warning on a pack of cigarettes, except here (unlike smoking, where the trial lawyers have made mockery of the whole point of having a warning), even if a reporter was fragged, there still wouldn't be any lawsuits allowed. (Forced to reckon with type 2 diabetes, hypertension, and premature ven-tricular contractions, I had recently lost fifty pounds and could now "man-age" these conditions. But as I looked around the room, I saw that there were more than a few fat guys with gray hair; they looked as worried as I felt. Still, in this game of chicken with the Navy, nobody seemed willing to jump from their vehicle quite yet, and I decided that this was my first experi-ence with peer pressure and combat.)

But the agreement's shortest paragraph was in some respects the scariest: "The media organization and the media employee understand and agree that the Government may terminate the embedding process at *any time* and for *any reason*, as the Government determines appropriate in its sole discre-tion" (italics and underlining in the original). It seemed that just as the col-lective eye fell on this item, Cdr. Werner was discussing a recent termination. A journalist (who was not identified) had violated the embed rules by dis-closing something (which was not specified) about a leaflet drop over Iraq; he or she was thrown out of the program, never to be allowed to return. (During the Civil War, humiliation was often used to punish breaches of trust: forcible wearing of signs such as "Thief"; having buttons or rank insignia torn off and then, in the presence of the entire regiment, being marched out of camp to the tune of the "Rogue's March"; even branding with a hot iron. While deeply resented, by all accounts, these penalties were effective.) The sudden silence in the room suggested that a lack of professional self-regard was not among the criticisms that some have of journalists. Indeed, I got the feeling that some of these guys would rather come home without a leg than be thrown out because they violated the disclosure rules.

The "Ground Rules" were the next agreement to be signed. Where the indemnity agreement was written to protect Uncle Sam's pocketbook, the ground rules were designed to protect lives. "For the safety and security of U.S. forces and embedded media," its preamble ran, "media will adhere to established ground rules." The first thing that struck me—and it was a powerful blow—was the second conjunction *and*, for unlike the editorial board of the *New York Times*, which can publish classified documents without worrying overmuch that their 43rd Street Manhattan offices will be struck by an enemy torpedo, a reporter on a ship is, as a smart-ass might say, in a different boat. For example, the "specific geographic locations of military units in the CENTCOM area of responsibility" is defined as "Not Releasable Information." Translation: Media can't tell anybody exactly where the ship is. Cdr. Werner says that "somewhere in the Persian Gulf" works, or even "somewhere in the northern Persian Gulf." But anything more specific runs the risk of alerting potential adversaries of our exact position. And should the ship go down, well, that means media, too. There are guaranteed to be no groans about this restriction on the public's right to know.

The following items were also considered nonreleasable. I provide this list verbatim so that readers can judge for themselves whether the Pentagon imposed onerous restrictions.

Not Releasable Information

- Specific number of troops in units below Corps/MEF level.
- Specific number of aircraft in units at or below the Air Expeditionary Wing level.
- Specific numbers regarding other equipment or critical supplies (e.g., artillery, tanks, landing craft, radars, trucks, water, etc.).
- Specific numbers of ships in units below the carrier battle group level.
- Names of military installations or specific geographic locations of military units in the CENTCOM area of responsibility, unless specifically released by the Depart-

ment of Defense or authorized by the CENTCOM commander. News and imagery products that identify or include identifiable features of those locations are not authorized for release.

- Information regarding future operations.
- Information regarding force protection measures at military installations or encampments (except those which are visible or readily apparent).
- Photography showing level of security at military installations or encampments.
- Rules of Engagement.
- Information on intelligence collection activities compromising Tactics, Techniques or Procedures.
- Extra precautions in reporting will be required at the commencement of hostilities to maximize operational surprise. Live broadcasts from airfields, on the ground or afloat, by embedded media are prohibited until the safe return of the initial strike package or until authorized by the unit commander.
- During an operation, specific information on friendly force troop movements, tactical deployments, and dispositions that would jeopardize operational security or lives. Information on on-going engagements will not be released unless authorized for release by on-scene commander.
- Information on special operations units, unique operations methodology or tactics, for example, air operations, angles of attack, and speeds; naval tactical or evasive maneuvers, etc. General terms such as "low" or "fast" may be used.
- Information on effectiveness of enemy electronic warfare.
- Information identifying postponed or canceled operations.
- Information on missing or downed aircraft or missing vessels while search and rescue and recover operations are being planned or underway.
- Information on effectiveness of enemy camouflage, cover, deception, targeting, direct and indirect fire, intelligence collection, or security measures.
- No photographs or other visual media showing an enemy prisoner of war or detainee's recognizable face, nametag or other identifying feature or item may be taken.
- Still or video imagery of custody operations or interviews with persons under custody.

Most of these items were self-evident except for the last two dealing with POWs, and they were required by the Geneva Convention: Prisoners may not be publicly displayed in humiliating ways. Everything else seemed intuitive; all doubts were resolvable just by placing oneself in the position of the pilot/captain/Army ranger/Seal and asking a simple question: If the enemy found out about this stuff, would it materially increase my chances of getting killed?

But not all reporters saw it that way. In seeking to distinguish themselves from one another, the Q&A phase became a race toward the most improbable hypothetical, with the winners receiving plaques that declare them officially educated beyond their intelligence. This is my pet theory on why press briefings open with good questions and then rapidly degrade in the quality of the queries. Tonight, some female Brit began pettifogging Cdr. Werner with a lot of "what if this" and "what if that" hypotheticals pertaining to nonreleasable items. Her intent was to figure out a way to impair security without violating the rules. Another idiot wanted to know if there was "some way" he could communicate with his editor during the rolling blackouts, in spite of the fact that one of the purposes of rolling the blackouts was to prevent that very kind of communication. By the end of the Q&A concerning nondisclosables, I found myself hoping that aircraft carriers had planks and that offending reporters would be forced to walk them.

The ground rules also specified a category of knowledge called "releasable information." Military epistemology is much like lawsuit deposition epistemology. In both, all things are theoretically "knowable," but true "knowability" is "confessability" (in the case of depositions) or "releasability" (in the case of military knowledge). In short, if you can't (don't want to) admit it during a deposition or if you can't (because you can't) release it under the Pentagon ground rules, it never happened. In the forest, the tree might have fallen in full view of an entire film and sound crew, yet it made no sound, indeed, never happened at all, either because you can't recall it (deposition) or you can't discuss it (military secret). This may seem confusing, but an old friend who specializes in defending serious tax cheats once told me that he had actually trained himself to forget things, so that under oath he was honestly able to claim that he didn't recall. And he really didn't recall.

The following information (the list is taken verbatim from the ground rules) is what could be recalled:

Releasable Information

- Approximate friendly force strength figures.
- Approximate friendly casualty figures by service. Embedded media may, within OPSEC limits, confirm unit casualties they have witnessed.
- Confirmed figures of enemy personnel detained or captured.
- Size of friendly force participating in an action or operation can be disclosed using approximate terms. Specific force or unit identification may be released when it no longer warrants security protection.

- Information and location of military targets and objectives previously under attack.
- Generic description of origin of air operations, such as "land-based."
- Date, time or location of previous conventional military missions and actions, as well as mission results are releasable only if described in general terms.
- Types of ordnance expended in general terms.
- Number of aerial combat or reconnaissance missions or sorties flown in CENT-COM's area of operation.
- Type of forces involved (e.g., air defense, infantry, armor, Marines).
- Allied participation by type of operation (ships, aircraft, ground units, etc.). After approval of the allied unit commander.
- Operation code names.
- Names and hometowns of U.S. military units.
- Service members' names and hometowns with the individuals' consent.

This list makes it pretty clear that, like my friend who defends tax cheats, journalists had to start remembering to forget things like too many specifics. Life was to be measured in "approximates," "generally," and "generically." The second principle seemed to relate to verb tense. Generally speaking, verbs that ended with the -*ed* suffix of past tense were more acceptable than verbs preceded by "are going to," "intend to," or "will take off at." In short, nothing that hasn't yet happened will ever happen.

I breathed considerably easier after reviewing this list, for the Navy would have no trouble from me. My law training coupled with twenty-five years spent in the high-litigation world of investment banking had taught me to never keep notes (they might be discoverable), check with lawyers before releasing any statement (in this case it would be the PAO), and engage in CYA role playing by imagining how my every statement would play if later recited to a jury of my peers: If it wouldn't sound right to them, it ought not be expressed. Cardinal Richelieu was supposed to have said, "I write no letters but keep all that I receive." I had been trained not only to write no letters but also to rarely keep any that I received. The latter might become evidence either of something that I was told or something that I should have known. Of course, while excellent principles of business, they are probably lousy for journalism. But is talk radio journalism?

There were more ground rules. A separate section was called "Wounded, Injured and Ill Personnel." The bottom line here was privacy and giving the Pentagon a chance to notify next of kin (NOK) before some hotshot journalist could surf his way to higher ratings on a red wave of American blood.

The rule was no names and no pictures of casualties until NOK notification, period. This restriction applied to the earlier of seventy-two hours or verification of informing the NOK. Also, there were to be no media in hospitals without an escort and no interviews or photographs of patients without their "informed consent." This latter phrase, beloved by lawyers everywhere, required that the patient "understands his or her picture and comments are being collected for news media purposes and they may appear nationwide in news media reports." This protected patients who were too sick or too stoned on painkillers from being injured again, only this time, instead of by the AK-47-toting Republican Guard, from a journalist with an eye on a Pulitzer.

The final section of the ground rules agreement was called "Classified and Sensitive Information." It was preceded by an important sentence in boldface, which, taken literally (as it should be), probably distinguishes the American military from any other armed force in the history of the world: **Media products will not be subject to security review or censorship except as indicated below.**

To a suspicious mind, "except as indicated below" is as forgettable as being kicked in the testicles; the trained eye will naturally dive for the fine print. But in this case, the fine print was a voluntary matter. The following is a verbatim example:

> The primary safeguard [against media dissemination of classified information] will be to brief media in advance about what information is sensitive and what the parameters are for covering this type of information. If the media are inadvertently exposed to sensitive information they should be briefed after exposure on what information they should avoid covering. In instances where a unit commander or the designated representative determines that coverage of a story will involve exposure to sensitive information beyond the scope of what may be protected by prebriefing or debriefing, but coverage of which is in the best interests of the DoD, the commander may offer access if the reporter agrees to a security review of their coverage.

There it is: The reporter who wants access to the good stuff agrees to give the military a prepublication look-see at the reporting. Now come the rules that only a country like America would even think of including. "Agreement to security review in exchange for this type of access," the next rule informs, "must be strictly voluntary and if the reporter does not agree, then access may not be granted." In short, no prepublication review, no access, but as long as the reporter isn't sitting in on a Strike-Ops session, he doesn't have to submit *bubkes* to the PAO. But what is the definition of a security review? Bright lights, tough questions, a rubber hose? Not quite.

> If a security review is agreed to, it will not involve any editorial changes; it will be conducted solely to ensure that no sensitive or classified information is included in the product. If such information is found, the media will be asked to remove that information from the product and/or embargo the product until such information is no longer classified or sensitive.

Moreover, the last item offered some insight into how tough our censors were: "Media products will not be confiscated or otherwise impounded."

I couldn't believe it. Reading this, I debated whether to write to my congressman and complain that the military was jeopardizing national security by giving too much access to the media. But my congressman is a left-wing Democrat, and I knew that it would do no good at all.

c. 2000
Elevator
Diplomat Hotel

After the meeting, I rode down the elevator with a well-groomed and traditionally garbed Arab gentleman and his abaya-cloaked wife. They smiled, and I wished them both a very happy new year in that this weekend marks the Islamic version of Rosh Hashanah. In flawless English, he courteously replied that, "I wouldn't know much about that. We are from Kuwait and we celebrate the Christian new year. Whatever the Bahrainians do . . . ah, well, it's different."

What I don't know about most things would fill volumes, indeed, will probably fill this volume.

March 7
A.M.

I stopped by Room 610 this morning for a "one on one" (i.e., to ask questions that I was too embarrassed to raise during the briefing) with the Navy

PAO. And the news was great: Before I could ask anything, Cdr. Werner said that tomorrow I'm off to the USS *Kitty Hawk* battle group! (But today, it's the effects of the smallpox vaccination. The scratch site is unbearably itchy, and I'm overwhelmed by periodic waves of fatigue.) I was also told that yes, there are areas on the ship designated for smokers, cigars are permitted, there are plenty of vegetarians on board (always good news for diabetics), and there will be several chaplains aboard. And if I'm very lucky, one of them might be a rabbi. And yes, there are plenty of self-operated laundry machines.

Now I had it all: the name of the ship that I would soon be calling home, a hotel Internet connection to do some research, and enough excitement to beat back the effects of the vaccinia virus proliferating through my system. Of course, the first thing brought to mind by "Kitty Hawk" was the sandy, wind-blown plain in North Carolina where the Wright brothers made the first piloted, engine-powered flight. But there were less commonplace memories as well, dimly recalled but also drawn from another era, one that I happened to live through but that, with the passage of nearly forty years, seemed just as antique as the image of two bowler-wearing Edwardians gluing an airplane together in a bicycle shop in Dayton. Flashing through my mind were grainy film clips of jet fighters taking off from the *Kitty Hawk*'s deck and bound for funny-named places that a 14-year-old kid can be excused for not remembering. They were the names of hills, jungles, and villages in Vietnam. And the memories went even further back. For some reason, whenever I tried to imagine the *Kitty Hawk,* a picture of President John F. Kennedy also came to mind. I wasn't sure why.

On-line, this last question was the first answered, and with it came a flood of not so much memory as of associations. The USS *Kitty Hawk* was commissioned on April 29, 1961—just a few months into the administration of JFK. I had no memory of that event (I was not quite ten years old), but something about it must have stuck—a random news story, something my Navy-veteran father told me, perhaps something I struggled to read in a newspaper or even a magazine. But about the associations I was very clear. The *Kitty Hawk* was launched at a time when American power was deployed unabashedly, when both Republicans and Democrats marched in lockstep to something called a bipartisan foreign policy. Mostly I associated the young president, hatless at his inauguration, with his declaration before the world: "Let every nation know, whether it wishes us well or ill, that we shall pay any price, bear any burden, meet any hardship, support any friend, oppose any foe to assure the survival and the success of liberty." It was only years later that I learned that these words, like most of Kennedy's more memorable statements, had been ghostwritten.

Reading through the *Kitty Hawk*'s history was like touring not only U.S. foreign policy for the last four decades but also the extent to which that policy was entwined with advances in military technology. By today's standards, the *Kitty Hawk*, with eight oil-fired boilers, was now superannuated by the more recently built nuclear-powered carriers. The *Hawk*, as it is sometimes called, is scheduled to be retired in 2006. Nevertheless, Kennedy may be gone, along with a bipartisan foreign policy, but the ship remains. Most of its four decades afloat had been spent in the Pacific. The Navy reports:

> From 1963 to 1972, *Kitty Hawk* . . . completed eight extended deployments, including six in support of American forces in Vietnam. During that period, *Kitty Hawk* was awarded a Presidential Unit Citation, a Meritorious Service Commendation, four Navy Unit Commendations, a Battle Efficiency "E" and many other unit awards.

The *Kitty Hawk* was then based in San Diego. But as old wars ended and new policies were developed to meet new threats, the *Hawk*'s mission (and the *Hawk* itself) also changed. In 1973, as Vietnam wound down, it was refitted from an attack carrier (which carried a CVA designation) to a multi-mission carrier (which dropped the *A* to retain just the *CV*). More than just alphabet games were involved. The Navy again:

> The "CV" designation indicated that Hawk was no longer strictly an attack carrier in that anti-submarine warfare would also become a major role. Hawk became the first Pacific Fleet carrier to carry the multi-purpose "CV" designation. The conversion consisted of adding 10 new helicopter calibrating stations, installing sonar/sonobuoy readout and analysis center and associated equipment, and changing a large portion of the ship's operating procedures. One of the major equipment/space changes in the conversion was the addition of the Anti-Submarine Classification and Analysis Center (ASCAC) in the CIC area.

This change resulted from the fact that during these years the Soviet Navy—in particular, their submarines—had emerged as the force to be reckoned with. Of course, land-based ICBMs were still there, but because their locations were known and even subtle changes in their deployment observable by satellites, they were, at least according to theory, vulnerable. But submarines—ours and theirs—didn't have fixed locations, couldn't be seen from space, and increasingly packed the nuclear firepower of land-based ICBMs. Having studied U.S. foreign policy in college during the early 1970s, I remembered the fears. Nuclear-powered submarines could submerge for months, even years, and were constantly on the move. Their existence, again at least in theory, threatened the doctrine of mutually assured destruction: If you didn't know where the submarines were, they might be able to launch, disappear, and launch again. Furthermore, missiles fired from Soviet subs based off the coast of the United States could hit many American cities within six minutes. Constant monitoring of these vessels thus became a top priority. Depending on how quickly the superpower politics of a given situation might deteriorate, it was best to know where these submarines were, should a preemptive strike be necessary. Indeed, it was a slender reed, but one's only hope was to kill them before they killed you.

The *Kitty Hawk*'s 1973 overhaul also brought other changes. In those days of Middle East oil boycotts, the ship's fuel efficiency was increased. The new Grumman F-14 Tomcat required more powerful catapults and larger jet blast deflectors on the flight deck. Changes came very quickly in the 1970s. In 1976 it went into dry dock again to increase storage space for munitions and maintenance; the advancing complexity of avionics required more and better facilities to service these increasingly powerful tools for navigation, flight operations, and weapons systems. New force protection was added; the Terrier missiles, designed to defend against hostile aircraft; were replaced by NATO Sea Sparrow missiles. Bombs and missiles became heavier and larger, so additional space and elevators (for moving them between decks) were added.

In 1979, the *Kitty Hawk* participated in another mission that presaged what would become a growing part of the American military mission: humanitarian assistance. Once again, the *Hawk* was afloat off the coast of Vietnam, but this time it was to assist boat people in rickety craft attempting to flee the socialist paradise. (For this mission and a similar one in 1981, the *Kitty Hawk* would receive the Navy Expeditionary Medal and the Humanitarian Service Award for its rescue at sea of many a forlorn refugee.) That same year, following the assassination of South Korean President Park

Chung Hee, the *Kitty Hawk* was ordered to the Korean coast to reassure South Korea of U.S. resolve, as well as warn the North Koreans not to be tempted by instability below the 38th Parallel. Later that year, the *Kitty Hawk* sailed to the North Arabian Sea to "show the flag" during the Iranian hostage crisis. But President Carter's idea of American resolve was to fly unarmed F-15s over Saudi Arabia as a warning to the Iranians, who, predictably, were unimpressed. Threats backed by flinches render even the most powerful aircraft carriers little more than overimposing steel tubs.

Compared with the first twenty years of service, the 1980s were slow years. The *Hawk* deployed here and there, honing its skills at launches and recoveries, systems upgrades and fatality-free cruises. In 1990, the *Hawk* underwent a SLEP (service life extension program), which the Navy claimed would add twenty years to its serviceable life.

It was just in time. F. Scott Fitzgerald once declared that there were no second acts in American lives. True or not, it has no applicability to warships. In 1992, the *Hawk* was ordered to Somalia as part of Operation Restore Hope. It was there only nine days before being ordered to make haste to the Arabian Gulf. Gulf War I, Round I, was over, but now it was Round 2, and Saddam's Iraq was already violating the provisions of the truce. Just a few days later (early 1993), the Navy reported that "the *Kitty Hawk* led a joint, coalition offensive strike against designated targets in southern Iraq." In 1994 it was back in Korean waters for the crisis created by one of Kim Jong Il's early attempts to blackmail the United States into providing light-water nuclear reactors (!) in exchange for promising not to build nuclear weapons. He had certainly found his mark in the persons of Mr. Clinton, but, as happened so often in the past, the USS *Kitty Hawk* was there, in the Navy's words, "providing a stabilizing influence . . . during a time of great tension in the Far East." In 1997 it was in dry dock for three months as part of a fifteen-month overhaul.

In 1998 the *Kitty Hawk*'s home port was relocated from San Diego to the Japanese port of Yokosuka. In the words of the Navy, this made it "America's only permanently forward-deployed aircraft carrier." Translation: If an Asian ally called 911, the phone would ring first on the *Kitty Hawk*. But the *Hawk* was always available for occasional Middle East duty and in 1999 was ordered again to the Gulf for the continuation of Gulf War I, Round whatever, to enforce the no-fly zone over southern Iraq. Her pilots flew 8,800 sorties during 116 days; some twenty tons of bombs and missiles were dispatched in 1,300 combat sorties. Then it was back to Asia.

For me, it's back to bed. I'm still jetlagged, and the smallpox shot on my left arm is actually *vibrating*. I feel slightly feverish. As I close the curtains on my hotel window, I notice that there are several taller office buildings nearby. I glance up at their roofs, wondering about snipers, and I instinctively move to the side. But I'm really too tired to care.

1400–1600
Hotel Room
Diplomat Hotel

I did several radio stints this afternoon. Beforehand, I turned on MSNBC to catch the headlines. I'm amazed by the differences in perspective between here and back home. Over here it's hyperfocus on details: schedules, rules, naval protocol, research on weapons systems, ships, logistics, and force protection. But in the States, it's the big picture, 24/7, grand strategy, the American version of the Great Game. On TV, entire armies move across impossible terrain, transported by suddenly appearing arrows and laser writers on maps so large commentators stand on mountain ranges and crush ancient cities underfoot. Retired generals tower astride the entire Middle East, a vision of the terrifying American Colossus that is the nightmare of so many Islamofascists. Of course, it's just TV, but expect to see one of Edward Said's clones make it the subject of a paper, soon to be coming to an academic journal near you.

When not dealing with the grand sweep of this or that, my talk show hosts want the straight scoop on rumors. I'm asked to comment on a report that Saddam Hussein will put troops in U.S. uniforms, have them execute Iraqi civilians, and then blame us. I have to say something (and I do), but in truth there's no way we'd hear any such report over here. The headline in this morning's *Bahrain Tribune* (the principal English-language newspaper in Manama) was "Israelis Slaughter 15 Palestinians," and that appeared in huge red letters. So I dress my trite response in a clown's suit ("Well, rumors and war go together like cigarette smoking and lung cancer") and then increase its bulk with the leaden credibility of history. Such rumors, I declare, have the flavor of early Civil War newspaper reports that a Confederate armada was approaching Boston Harbor. Perhaps more usefully, I opine that one by-product of Rummy's embed program is that the International Criminal Court has probably been replaced by hundreds of reporters, and if Saddam wants to fabricate a massacre, he'll also have to produce Western journalists who saw it happen. (Rumsfeld has trumped them all with the promise of a reality TV show that will be second only to a live feed of Armageddon. In this war, perhaps more than in any other, if it isn't reported, it never happened.)

1800
Conference Room, Diplomat Hotel

Drats! At this evening's briefing, Cdr. Werner announced that there won't be any flights to the *Kitty Hawk* tomorrow. No reason given and none asked for. But the new departure date is Saturday morning. Downside: one more day in Bahrain. Upside: one more day in Bahrain. I'll sun myself, get my laundry done, do some work, some radio, and, most important, continue recovering from the smallpox vaccination's large fatigue.

But what am I going to do about *Shabbos* tonight?

c. 1900
Lobby, Diplomat Hotel

I'm having a long cigar and drinking mint tea. This high-ceilinged, well-lit lobby offers clusters of comfortably low couches that surround beautifully inlaid teakwood coffee tables. In the center of the lobby is a pianist playing what to me sounds like live Muzak. Gen. Ulysses S. Grant once said that he knew but two tunes: "Yankee Doodle" and that which wasn't. Alas, me, too. I'm joined by several "gentlepersons of the *Times*," including one who introduces herself as a Ms. Clemson. They are nice young people. I listen to their pleasant banter and limit my contribution to trying not to blow cigar smoke their way. Yet I stay, listen, and learn. What I discover is a peculiar sociology of the media—the presence of a self-reifying group that actually shapes the filter through which their experience must pass.

They discuss when the war will start. Each person makes a statement "I think this," which is then quickly followed (in one form or another) by a question: "What do you think?" Somebody replies, the group chews the matter over, and then another person declares, "I think this." Soon, all declarations had been modified along these lines: "You may be right. Well, in view of that, this is what I think." After a few minutes of friendly discussion, a consensus is reached. I have no doubt that if each of the *Times* reporters is now sequestered and told to write a story about when the war would start, they would all say the same thing.

There's nothing sinister about this. Humans are gregarious by nature and, all things being equal, strive for compatibility. But it showed me that some of what passes for news contains only a part of what Sgt. Joe Friday wanted to know when he solemnly asked his female subjects for "Just the facts, Ma'am." Another part of "the news" is also the product of social interactions among small groups of people. Martin Rudwick analyzed this phenomenon in his micro-history of how a long-forgotten dispute was settled among a small group of geologists in England during the early nineteenth century. In *The Great Devonian Controversy: The Shaping of Scientific Knowledge among Gentlemanly Specialists*, Rudwick concluded that "scientific knowledge making [was] ineluctably and intrinsically social in character, not (or not primarily) in the sense of pressures of the wider social world, but in the sense of intense social interaction among a small group of participants." In other words, the scientific findings (trying to date rocks) of this particular group of people were as much a function of their struggle to harmonize personal social conflicts, clashing ambitions, and professional jealousies (to name a few) as they were about the empirical evidence. How we come to know what we think we know is socially constructed.

I must keep this in mind the next time I decide to bloviate about the liberal bias of the *New York Times*. This view is confirmed later when I read a story filed by one of these reporters. Despite the war, she still thinks the enemy is Sheriff Bull Connor, and so she writes an article about a Muslim sailor who claims he's being treated unfairly.

March 8
0500
Hotel Room, Diplomat Hotel

During the past six hours I've done two ten minute spots on talk radio. It's pure entertainment and completely forgettable. For most people, it's an appetizer of chewing gum for the drive home, followed by a (very) light entrée of TV news once they've arrived. One host asked me if the media were a bunch of "traitors." Only if there was a story in it, I replied. Another one wanted to know "what the mood was like on the streets of Bahrain." He must've been nuts if he thought I was going to stick a microphone into the faces of people who, from a few of the looks I've gotten since arriving, hate our guts. Besides, it's discourteous.

Smallpox fatigue has given way to a speedy feeling, and I can't get back to sleep. So I do the next three best things: light a cigar, order mint tea from room service, and go on the Internet. Of course, it's back to researching the USS *Kitty Hawk*. Having learned something of its past, it's time to learn something about its present.

This ship's dimensions cannot be easily visualized. The flight deck is 4.1 acres and measures 1,065 feet or 3.56 football fields in length, with its widest point at 273 feet. With an average displacement of eighty-six thousand tons, it draws only 36 feet (giving a sense of how wide it is), and it towers some 201 feet above the waterline. This rectangular mass contains eight separate decks down (i.e., below the flight deck) and eleven levels up (i.e., in the "stack," the pile of levels that rise above the flight deck on the starboard side). Incredibly, the *Hawk*'s four steam-turbine engines, powered by eight boilers, give it a top speed of more than 30 knots (34.5 miles) per hour. This is accomplished by four screws, each 21 feet wide. Each anchor (there are two) weighs 30 tons, and *each link* in the anchor chain weighs 360 lbs. These links form a chain some 1,080 feet in length.

Numbers tumble off my computer screen. The *Hawk* carries four million gallons of fuel and can generate fourteen million watts of electricity. The crew, including the air wing, numbers approximately fifty-five hundred men and women. To feed this crowd, seventeen thousand meals are served daily. They include four hundred to six hundred gallons of milk, eight hundred to one thousand loaves of bread, ninety-six hundred to twelve thousand eggs, and three hundred eighty thousand gallons of fresh water, distilled daily. Medical care is provided by four doctors, five dentists, and an optometrist; there are four operating rooms and a sixty-five-bed hospital. Balm for souls is provided by three chaplains during twenty-one separate denominational religious services, legal advice is given by two lawyers, sailors can work out in one of five exercise facilities, and hair is cut in two barbershops. There is one U.S. post office, which handles an average of 2,500 pounds of mail each day, and one laundromat. The closed-circuit television system has six chan-nels. There are twenty-four hundred telephones and fifteen hundred com-puters on board.

How do I understand all of this? I think of this vessel as if I were still an investment banker analyzing a corporate entity. With about five thousand five hundred employees, the *Kitty Hawk* has a current average annual payroll of $145 million. (This gives some notion of wage inflation; in 1961, the ship cost a mere $265.2 million; in other words, today, every eighteen months the government pays out in salaries the original cost of the ship.) To keep this leviathan stocked requires an inventory of approximately sixty thousand separate items, and 18,000 pounds of these are received on board every day, everything from JDAMs (joint direct attack munitions, number classified) to soda pop (average daily consumption is five thousand forty cans). The number of accounts payable serviced on-ship (as distinct from those handled by the Pentagon's bean counters) is more than five thousand five hundred.

It struck me that the most remarkable thing about an aircraft carrier wasn't its weapons or dimensions but the fantastic management challenges it posed—challenges not entirely different (in principle) from those faced by many midcap manufacturing companies listed on the *Standard & Poor's 500*. Thousands of people to be directed, tens of thousands of tasks to be performed and monitored, hundreds of thousands of supplies to be ordered, shipped, taken aboard, sent, and then, finally, an end product—the projec-tion of American power abroad—to be delivered. Granted, the aircraft car-rier produced war—or peace—rather than widgets, but as a monument to organization, it bore a peculiarly American stamp. I wondered to what the captain of the *Kitty Hawk* might be compared. Was he just a CEO in uni-form?

Peaceniks might not like it, but when combined with its power and tech-nology, the aircraft carrier was perhaps one of the highest forms of American civilization.

They were our own great pyramid of Giza.

1800
Conference Room, Diplomat Hotel

Tonight's briefing was relocated—for security concerns, somebody whis-pered to me—from the very public first floor to the eighth floor, accessible only by elevator. Because I've attended a briefing before, and I've already been assigned to a ship, I will be excused early. Tonight's crowd is chatty, excited, nervous, and also, at fifty or sixty people, double the number from last night's.

"I would like to direct your attention to Ground Rule three," Lt. Cdr. Werner begins, speaking loudly. "Media embedded with U.S. Forces are not permitted to carry personal firearms." He looked around the room. The chat suddenly stops. Werner gave a moment for his declaration to settle in. "That means no firearms," he continued. "No handguns, no rifles, no knives larger than a pen knife, no mace, and no pepper spray. Now," he asked, "did any of you bring any personal weapons with you?"

This crowd was so surprised by the question that nobody even bothered to answer "no." But the silence lasts just a moment longer than the "I'm surprised anybody would ask me that" variety of wonderment. Werner's question had suddenly put the "D" word on the table, as in *deadly, danger-ous*, and, ultimately, *death*. It reminded everyone that they were noncomba-tants heading off to war and that their sole protection was little more than a few words on a scrap of paper negotiated by infidels in Switzerland a very long time ago.

Frankly, I would like nothing better than to take Werner aside and whis-per, "Yeah, I've got a personal weapon. I've got a whole friggin' arsenal. Here's my Walther PPK, my Smith & Wesson .40 Caliber Tactical, and, for backup, I've got a Smith & Wesson 2$^3/_4$ inch barrel .38 Revolver." I do own those guns but, of course, didn't bring them with me. Journalists are noncombatants, and I remembered that during the Afghanistan War, one TV reporter got into hot water when he disclosed that he was packing heat during the Battle of Tora Bora. War correspondents die on the job for many reasons and certainly don't need to add to the possible causes of death: "Enemy had probable cause to believe he was packing." But here in Bah-rain, surrounded by hostiles and feeling like the only Jew in the Gulf, I sure would have felt better with a comforting bulge under my left shoulder. Irra-tional, of course, but there it is.

The rules for packing up and getting out to aircraft carriers are also dis-cussed. Cdr. Werner reviewed a memo he had sent a week earlier. The first instruction promised a moment of ready-room drama that suggests that getting to an aircraft carrier in almost wartime isn't like taking the Boston–New York Shuttle:

Once we schedule a flight to your ship, we'll ask you to meet us in the lobby of the Diplomat for transportation to the aviation unit. When we provide the time, we must insist that you be there on time. Due to the dynamic nature of carrier-based aviation, you most likely won't learn your meeting place until late the night before, so please remain accessible, flexible and ready such that we can contact you and get you there in time.

It's clear that there won't be any smiling Skycaps, tip-me valets, or itchy-palm baggage-handling services: "You will be responsible for toting your gear and personal belongings while on board." There's no need for an excess luggage policy because none is permitted: "Travel light to the carrier. Take only what you need, and recognize that large pieces of luggage and camera gear are tough to move through narrow passageways." The trip over is not a photo op either: "There is absolutely NO photography/filming at the military aviation unit. The local officials will take your camera(s)." And nobody gives a rat's anus about your comfort or convenience: "Be prepared to wait. Showtimes at the Aviation Unit are generally two hours before take-off. We appreciate your patience and understanding as we negotiate getting you out with the myriad of other parts and people heading out." In short, Werner clarifies policy: Take a number, sit down, and shut up. Perhaps it's not much different than the Boston–New York shuttle—just more honest.

Arrested Landing

March 9
0600
Room, Diplomat Hotel

Up WITH A START, shower, dress, check, and check again all of my stuff against the Navy's "What to Pack" list. This list, provided verbatim here, could just as easily have served for one of my kids' summer camp, adding just a hint of entering a war zone:

Shower shoes
Towel(s)
Undergarments
Soap, shampoo, tooth brush, tooth paste (essential toiletries)
Shaving items
Soiled laundry bag
U.S. Dollars for means and souvenirs
110-Volt adaptors for U.S. electrical outlets
Aluminum foil/mylar covering for cameras (radar protection)
Duct tape
Floppy disks/CDs/zip disks (the ship will not provide disks for data transfer)

To this, I added my own items:

Diovan HCT (anti-hypertensive and diuretic)
Lipitor (cholesterol killer)
1000 mg. Vitamin E

81 mg. Aspirin

One-a-Day "Over Fifty" vitamins

Two boxes (50) Romeo and Juliet Belicoso cigars (Habana)

New pair Converse High Top black canvas gym shoes, known to my hipper-than-
thou children as Chuck Taylors.

Satellite telephone

MP3 voice recorder

Laptop computer

Cigarette pack–sized digital camera

Books, papers, memos, articles, pencils, pens, Post-Its, scratch pads, orders, cer-
tificates, list of rules, addresses, telephone numbers, calculator, passport, plane
tickets, maps, matches, assorted wires, clips, and floppies

Then it's down the elevator and ready for duty at the crack of 9 A.M.
"Duty," of course, means boarding a bus to what CPIC calls "the aviation
facility." This means airport, and we are advised about two rules: Don't
bother asking where it is, and don't take any photographs once there. The
reason, of course, is security. Cdr. Ward asks if anyone has ever heard of
Khobar Towers. Hearing that name gives me pause. Khobar Towers was an
apartment building in Saudi Arabia used for housing U.S. troops when it
was blown up by terrorists, killing lots of Americans. "For weeks before that
attack," Ward explained, "there were all kinds of shady characters outside
of Khobar taking pictures. We learned that it's better not to advertise the
architecture where we can help it."

After a pleasant ride that concluded with a curvaceous negotiation of an
obstacle course of strategically placed Jersey barriers, we finally arrived at the
"aviation facility." This was not your average airport; indeed, from the
street, it didn't look like an airport at all, merely a scattering of nondescript
buildings amid a wider scattering of nondescript buildings. This wasn't just
military drab. It was low profile, invisibility being ever the first line of
defense. But when we hopped off the bus, I was greeted by a sight that filled
me with joy: a five-foot wall of sandbags, behind which were three Navy
security men wearing desert camo and toting M16s. I wouldn't dare ask, of
course, but they looked for all the world to be locked and loaded and "good
to go." As a staunch Second Amendment man, I've proudly spouted the
NRA slogan, "Guns don't kill people; people kill people." This afternoon,
I make my own amendment: "And guns in the hands of good people can
be used to kill bad people, who might otherwise kill me."

Once inside the airport, I suddenly felt a pleasant, even mildly exhausting rush of relief. For four days, I had been pursued in my imagination by a host of terrorists, kidnappers, snipers, Arab security services, common thieves, and every other sort of bogeyman that a White, middle-class guy like myself could conjure during the decades spent watching things explode, burn, or simply lie dead in the street, all of which fairly summarizes American news coverage of the Middle East. Now I felt safe. Now I was going into a potential war zone.

Passports checked twice, bags and person x-rayed, I followed some arrows and soon found myself standing in a large waiting room that resembled the bus terminal of any big American city. Men and women, some in uniform, and some not, sat or slept on long rows of benches that had been thoughtfully ordered without armrests. At the opposite end of the room was a large-screen television that had just begun showing the movie. . . . *Black Hawk Down*.

I wondered if showing this film on the brink of war was wise. *Black Hawk Down* is a straightforward retelling (subject to Hollywood's usual inventive requirements) of the 1993 American disaster in Somalia: A failed attempt to arrest a local warlord, a handful of U.S. Rangers trapped in the city of Mogadishu without adequate armor and facing a reckless and determined enemy who numbered in the thousands. The result was a nightmare for the soldiers and a political disaster for the feckless Clinton administration. It ended in a shameless piece of political theater in which gangster chief Mohamed Aidid (the erstwhile arrestee) had the bodies of eighteen dead American soldiers dragged through the streets as crowds cheered and video cameras rolled. The sequel proved that a faraway tribal chieftain understood the political sensibilities of an American president, who was supposedly astute in nothing but political sensibilities. The U.S. forces withdrew, and the people of Somalia resumed dying under the auspices of Aidid.

I took a seat and edged closer to the screen to better hear the movie. Some of America's most memorable war films aren't about victories at all but rather defeats. In fact, some of the best are about defeats. During World War II, movies such as *They Were Expendable* (the fall of Bataan and Corrigedor), *Wake Island* (the Japanese occupation of Wake Island), and *Bataan* celebrated the triumph of the spirit over defeat. More recent years have seen *Tora, Tora, Tora* (Pearl Harbor), *Glory* (decimation of Civil War Black unit at Battery Wagner), *A Bridge Too Far* (Operation Market Garden, World

War II), *Apocalypse Now, Deer Hunter, Full Metal Jacket*, and *Platoon* (Vietnam). Even the more triumphalist movies are mixed affairs in which a Moses-like hero, leading his men to certain victory, is himself unable to cross into the Promised Land: *Sands of Iwo Jima* (protagonist John Wayne is killed before final victory), *Saving Private Ryan* (protagonist Tom Hanks is killed in the last few scenes), and *The Fighting Seabees* (John Wayne is killed in the last few scenes). And, of course, there is the father-of-all defeat movies, *Gone with the Wind*.

This has become a trope, largely because notions of Judeo-Christian martyrdom, ranging from the nationalistic variety of the Maccabees to the more universalist martyrdom of Jesus and various disciples, are so deeply embedded in the American consciousness of communal death, that is, the deaths of those who die in a representative capacity; in dying, they "represent" larger values of freedom, decency, toleration, and the like. Depictions of these deaths, or the disasters that produced them, are quite literally reenactments of the triumph of the Passion of Christ, mixed up with the Maccabean story of Elazar. In 1863, Ralph Waldo Emerson wrote "Voluntaries," a poem inspired by the death of twenty-five year-old Col. Robert Gould Shaw, who even while alive was described by John Greenleaf Whittier as "the very flower of grace and chivalry . . . beautiful and awful . . . an angel of God come down to lead the host of freedom to victory." Shaw was killed while leading his Black troops up the sandy walls of Battery Wagner, and Emerson has martyr-Jesus lurking between the lines:

> So nigh is grandeur to our dust,
> So near is God to man!
> When Duty whispers low, *Thou must,*
> The youth replies, *I can.*

Thirty-four years later, the famous bronze frieze by Saint-Gaudens depicting Shaw on horseback leading his Black troops was dedicated. It bore the poetry of Shaw's kinsman, James Russell Lowell, which closed with these lines:

> But the high soul burns on to light men's feet,
> Where death for noble ends makes dying sweet.

Ninety-three years after this, the movie *Glory* was made, which is really the Saint-Gaudens monument filmed for the big screen. It maintains the hagiographic (and somewhat historically accurate) tradition. Shaw's status as a martyr is unmistakable: At his death moment, shot through the heart by a Confederate rifleman, he pauses, arms outstretched Christlike, before tumbling backward into the moat surrounding the fort. The next morning, Shaw's body was thrown into a burial trench with those of his men. When asked where Shaw's body was, a Confederate officer replied, "We buried him with his niggers." In that officer's eyes, it was the final insult. But to a North whose discourse about the war was often framed in a biblical context, it was no insult but an embodiment of one of the more famous "reversals" in the Gospels, of which Mark 9:35 is typical: "Whoever wants to be first must be last of all and servant of all." In short, by being buried with "his niggers," many in the North understood that Shaw was taking his place with the least and would thus rank first in the eyes of Heaven.

The church historian Eusebius declared that martyrs were the seeds of the church. A historian of wartime home fronts might also declare that martyrs are the seeds of morale. Nothing so congeals a group than to see one of its own struck down. Of course, in part the trope survives because religious discourse survives. What's different is that today the discourse thrives as a vast, enriching, but largely subterranean current, which is derided when not entirely ignored by a largely faithless or skeptical elite.

c. 1200
Waiting Room, Aviation Facility

It's time to go. A man hands me a necklace-style life preserver and something called a "cranial"—two pieces of plastic stitched to a canvas helmet with hearing protectors and goggles. No one is allowed onto the tarmac or into the airplane unless garbed in these things. Our motley troop—perhaps ten journalists and 15 sailors, mostly teenagers, lugging their duffel bags—are led out across the sizzling tarmac, whipped by gasoline breezes but strangely silent because of the hearing protectors. It is stop and go. We walk a few yards, stop to allow a vehicle to pass, walk a few more yards, stop again to allow an airplane to be towed past our front, and then start walking again.

The plane that will take us to the *Kitty Hawk* is a C-2, a fixed-wing, folding-tipped, twin-engine propeller craft. It's snout-nosed, loads from the rear via a platform, and has twenty-five or thirty seats, all facing the rear. The plane is painted drab gray. Indeed, every plane on the tarmac is painted drab gray, with black numbers and letters on wings and tails and fuselages. But up close, on the inside of the plane's loading platform, I find that some distinct personality has seeped out of the sameness.

Discreetly stuck to the metal innards are colorful travel and bumper stickers, the kinds of things people put on their cars or suitcases to let the world know where they've been. And these guys have been everywhere, at least around the Pacific Rim: bars in Australia, restaurants in Singapore, water ski rental shops in Japan, and hotels everywhere.

And one glance at the crew explains a lot because the pilots and ground crew, technicians, and fellow passengers are all much younger than I am. Many of these sailors are the same ages as my children, and obviously enjoy the same things. This was neither my first nor my last encounter with the fact that the military is managed by the old but run by the young and, by the looks of things, the very young.

Stepping onto the platform, I eyed the pilot carefully. He struck me as late twenty-something. In civilian life, I prefer my pilots to be like my physicians—tall, urbane, silver haired fellows who do what they do with a confident wink and a nod and leave all the fretting to me. However, I am now in the world of young bucks—guys who look like they've just walked off the set of *Top Gun*. But when I look past the gelled hair and fancy sunglasses, they seem to carry themselves with an unexpected confidence. This is a new and welcome observation (especially for a passenger about to board a fast plane destined for a short landing) and contrasts sharply with the slackers, dressed-down, self-absorbed, and "serious" youths I've learned to live with in my graduate classes at Harvard. I cannot avoid the word: From the enlisted kid who helps me up the ramp with my bags to the pilot who briefs us on the flight, these are good boys, *mensches,* as my mother of blessed memory would have called them.

Military aviation lends new meaning to no frills. Two rows of two seats are bolted to a metal floor; no soothingly colored plastic skin covers the interior of the airframe. Bundles of wires, ducts, and foil insulation stuff the insides. There aren't any instruction cards, barf bags, or glossy in-flight magazines to while away the time aloft. In fact, except for two small peep hole type openings toward the rear of the plane, there aren't any windows either. But we are given verbal instructions. As the loading platform is raised, one of the flight officers instructs us on how to snap on—and in an emergency, get out of—the over-the-shoulder harnesses that keep us tight in our seats. Shouting above the din, he also shows us the hand signal that will precede by a few seconds the most feared part of the flight—the arrested landing. In case anyone misses the hand signal, a lighted panel reading "ARRESTED LANDING" is bolted to the ceiling at the rear of the plane. It will flash 20 seconds or so before we land (or, in the blunter parlance of carrier aviation, "recover") on the flight deck.

A week earlier, all media embeds posted to carriers received a lengthy E-mail from CPIC that discussed arrested landings:

> You will be making an arrested landing on the carrier, causing the plane to decelerate to a complete stop in less than four hundred feet. Because physics dictates that objects in motion tend to stay in motion, the aircraft—and you safely strapped into said aircraft—will stop. Whatever you're holding will not. All bags—especially cameras—are hand-packed by Navy crewmen on your flight.

Oddly, although Alyson was concerned about many aspects of this adventure—flying commercially into a war zone, staying at a hotel in Bahrain; in fact, in time of war, being anywhere outside the city limits of Concord—it was the arrested landing, probably the most potentially hazardous aspect of the trip that she found most appealing. But then she likes to ski down steep mountains and ride fast horses; I don't like to do either, and I was damned sure that I wouldn't like an arrested landing.

The hour's flight was smooth if noisy, but the harness system began to chafe against my torso. Then the flight officer stood up and twirled his index finger, the signal for landing. Above him, the panel lit, the plane banked steeply, first one way, then another, then the nose went down, and my eyes widened.

Then we touched down. It was fast, hard, and silenced all my complaints about the harness. My body shot forward, followed instantly by my gastrointestinal system, the contents of my heart and arteries, and my ocular fluids. I tasted parts of me that were never meant to be tasted; hyperventilation was a waste of time as, for a split second, there was no traction in my chest muscles. And then we stopped. The engine seemed to ease off, as I slumped into my seat.

There was no time for a mental victory lap. After landing on a carrier, planes quickly discharge their contents and taxi off the active runway. Other planes are likely to be landing or wanting to take off, and the flight deck is at best a two-runway operation. We taxied for a moment before the loading platform was lowered, filling the fuselage with the exhaust-filled air that seems to permanently envelop the flight deck of an aircraft carrier.

Standing outside the C-2, I knew I had arrived at the center of a universe. All was pulsating energy and seeming confusion. Even through the cranial, the noise was deafening; the visual montage was overwhelming. People were walking and running, blurs of red, green, brown, and white uniforms; planes were firing up or winding down their engines, being towed on deck or taxi-ing hither and thither; low yellow vehicles were towing things in every direc-tion; a profusion of painted lines on the flight deck seemed to lead nowhere and told me nothing. I looked up. Towering above all was the stack of com-mand-and-control decks, and rising with them was a bewildering array of spinning radar dishes, bizarre-looking antennas, wires, cables, ladders, flags, white domes, and crow's nests. The artificial winds of jet blasts whipped the deck and me too.

At first, I couldn't have proved I was even at sea. Sure, the ocean was visible off the side of the ship, but the sheer area of the flight deck, the seeming terra firma of the runway, the height of the stack, and the number of loud, large objects being carted or taxied about suggested that this was a large pier or even a seaside airport, in any case, still attached to solid ground. Of course, it wasn't. It was a boat, same as a rowboat, but bigger.

"Welcome to the *Kitty Hawk!*" A tall, thin young man was literally shouting into my hearing protectors, his mouth less than an inch away.

c. 1600
Wardroom I

Wardroom I is one of two officers' dining rooms. The floor is a lighter-than-navy blue linoleum, which marks this room for officers only. (There are a number of such areas throughout the ship—p-ways, ladders, berthing rooms, heads—reserved for officers. These are identified by blue floors, blue plastic curtains, and/or a sign that reads, "Officers Country.") This room (in fact, every room on the ship) is bathed in fluorescence, which, in the absence of any portholes or windows, becomes an alternative sun. Ward-room I is furnished in the style of a pleasant country restaurant, sans the country: Small tables fill the room, with condiment bottles clustered in their center, and booths line the walls. The ceilings are low; in fact, the ceilings are low in most rooms on the ship. And like the C-2 that brought us here, there is no skin to conceal the myriad pipes and bundles of wires that carry steam, water, and power to every square inch of this vessel.

We're between mealtimes now, but the wardroom, while empty of diners, is still full of people, and not just the media who are waiting for their orientation. There are people passing through, people pushing mops and buckets, people wheeling equipment and supplies, people stopping to stare, and others who just seem to be around.

About ten media people arrived on the boat today; some twenty others were already here. We have three Navy handlers, who won't, in fact, be handlers at all—more like go-to guys. The senior go-to guy is Lt. Brook De Walt, who runs the *Kitty Hawk*'s PAO. A thin man in his thirties, just the age for ambition, I'd say, the lieutenant knocked around in civilian life for a while before deciding to join up. He donned the Navy blue relatively late in life (late twenties, that is) and knew what he wanted to do—public affairs. PR guys, are still PR guys, however, whether in or out of uniform; in my first life as an investment banker, I dealt with plenty of them, from crisis management types to publicists seeking to spin stories, place client "news," or do things like vet environmental charities on behalf of CEOs looking to sidestep some late unpleasantness about their company's dumping tons of PCBs into a local river. PR guys tend to come in two sizes: There are the oleaginous ones who are veiled control freaks but manage to persuade clients that it was their idea from the get-go, and there are the oleaginous ones who are unveiled control freaks and don't give a rodent's *derriere* what the client "thinks," because they believe that they are the deus ex machina and confident that they can handle matters. Lieutenant De Walt is of the latter class.

This orientation isn't really about "finding our way"; trying to explain how to get anywhere on an aircraft carrier to a bunch of subnovitiates like us would be like trying to explain to a 10-year-old what a pain in the ass the monthly mortgage payment is. Lt. De Walt makes clear that learning our way around is something we'll just have to experience. To my surprise, he encourages us to do just that. "Get lost," he insists. "It's one way to find your bearings." What this orientation is really about are the rules. And to my further surprise there aren't too many of those, considering that we're on a ship of war on the brink of war.

The first set of rules falls under the category of intuitive self-preservation, at least for those who wish to live to see their grandchildren. "On the flight deck," Lt. De Walt explains slowly and with grade-school locution, "you are standing on the most dangerous four-and-one-half acres on this earth. You will not be allowed on the deck without an escort. You must wear long-sleeved shirts, the cranial, and the life vest. You must not bring anything that can blow or be sucked off of your person and wind up in a jet engine. That means no pens, pencils, jewelry, loose papers, or anything else along those lines."

For safety reasons, we must also be escorted to enter the engineering areas of the ship, such as the boiler and engine rooms or the magazine (where the bombs and missiles are stored).

The second set of rules falls under the category of preserving the life of somebody else, namely, the pilots. "Under no circumstances will you be allowed to snap pictures using a flash anywhere outside the skin of this ship. That especially means on the flight deck, the fantail, and the hangar bays when the doors are open." I vaguely remembered something about this from my own private pilot days twenty years before. It may seem odd, but it's true: The flash of a camera, if it strikes the pilot's eyes at a certain angle, has been known to cause the same temporary blindness as any other flash too close to the eye. The greatest risk is during night operations.

These rules also include an absolute prohibition on photographing open panels on airplanes. We are to be given virtually unimpeded access to the hangar deck, really a floating garage for airplanes, an assembly hall, mail room, delivery gangway, and sort of the public square of an aircraft carrier. But also serviced here are the airplane's sensitive electronic systems, including fancy radars, electronic countermeasures, navigation, and weapons guidance systems. These are accessed through detachable metal plates on the skin of the aircraft—the open panels. It's secret stuff that the Navy isn't eager to share with adversaries.

Listening to all of this heightens my paranoia. Putting on my James Jesus Angleton hat, I look around the room and wonder about my colleagues. I start by wondering about myself. How does the Navy know that I'm not a spy? All journalists are, in a sense, spies. All the Defense Department wanted from me was my Social Security number, and I wasn't questioned further.

Two matters seem obvious: For the Pentagon, the advantages of getting its story told, of waging war on this new battlefield of information, far outweigh the risks of espionage; second, for me, it is evidence that I have led a life that, from the standpoint of counterintelligence, is flat and uninteresting. In an odd twist of the Munchausen syndrome, I begin to wish that someone had questioned my neighbors or dropped by my house for a chat about that mysterious "trip" I once took to Cairo via Damascus, Aden, and Kabul.

Next discussed are items involving "operational security." If the sign on the door says "restricted access," that means don't enter. Lt. De Walt then hands us a list titled "List of Restricted Spaces." I stare blankly at most of these, clueless as to what some are or what the abbreviations mean, and I am certainly clueless as to where they are, although for several of them I intuit why I can't go there. "Unlimited access to the following spaces is not authorized," the preamble instructs. "For scheduled access to any of the spaces listed below, coordinate with PAO." The list:

Bridge
Echo Papa
TFCC
CDC
CATCC
CVIC
Weapons magazines [this I immediately get]
Flight Deck [this, too]
Ready Rooms (All)
Berthing Spaces [I get this]
Senior leadership office spaces [this too]

Lt. De Walt becomes emphatic about the next point: The ship's exact position can never be communicated to anyone off the ship. In reporting, we cannot be any more specific than, for example, "somewhere in the North Persian Gulf." And the big no-no, the thing that is guaranteed to get us tossed off (or, in an earlier era, keelhauled or hung from a yardarm) is an absolute prohibition on disclosing future or pending operations. As a practical matter, this means that if we know planes are taking off on a mission (implied in the stricture is that we also know something about the mission), we cannot tell anyone off the ship until the planes have returned safely. In short, to use Lt. De Walt's word, no stories may be filed that contain the word *gonna*.

Technology has made this a potentially serious risk. Most reporters came with satellite phones, and this means that the time elapsed between composing and filing a story is only minutes. In the case of my media, talk radio, where nothing is really composed, only yakked, that time can be reduced to seconds. But technology also cuts in favor of an adversary. Filing a story doesn't necessarily mean instantaneous publication; broadcasts and newspapers have cycles, and editors sometimes agree do hold items. But Lt. De Walt pointed out that sat phone signals can be intercepted by an enemy, who would then have advance knowledge about the mission. (I can't avoid being a wiseass here. "Yeah," I volunteer, "and I hear there are several French and Canadian ships in the area.")

What's interesting about these rules is that the Navy isn't mandating prior restraint. This comes damn close to an honor system, and Lt. De Walt says as much. "We're not going to prevent you from filing stories," he warned, "but if you're caught communicating when you shouldn't be or disclosing any 'gonna' items, you're out of here. And that means you and your news organizations will never again be allowed to set foot on another Navy ship." That threat is probably credible for the Talk Radio News Service. But over the long term, I'm not sure that organizations as influential as CNN or Fox News would have much to worry about.

The Navy is also implementing something new—rolling blackouts. In the past, blackouts—the prohibition of any ship-to-shore broadcasting—were imposed from the commencement of active hostilities until the PAO determined that the element of surprise was no longer an issue. But during the 1991 Gulf War, the Pentagon figured out that a mother of all blackouts was itself a signal to shore-based editors that something was up. Reporters who had been in daily contact with their editors were suddenly not heard from, and home offices were able to draw their own conclusions. To avoid such obvious clues, blackouts were now going to be imposed randomly. The code name for all of this was "River City," and when we heard those words broadcast over the ship's public address system, we were to consider ourselves blacked out until the words "End River City" were heard. (Why "River City" was chosen as a name was a mystery to me. I assumed that it

was taken from Robert Preston's song in the 1962 movie *The Music Man*—
"We got trouble right here in River City"—but when I mentioned this to a
twenty-something PAO staffer, he drew a blank.)

There were also rules requiring appropriate dress. CPIC had given us a
list of these before we arrived, and Lt. De Walt reviewed them again. For
anyone paying attention, this list contained many clues about what shipboard life would be like, as well as what is expected of civilian embeds living
cheek by jowl with naval personnel:

> Shorts, tank-tops, sleeveless shirts, and dresses/skirts are prohibited.
>
> Sandals, flip-flops or any open-toed shoes are prohibited. Sneakers or boots
> are okay, but wear something protective, yet comfortable—you'll be standing
> on hard steel and climbing many ladder wells.
>
> Appropriate cover-up (i.e. bathrobe) for transiting to/from bathing facili-
> ties (Essential for mixed-gender ships).
>
> Warmer sleepwear during the winter months, as staterooms are still air-con-
> ditioned.
>
> Clean set of dinner clothes. For example, khaki trousers or nice jeans and a
> polo shirt or blouse is recommended, as you may be eating meals with officers
> in the wardroom.

These were the items for embeds on naval ships generally. For those embedding on aircraft carriers, additional items were required:

> Rugged pants or trousers such as denim jeans or cargo pants.
> Long-sleeve shirt.
> Sturdy shoes, preferably with rubber soles.

So there it is. Safety and decorum. *Ubi homines sunt modi sunt.*

c. 1800
Media Room

It is literally true that the media room is our battle station. When general
quarters is sounded, every person on this ship has a place they must be
within four minutes of the announcement. Presence is also required when
man overboard is sounded. Who that man (or woman) might be is then

determined by an enormous deduction: All fifty-five hundred crew members, gathered in groups at their various stations, are counted, and anyone not counted is searched for. We are told that, yes, men (no one asked about women) do occasionally go overboard. Some are crazy and jump; others are blown off by jet exhaust, high winds, or a pitching deck.

This room is where the ship's live, closed-circuit broadcasts originate. Like most other rooms on this vessel, it is small and crowded with things. A blue curtain covers one wall, in front of which is a pleasant-looking "desk" of light wood, the same type TV anchors sit behind to give the illusion of an office; it is an image most viewers associate with "work." There is a television camera, hooded and shunted to the side, and shelves on a wall filled with videotapes in a room no larger than a clothes closet that has been soundproofed and is used for producing finished product. Right now, the crew from Sky Television is in there, editing their daily runs before sending their work home via satellite or Carrier Onboard Delivery. The media room also has klieg lights, so hot that they nullify the air conditioning. Add to this the fact that in a room built to comfortably hold five maybe ten people, about thirty-five are now crammed in, each with a different concept of personal hygiene.

Before us stands Lt. Cdr. Mike Brown. Unlike Lieutenant De Walt, who wears a navy blue jumpsuit, Cdr. Brown is dressed in properly creased and perfectly tailored brown khaki. Of course, I don't know whether his uniform is tailored or whether I'm just a lumpy older man jealous of a lithe younger one (wearing clothes that actually fit, an experience I haven't had for years). Cdr. Brown looks to be in his mid- to late thirties and is also a PAO, but with a different boss than Lt. De Walt's. The latter "works for" the *Kitty Hawk*, but Cdr. Brown is on the flag staff, which means he "works for" Adm. Matthew G. Moffit who is stationed on the *Kitty Hawk*. Brown is a candid man, and he describes his job as trying "to make the Admiral look good."

What he and De Walt actually do is provide access. But before receiving access, we must first be made shipshape. It is here that we are introduced to a new restriction—pilot interviews. This is a sensitive topic for many reasons. The pilots are the spear's point of the aircraft carrier. It's why the ship is here; in fact, it's why the ship is a ship at all—to launch jet fighters whose weapons are the razor's edge of American power.

2000
Signal Deck

I have donned the cranial and vest and, together with the new media embeds, proceed single-file to the signal deck to watch nighttime flight operations. Jet lag, excitement, old age, too much coffee, and too many cigars have finally caught up with me. By the time we climb what seems like a hundred ladders each with a thousand steps, I'm out of breath. But once outside, I find that it was worth all the trouble. The signal deck towers above the flight deck of a ship whose dimensions are not easily visualized; even here, I can see only a portion of the 1,065-foot-long (equal to 3.56 football fields) flight deck. I've already noted its huge dmensions, and tonight, every square inch of the deck is being used for something.

The *Hawk* carries more than seventy-five aircraft, six or seven of which are currently being prepped for takeoff. Each plane taxis to a point midway on the flight deck, where it is attached to a steam-powered catapult (the *Hawk* has four) that shoots 263 feet forward, the effective takeoff length of the runway; planes are literally snapping into the air. At the moment, an F-14 Tomcat is being centered on the catapult; in another moment, a panel called the jet blast deflector rises just aft of the plane. This deflection redirects the engine thrust, both protecting the runway behind and adding to the power of the takeoff roll. Just how powerful is best seen at dark. The F-14 before us unleashes a horizontal, rolled sheet of white fire that quickly becomes an extension of the airframe itself. The noise, the gestures of the ground crew, and the length of the fiercely burning exhaust all increase in tension until final release, and the plane shoots off the deck. If the visuals aren't convincing, consider the physics: an F-14 Tomcat has a maximum takeoff weight of 74,349 pounds and gets only 263 feet to reach its minimum takeoff speed.

A plane takes off, another plane lands—and does so on exactly 120 feet of runway. This is accomplished by four so-called arresting gears, which are cables strung over the runway and attached to pistons beneath the deck. When landing, a plane not only lowers its wheels but also drops a tail hook from beneath its tail section. This hook literally catches one or more of the cables as it touches the deck, and the plane is actually jerked to a halt.

But the most impressive part about tonight's tour of the signal bridge is watching the movements of the deck crew. These men and women service the jets; they load, fuel, arm, taxi, and inspect them, among a hundred other functions. Multi-colored blurs of t-shirts scramble about. Some run, some walk, some crouch, some lie prone, some gesticulate wildly with their arms, and some stand still. At first it looks chaotic, but after several repetitions, the chaos quickly gives way to an impression of ballet, only driven by function and not form.

Tired as I am, bundled in a long-sleeved shirt and a tight-fitting vest, hearing stifled by the cranial, mouth closed by the fruitlessness of speech amid the roars, and eyes shuttered behind goggles, it seems I have only two senses left: a nose for the pungent odor of jet exhaust and a mind filled with pure wonder.

I'm not tired anymore. Watching my tax dollars working this way is more stimulating than, say, watching them paid to politically wired contractors in Boston's Big Dig project. As we file down the stack to the PAO to return our cranials and vests, I'm overdue by many, many hours for a cigar.

2345
Wardroom II, Sailors' Phone

It's time to file my first shipboard report. Tomorrow I'll try the satellite telephone, but tonight I'll just dial up the States and leave a recording. My instructions are that my spiel should not exceed thirty seconds.

Officers (and media) make these calls from the second of the two rooms that comprise the Wardroom II suite. The larger of the two spaces is the dining room, but just off that is a smaller room, lit by intentionally weak lights, furnished with long sectional sofas upholstered in navy blue cloth, and decorated with traditional nautical fixtures—brass portholes on the doors instead of rectangular windows, brass hooks against the far wall on which officers' hats may be hung during conferences, and brass pulls on the doors and cabinetry. But this stuff is pure atmosphere. What makes this room popular is the large-screen television on one wall and the three telephones next to the sofas. Two are called sailor phones. Pick them up, and an AT&T operator is at your service. The third phone is used for internal calls.

At the moment, the television broadcasts ten seconds of news for every 20 seconds of wavy, parallel lines that distort the image, although the voice is still audible.

"We must be turning," somebody said, referring to the fact that when the ship turns, certain of its antennas often lose signals. Throughout the boat, TVs go haywire and the sailor phone becomes comatose. But in spite of the turn, the sailor phones work, and there is no River City restriction.

"Better call fast, chum," one old codger says to me. "That phone could blink out at any minute."

There's no telephone booth privacy in this room. People sit in the open during calls to wives, mothers, and lovers; words of passion and loneliness, frustration, bitterness, and longing pass in semiwhispers, audible but studiously unheard by anyone else in this room, for there is a careful etiquette of ignoring others' telephone conversations. It is partly self-protective; gossip, comments, and smirks at others are sure to earn you the same treatment when it's your turn to pour your heart out to a loved one.

But I'm not calling a loved one. I'm calling two pieces of digital recording equipment, one owned by Talk Radio News Service and the other by American Urban Networks. Thirty seconds of material won't be difficult, chiefly because I have nothing to say—at least nothing that fits into that time frame. Broadcasting time frames are the analog to newspaper pages. They are quite literally the boundaries of the world that the radio station seeks to invent. I say *invent* because seeing a series of stories on one page or contained in a single newspaper, or a chain of incidents related or pictured during a broadcast, suggests a connectivity between people and events that may not exist. Benedict Anderson makes this point eloquently in his book *Imagined Communities*. Would the nation-state have been conceivable in the absence of print capitalism's willingness to frame the damn thing, publish maps, breath life into it, and create a connection between people who don't know and will never lay eyes on one another?

This matters at the moment because it suddenly dawns on me what my real mission is. Unless I know where Jimmy Hoffa is buried (I don't have a clue), what the people back home want to hear aren't facts, little stories, or self-inflated insights. What they want is the immediate experience of connecting to a looming war that is different than past wars. Other wars lasted for years, and everybody knew an uncle, brother, husband, wife, boyfriend, lover, sports idol, or movie star who wore some kind of a uniform. But this war is being waged by a relatively small force of volunteer professionals. And if the war lasts the couple of months that Rummy and Company are publicly predicting, there won't be much time for the public to bond with the conflict. As part of Anderson's imagined community, it is in the nature of patriotism to demand a bond.

So instead of "color" being a mere adjunct to the story, I have concluded that color is the story, because that's what the listeners want from this war. In the case of talk radio, they want a quotable voice that gives them a bridge directly to the scene. So I write up and file the following:

> I'm reporting from the deck of the USS *Kitty Hawk,* the oldest United States aircraft carrier still in active service. This formidable warship is a beehive of 24/7 activity. Lately, there is a sense of increasing preparation for war. Gunners practice firing the deck's fifty-caliber weapons; F/A-18s practice bombing runs within sight of the carrier; the crew drills for the possibility of a chemical or biological weapons attack. Protective suits are donned and gas masks are carried by all sailors. Yet while the *Kitty Hawk* may be sailing close to the eye of the storm, there is a sense of calm as the crew performs their well-practiced evolutions. Still there is no mistaking the increased tensions. Sidewinder and Phoenix missiles are stacked for easy access; and long lines of sailors form outside the smoking areas of the ship, awaiting permission to enter a well-earned nicotine break. Sailors puff away while just overhead F/A-18s, F-14s and EA-6 Prowlers are catapulted into the night sky going about their business to enforce the no-fly zone over Iraq. Time will tell about the war, but there is a pervasive sense that the time is growing very short.

Every statement is true, and at the same time, the passage is a complete construction. Otherwise unlinked events are linked. Jets fly, guns fire, people smoke, the ship sails, and I not only arrange the sequencing but also I'm the only one claiming that any of these events are related. It is equally true that simultaneously with the events described in my broadcast, ocean waves rose, metal paint chipped, onboard vending machines failed to dispense soda pop, and some people cleared their throats.

Journalism is no first draft of history; it's more like a Rohrschach inkblot.

CHAPTER 6

The Smoking Sponson

He never uttered an oath, nor a word of low or indelicate character; he abstained habitually from tobacco in every form, and from ardent spirits, wine and beer.

> *Adjutant Stearns*, containing a eulogy for Frazar A. Stearns, Adjutant, 21ST INFANTRY, 1863

It is doubtful if any single item except food, water, and letters from home was so highly cherished by Johnny Reb as "the delightful weed" . . . nor is it any wonder that many Rebs, who had resorted to everything from singing to smoking to make army life tolerable, should, on reaching home at war's end, inquire first, after the round of embraces, as to the prospects of the tobacco crop.

> Bell Irvin Wiley, *The Life of Johnny Reb*

Sponson, n.
*Also **sponsing, sponcing**. [Of obscure origin.]*

1. One or other of the triangular platforms before and abaft the paddle boxes of a steamer.
2. A gun platform, standing out from the side of a vessel.

> *Oxford English Dictionary*, 2002 Edition

March 10
0001
Enlisted Smoking Sponson

ON THE SPONSON, conversations are measured in cigarettes. Only so many people can fit on this deck—maybe seventy—and sometimes, like tonight, there are many times that number wanting on. A perpetually renewing line snakes its way across the wide hangar deck, and sponson etiquette requires that, once admitted, by all means, talk, laugh, listen, circulate, or keep your own counsel, but smoke, because somebody else is waiting to do just that. A security guard is posted at the sponson portal, and as one smoker leaves, he waives another through.

It took me an hour to find this place. Its location is no secret, of course, but I wandered lost among the decks and ladders, the frames and workspaces that compose this steel city (which is, it is trite to say, like a city, but unlike most, this city has no homelessness or unemployment). I feel like one of the ambulatory schizophrenics who wander the streets of cities ashore, talking incoherently to every passerby, none of whom knows how to answer my crazy questions. This is because they know the directions *too* well and assume that everybody else on board also has their genius. The dialogue amounts to an extended tautology:

"Excuse me. How can I get to the smoking sponson?" I ask.

"Easy, Sir," comes the invariably affable reply. "Take this ladder to 04 deck" (or 03 or 02 or spit-in-my-shoe deck) "and then take the first ladder between frames 134 and 194" (or "open the door and lay on the floor," says Barnacle Bill the Sailor), "then down one ladder or up one ladder or a lateral ladder" (and with all these ladders you won't get fatter), "and then poof, you're there!"

It turns out that the sponson is one of the easiest places on ship to find. It's on the same level as the hangar deck, which is, from the standpoint of its architecture, the center of an aircraft carrier's universe; all other decks are located by their relation to the hangar deck. A ship has no north, no south, no east, and no west; as it plows the trackless seas, its only referent is its own structure, and all other points change by the second (unlike the addresses of stationary objects such as houses and office buildings). Aircraft carriers rarely move in reverse, so one can posit a forward (bow) and a rear (stern); given this, one can also define a left (port) side of the vessel and a right (starboard) side.

But on a ship as large and complex as an aircraft carrier, this is almost too elementary to be useful. There are no portholes below the hangar deck, where much of a ship's life is lived; with no visual outdoor horizon, there is no intuitive sense of the ship's direction; without knowing which end of the ship is front or rear, identifying the points of bow, stern, port, and starboard becomes more problematic.

Putting aside the trivial question of orienting lost and expendable civilians, knowing precisely where you are at all times on ship is an indispensable piece of self-awareness for a sailor, in its way as critical to your well-being as not walking into a propeller or being blown overboard. For starters, there's the daily commute between a sailor's berth and work; there's knowing the location of the doctor, the baker, and the eyeglasses maker, not to mention the mess, the ward rooms, and the head. But these routine journeys are eventually memorized. Where the ability to instantly conceptualize location matters is when a sailor is in an unfamiliar place on board (and it is a striking fact that very few sailors have been everywhere on an aircraft carrier) and an emergency sounds, requiring the sailor's presence (as well as that of fifty-five hundred other people) at the muster station. Then sailors have to know precisely where they are and how to get where they're going—and do it in less than four minutes.

To help sailors know where they are, the Navy created addresses of frame references and numbered decks for practically every location on the ship. These are posted on bulkheads throughout the ship and called bull's-eyes, which are to the novice absolutely indecipherable three-tiered sets of letters and numbers whose precise meaning is known only to the mystagogues. To the rest of us dummies, it looks like the kind of math problem that would have stumped the protagonist in *Good Will Hunting*. Here is an illustration from the "Welcome Aboard!" pamphlet given to all newbies on the *Kitty Hawk*:

03–137–3-Q

137–140

X-1

The explanation that accompanies this example defies paraphrasing, so I quote it in full:

The first two numbers in the top row (03) represent the deck or level. Each deck above the hanger bay is number 01–010, ascending.

Each deck below the hanger bay is numbered 2, 3, 4 etc., descending.

Therefore, 03 represents the third deck above the hanger deck.

The second set of numbers (137) represents the forward most frame in the space from the front of the ship to the back. Beginning at the front, and running all the way to the back, there are cross sections called "frames." There are 247 frames on KITTY HAWK. In the example, frame 137 is a little more than halfway back toward the back of the ship.

The third (3) represents your location in relation to the ship's keel or centerline. Odd numbers are on the starboard (right) side of the ship, even numbers are on the port (left) side, and 0 represents the centerline. The higher the number, the further outboard you are.

The letter of designation (Q) identifies workspaces. The letter (L) identifies berthings, staterooms, sickbay spaces and the letter (T) identifies escape trunks.

The second row of numbers (137–140) represent the frames that are encompassed by that space. This gives you an idea of the space's size.

The final row of letters and numbers (X-1) tells you which of the ship's divisions or departments are responsible for the cleanliness and maintenance of that space.

For now, all I get is the part about the deck. Using the handbook's example, it means I have to walk down three ladders to smoke.

For all of the cutting-edge aircraft, fancy equipment, and high-tech avionics awaiting service on the hangar deck, this is a place that, oddly enough, might have been more familiar to Americans fifty or one hundred years ago than is the case today. The reason is that the hangar deck is really a factory, the kind of place where our ancestors forged iron, rolled steel, built automobiles, and stamped metal. It is a concourse-size space filled with the thundering sounds of banging, drilling, hammering, welding, metal-on-metal screeching, slapping, and whacking. It smells like grease, fuel oil, and exhaust; people are walking to and fro, shouting, climbing up and down ladders and over aircraft, comparing notes, looking for tools, carting nondescript boxes from space to space, trucking about 2,000-pound bombs, sorting mail, hanging out, or just walking in shorts and t-shirts to and from the exercise room overlooking this deck. This is not a suburban office building or glass tower high-rise where the loudest sound is the nearly silent HVAC system and the biggest complaint is carpal tunnel syndrome. As one walks on this very dangerous deck, the stakes are high. A sandwich-board sign has been erected by the propeller engine of an E-2C Hawkeye. In black letters, it features a huge skull and bones and reads "STOP! WALK AROUND PROP ARC" with an arrow pointing to the right. And it's there for a reason. I have been told that in the past, guys have walked into spinning propellers and had their skulls halved like an apple.

This is where the planes come to be fixed and where supplies are loaded from docks while in ports and from other ships while at sea; it is where the mail is sorted and where huge boxes with unmarked contents are stacked in towers reaching toward the ceiling. It is home to welders, lathe operators, electricians, engine specialists, wizards of avionics, and a thousand other specialties. Neatly uniformed ship's security cordons off sections for safety reasons (for example, when ordnance is being moved about) or just patrols the deck like city cops on a beat, ensuring that things move smoothly. All is bathed in mercury-vapor yellow fluorescence; more than an artificial light, it is the light from another star illuminating an alien planet. And the greatest hazard is unmarked. The airplanes are fastened to the deck with guy wires and their wings are at eye level. These hazards have no warning signs. I follow the person in front of me and duck when he ducks and sidesteps when he sidesteps. The greatest enemy on an aircraft carrier isn't some turbaned jihadist. It's simple carelessness.

"Got a light?"

"Yeah."

"Where are you from?"

"Rome, New York, it's upstate. . . . Los Angeles . . . Texas . . . Wyoming . . . Washington, state of . . . Troy, New York, man, the asshole of the East . . . Brooklyn . . . Dayton . . . San Diego . . . Nowhere and everywhere, dude, I'm a Navy brat. . . ."

For some reason, no planes are taking off or landing at the moment. The soft red glow of the sponson's smoking lamps, the lower decibels of normal conversation, and the continuous but quiet sounds of the *Kitty Hawk* parting the Gulf waters oddly make this crowded deck as relaxing as the solitude of a mountaintop. My cigar takes forty-five minutes, or about the time it takes to smoke ten to twelve cigarettes. This means that I can have about as many brief conversations with different people. "Got a light?" is one conversation starter. Yes, I carry a lighter and always have a light. "Where you from?" is what I ask and am often asked in return. "What's your job?" I inquire; interestingly, they already know what my job is. Scuttlebutt races ahead of mere introductions. The only question I usually get is "Which of the media are you with?" When I reply, "Talk radio," it just as often draws a blank. Besides talk radio being a relatively new form of media (a decade old, perhaps), the *Kitty Hawk* is based in Japan, and some of these sailors aren't in the States long enough to follow Rush Limbaugh; most were at sea when Bill O'Reilly from Fox News' *The O'Reilly Factor* started his radio talk show; many know of Sean Hannity from Fox's *Hannity and Colmes* television show but don't know that Hannity also does radio on WABC in New York City.

This deck is a jutting triangle located underneath the flight deck (which is actually some fifty feet above). The deck rail is made of rope, but it's secure enough to lean (slightly) over and gaze at the water. A few feet to my right is a .50-caliber machine gun silhouetted against the night sky, its barrel raised almost perpendicularly to the deck in a mock salute to this uneasy peace. The *Kitty Hawk* has nine of these guns, known formally as the M2HB. They are one of several business ends of the *Kitty Hawk*'s close-in force protection. Recoil-operated and air-cooled, the M2HB measures more than sixty-five inches; about forty-five inches of that is the chrome-lined barrel. With a cyclical rate of fire between four hundred fifty and five hundred fifty rounds per minute and an effective range of about two thousand yards, this gun can control most small craft within range. It's just too damn bad that one of these wasn't trained on the Al Qaeda–captained motorboat that slammed into the hull of the USS *Cole* in Yemen.

"Seen one of these up close before?" a young sailor asks, referring to the .50.

"No, not like this," I reply. He takes a last drag, flicks the butt over the side, and lights up another cigarette.

"Do you ever get nervous out here?" I ask.

"What, scared?" He seemed incredulous that I would ask. Not because I was prodding him for some unmanly confession—rather, I think he thought it was just a foolish question.

"Look, you can't be any safer than we are standing right here," he said confidently. "We're in the center here, man. We got a whole carrier battle group surrounding us. Just because you can't see them don't mean they're not there. And they got one job—looking after this boat."

"How many ships in our battle group?" I asked

"Hey," he shot back, "if I told you, I'd have to kill you right afterwards." I laughed and he smiled.

"Seriously, man, I don't know for sure. Five or six, maybe. But even if I did know, it's something we don't talk about. That stuff's above my pay grade."

"What's your job here?" I asked.

"Aviation machinist's mate," he said proudly. "Here, you'll know us by this." He pointed to a monogrammed silver airplane propeller and wings on his blue uniform. "I like to think of it as the most important job on this ship. Without us, planes don't fly. No planes, no aircraft carrier. No aircraft carrier, and the Prez's got nothing to get the job done."

"So you like the Navy," I asked.

"I don't know. Ask me tomorrow."

"Why'd you go into the Navy?" He looked into the water for a moment, suddenly less flip.

"When I graduated from [high] school," he finally said, "I didn't have much of a future in Tacoma. My mother works and we got no money for college. Navy'll help take care of that, though."

We shook hands and he left. In a moment I was talking to two other guys.

"What are your jobs?" I ask. These kids were pals and seemed happy.

"Aviation structural mechanics."

"Both of you?"

"Yeah. When I have to check out a wing, my shipmate here gets on his hands and knees so I can step on him to get up there." These two were ribbing each other more than me.

"Why'd you enlist in the Navy?" I asked both boys.

"Out of high school I was just another dude with a reading problem," one replies. "But in here, man, I'm still not the best reader in the world, but give me an aileron to check out, and I can tell you whether or not that plane's coming back," he beamed. "And I hear that companies like Boeing and Lockheed are willing to pay a lot of money for guys who do what I do."

I looked at the insignia on his lapel. It was two crossed hammers and two wings.

"What brought you to the Navy?" I asked a tall, slender kid who had just bummed a light. He smiled.

"Back home, a lot of people were surprised," he replied. "I finished high school near the top of my class and put in a year of college. But it was a struggle to make tuition. My folks are separated, and the scholarships weren't there. After I'm out, I'll be getting some help from Uncle Sam."

"What do you want to do after you're out?"

"Do you know what I do here?" he asked, pointing to his lapel. I stared at the insignia and tried to remember the enlisted ratings chart from *All Hands* magazine. It was a silver ship's wheel. I couldn't remember, so I took a guess.

"Steering? Navigation?" I asked lamely.

"No, man," he said, "this is Quartermaster's Department. As far as I'm concerned, we run this boat. Knowing how to keep track of the inventory guarantees that everybody's got enough food, toothpaste, you name it." He paused for a moment, resting with his thoughts. "You know," he finally said, "Hell if I knew why I was in college. But I know now why I'm going back."

"Why?"

"Accounting degree. I have a talent for numbers. There's a lot of money out there for people who can do what I do."

"Indeed, there is," I said, remembering a host of faces during my 25 years in the investment business.

There were other conversations just like these. Some liked the Navy, some hated it, and some were ambivalent. But everyone seemed to share—more or less; some early in conversation, some later; some with acute conscious-ness, and some who had only a vague awareness—at least three things: first, a disappointment with the public schools; second, large ambitions; third, whether or not they liked the Navy, all seemed proud of what they did here. All believed their jobs to be indispensable; all believed that these were useful stepping stones to something else, something better, and something much better than what, sans the Navy, would have awaited them in civilian life. There were no lifers here in the stereotypical sense of cud-chewers who "found a home in the service" and looked forward only to doing mindless tasks and collecting their pay. The people I met who wanted to make the Navy a career were very ambitious of promotion to chief petty officer or commissioned officer. They wanted these for the respect (and self-respect) they conferred, for the higher pay and privileges, and for the increased man-agement and job training that came with the higher grade. The rest—and these were the majority—did not intend to spend their lives in uniform. But listening to them, I realized that the *Kitty Hawk* wasn't just a warship. It was a floating university, a seagoing career counseling office. And the Navy could also be a personal counseling office.

"Two years ago," one sailor explained, "I was sitting in my high school principal's office because I said, 'Screw you' on a dare to one of my asshole teachers. Today, I fix ejection seats on F/A-18s. When I was a kid, if I screwed up, I'd get a few giggles in class. You know what happens if I screw up today?"

"What?"

"A pilot dies."

This was a prevailing sentiment, something not often found among their civilian peers—accountability. It came down to trust. Once they proved themselves in basic training, the Navy was prepared to trust them, and as far as I could tell, these kids responded by discharging that trust very seriously. All were aware that countless others depended on what they did, sometimes for their very lives. And what they did may have been only a cog, but at sea, any cog that fails eventually stops the ship. Unlike the civilian world, where politicians and others regularly devalue many forms of work—entry-level employees are "burger flippers," financiers and CEOs are "fat cats," government workers are "bureaucrats," and so on—here, all employment, high and low, is connected (as it is in civilian life) and the people who do the work are made to understand the connectivity (which the civilian world fails to do).

Imposing accountability—expressed in a more gendered age by the phrase "the military will make a man out of you"—is how American society traditionally understood Army or Navy service. Unlike today, social class and education seemed to have less bearing on these attitudes. After three years of Civil War service and three serious wounds, Boston Brahmin Oliver Wendell Holmes Jr. (Harvard, 1861) was confident enough to write to his parents, "I started in this thing a boy [and] I am now a man." In an unusually confident voice, he went on to discomfit his famous poet-father by announcing his intention to leave the service when his term was up. "I honestly think the duty of fighting has ceased for me—ceased because I have laboriously and with much suffering of mind and body earned the *right*." Three years before, Holmes's comrade Henry Livermore Abbott (Harvard, 1860) stated that his own patrician background lacked something. "I felt that I had never done any thing or amounted to any thing in the whole course of my existence," he wrote to his mother in 1861, "and that there was no better prospect [than enlisting]. . . . I couldn't help concurring with every body else, and got so disgusted with being nothing and doing nothing, and resolved if I couldn't do much, to do what so many other young men were doing.'' Abbott did not survive the war, but at his death, he was acknowledged as one of the most distinguished field officers in the Army of the Potomac. And most biographers of Holmes Jr. believe that his subsequent career as one of the molders of modern American jurisprudence would have been impossible without his Civil War experience.

However, the fact that everybody says virtually the same thing about the pride they take in their jobs and their hopes for the future made me wonder about the extent to which a volunteer military is, by definition, self-selecting. Before going overseas, I had picked up several Navy recruiting brochures. I looked at them later and was surprised by how the attitudes I had encountered on the sponson seemed to correlate with the qualities solicited by these materials.

One brochure, "Who Better to Describe Navy Life Than Someone with a Life in the Navy[?]" seems to tell the whole story. The title is a clever play on the well-known taunt to "get a life" that is often directed at people thought to have few interests and few things going for them. One can argue that by itself, the title will appeal to those who feel that the "life" they have is not, to paraphrase the Army recruiting slogan, "all that it can be."

The brochure features color photographs of four smiling young sailors, relaxed at their workstations; next to each is a one- or two-sentence quotation about their lives in the Navy. These blurbs presuppose many things in the reader: ambition, some disenchantment with civilian life, and, by implication, a conviction that the Navy can remedy the deficits of lousy public schools, outrageously expensive college tuitions, unsettled homes, and class prejudice:

> "I'm only twenty years old. I'm in charge of a $32 million piece of equipment."—Airman Josh Stehr, shown in his cranial and yellow shirt on the flight deck.
> "The two years of training I've gotten would have cost me close to $25,000."—Electronics Warfare Technician Casey Bowman, shown sitting in front of various screens and other gadgets.
> "The best thing about the Navy is that you get to travel; I've been to France, Spain, Portugal, Israel."—Radioman Wayne Holloman, shown in his white uniform with an unidentified but probably foreign skyline in the background.

"Steering a $1 billion ship is amazing. I expected a lot of things from the Navy and so far I'm getting all of it."—Seaman Alejandro Saa Zamorano, shown in his white uniform sitting in front of an unidentified computer screen.

Here's the subtext of these blurbs:

"I'm just a kid who, before enlisting, wouldn't have been entrusted with a garden hose. I join the Navy, and hey, these guys actually trust me enough to give me an airplane to look after. *Me*. And the smile on my mug tells you that I like being trusted. And my willingness to pose for this ad tells you that I'm happy to return the favor to the Navy."—Airman Josh Stehr

"Twenty-five grand is actually less money than some Ivy League asshole's rich daddy pays to entitle him to screw off in Harvard Yard for four years before taking a safe job starting at $75,000 a year. But for guys without rich daddies or mommies, the Navy (unlike that shitty public high school I attended), actually gives me skills that would otherwise cost me the big bucks I never had as a civilian. Is that a deal, or what? I mean, what the hell have the editors of the *New York Times* done for me lately?"—Electronics Warfare Technician Casey Bowman

"Hey, every time I turn on the TV, some rock star/celebrity/politician-on-a-junket is stepping off an airplane yakking about the five-star hotel they just left in places that guys like me only get to see on *Entertainment Tonight*. I want to at least see these places before I die, and OK, an aircraft carrier isn't the Savoy Hotel, but given a choice, where I travel is more important than where I stay. This could be the last chance in my life to do these things before the mortgage and the kids show up. I deserve a shot too."—Radioman Wayne Holloman

"Steering this $1 billion ship is a metaphor for taking control of my life, which was, prior to enlisting, rudderless. Now they trust me to do this. *Me*. And believe me, if I can steer this ship, I can manage your business, handle your money, and, most important, handle myself. A thousand sessions with a Park Avenue shrink would never have given me this kind of confidence."—Seaman Alejandro Saa Zamorano

Two other things strike me in conjunction with my first time on the sponson. Of the four blurbs, only one echoes the famous recruiting slogan of the past: "The Navy: It's Not Just a Job, It's an Adventure." The other three are explicit or implied appeals to the qualities that overlap personal development and material self-interest: training, responsibility, management skills, life direction, and self-esteem. Many of the kids who show up at the recruiter's office already know two things: There's something they haven't gotten out of life, which for most of them consists of their public school, hometown, or their family, and the Navy offers that something. Add to that my sense of the *Kitty Hawk* as a seagoing university, career and personal counseling center, and an important center for remedial education.

But perhaps the most salient fact about the men and women I've met aboard the *Kitty Hawk* was best expressed by Sir Winston Churchill in *My Early Life: A Roving Commission*. From Sandhurst to Parliament by way of the Fourth Hussars, Cuba, India, journalism, the Battle of Omdurman, and a harrowing escape from an Afrikaner POW camp during the Boer War, Churchill concluded, thirty years after these adventures: "Twenty to twenty-five! These are the years!"

Living Spaces

0500
SEAL Berth

THE MEDIA IS QUARTERED in the SEAL berth. Only one ladder down from the hangar deck, this is the space where Navy Special Forces, whose stay is usually brief but busy, are housed. Like every other space on board, it's small and tight, but unlike the other spaces on this ship, it's messy and it smells. That's because its present tenants are a bunch of male journalists who are less than fastidious about personal hygiene. Too, like most overpaid civilians, they (we) are accustomed to having somebody else pick up after them (us). Dirty laundry is stuffed in every corner; shoes and sandals litter the floor; laptops, sat phones, digital recorders, and camera equipment are scattered everywhere. It's chaotic, but it's my home.

This space is divided into two rooms by a row of ceiling-high storage lockers that are arranged to form a narrow passageway connecting two spaces. The first room, which is just to the right of the ladder well, contains a long table on which are crammed five desktop computers. Across from the table is a two-cushion-wide leatherette couch that has seen better days. Bracketed in the right-hand upper corner is a small television set. The passageway connects this room with the sleeping space. Its walls of metal storage lockers are intended for personal items. Behind these ersatz walls are twenty-four racks—Navy lingo for beds. But *rack* is a more accurate term. Almost identical to the old stacked sleeping compartments in Pullman railcars, the racks are just over six feet long, three feet wide, and maybe eighteen inches high. In other words, no tossing and turning at night, no sitting up in bed, no stretching legs or arms; indeed, whatever one does in bed must be done either flat on one's stomach or on one's back—there is no middle ground. The mattress is about three inches thick, and a curtain slides across the entry slot for privacy.

As with the old Pullmans, the racks are stacked three high like a tall dresser but without the drawers. The sleeping section of the berth is itself divided into two narrow passageways, with six racks on each side. Beneath each rack is a locked storage compartment a few inches high that runs the length of the bed and the width of the mattress. All in all, it's an excellent preview of what it will be like when I'm dead and in my coffin.

I'm up this morning on three hours' sleep, but it's not because of the racks. Sleeplessness on these ships is a fact of life—a loud noise, a foot in my face, a bright light, the smell of fuel oil—I must accept this or go ashore. I'm anxious for a look-see at my colleagues, but first is a reminder that the housekeeper doesn't come Mondays and Thursdays. As I stumble out of bed in my underwear, a young man neatly turned out in a woodland camo uniform is standing in the passageway.

"Sir, excuse me," he says in a polite but slightly irritated tone. "Does this belong to you?" He pointed to a suitcase that somebody left in the middle of the floor.

"Uh, no."

"Well, Sir," he continues, "it's important to keep the p-ways clear just in case you have to exit or egress this space in an emergency."

"Of course," I replied, and I quickly moved the suitcase to the side. I was old enough to be his father, but he was looking at me in a way that he probably never looked at his father. I felt embarrassed. Sloppy. Soft. Weak. He explained that he was from ship security—the onboard cops—and it was his job to inspect our quarters and keep them safe and clean. This was done several times a day, and he politely explained that "it's nothing personal against you gentlemen from the media because on a ship, everybody's quarters, every space is inspected several times each day."

For years I had been chasing after my children to pick up after themselves. Now it was my turn for children to chase after me.

0520
Officers' Head

Up the ladder to 3 deck on my way to the head, and the first thing I see is a real eye-opener, worth at least a quart of black coffee this morning. Neatly stacked right outside my hatch were six Sidewinder and perhaps a dozen Phoenix missiles. Both are air-to-air missiles, made to be fired by jets at other aircraft. The Sidewinder, named after a snake, is 9.6 feet long but only five inches in diameter. It weighs what I do, 190, but unlike me, it travels at supersonic speed, powered by what the books describe as a "high-perform-ance, solid-fuel rocket motor." It's tipped by a 20.8-pound blast fragmenta-tion warhead—not much as explosives go, but then not much is needed for a heat-seeking missile intended to detonate in or near an enemy aircraft engine. It's used by the F-14, F/A-18, AV-8, and AH-1 aircraft.

But the Sidewinder is meant for targets that can be seen by the pilot; not so the Phoenix. It measures 13 feet long and is 15 inches in diameter; with a range in excess of 100 nautical meters, the pilot only has to "see" his adversary as a stream of electronics on his radar screen. And the Phoenix, besides being bigger, is heavier. It weighs 1,024 pounds and carries a 135 pound high-explosive warhead. Traveling in excess of 3,000 miles per hour, the Phoenix is a supersonic death sentence, usable in what the Navy describes as an "all-weather, heavy-jamming environment."

The sight stops me in my tracks. A couple of kids, wearing the red, long-sleeved t-shirts of the ordnance crew, are using a dolly to maneuver a Phoe-nix into place. One of them, a mustached young man, notices that I'm star-ing, and he grins at me.

"Sir, can you believe what I'm doing here?" he asks. "Hell, a year ago, my mother wouldn't even let me get my driver's license!"

His remark focuses everything. This awesome weapon of war, the USS *Kitty Hawk*, this last link in a long chain of older men that directly connects the Oval Office with the most junior sailor, is run by younger men and women who, only several years before, were children. Later, I reach into my pocket and pull out a folded sheet of paper that Lt. De Walt gave me yester-day. Intended to explain to the media not only who's who but also who's where in the Navy's hierarchy, it's entitled "X-1 Division Chain of Com-mand," and it's worth reproducing in its entirety. It makes the connection.

The bottom slots are filled by twenty-somethings, a few just over thirty, maybe.

X-1 Division Chain of Command

President of the United States
George W. Bush

Secretary of Defense
Donald Rumsfeld

Secretary of the Navy
Hansford T. Johnson (Acting)

Chief of Naval Operations
ADM Vern Clark

Commander, Pacific Command
VADM Thomas Fargo

Commander, 7th Fleet/Carrier Group 5
RADM Matthew Moffit

Commanding Officer	*Command Master Chief*
Capt. Thomas A. Parker	CMDCM (AW/SW) Marvin Dublin

Executive Officer
CDR Gary C. Peterson

Department Head	*Department LCPO*
Lt. Vincent Ortiz	NCCM (SW) Wilfred Cotto
Division Officer	*Division LCPO*
Lt. Brook De Walt	JOC(SW) Maria Mercado
Division LPO	*Print Shop WCS*
JO1 (SW) Bell	L11 (SW) Morales

In any organization, one expects to find the gray hair at the top. 'Twas ever thus. But few organizations have the youngest people toting bombs, landing airplanes, overhauling jet engines, and just about every other kind of skilled, dirty, and dangerous job to be done on a warship. I begin to see what the Navy does for these kids that civilian society doesn't. In so many ways, the Navy simply *trusts* them.

My nightshirt and plastic sandals are the most important things in my duffel bag. To get to the closest bathroom, I have to climb the ladder and walk the length of a football field down a crowded p-way, passing hundreds of men and women, most of whom are uniformed and on their way to work, while I've got a bath towel slung over my shoulder, sleep still in my eyes, and sandals slapping the linoleum decks. I feel like a street bum, always dressed for the wrong season. At first I avert my eyes from people I pass in the p-way. But after walking 50 yards or so, I realize that it is they who are averting their eyes from mine. It's because I'm not the only one forced to take this Walk of Shame. In fact, I am passed by several others headed for the showers. Not looking at what others don't want you to see is a subtle form of ship's courtesy and necessary for fifty-five hundred people sharing a tight space.

Walt Whitman famously prophesied about the Civil War that "the real war will never get into the books." What certainly never got into the books was any discussion about bathrooms. The Revised Army Regulations of 1861, which specified every conceivable rule governing Army life, remains vague about one feature essential to maintaining a military: toilets. The regulations refer to them discreetly as "sinks" but never define what they are. Their purpose was only hinted at in Paragraph 522 of Article XXXVI. After specifying where these mysterious trenches must be dug ("150 paces in front of the color line"), the paragraph declares: "A portion of the earth dug out for sinks [is] to be thrown back occasionally." Looking up the word *sink* in the 1853 edition of Noah Webster's *American Dictionary of the English Language* doesn't help much: "SINK, *n.* [Sax. *sinc*] A drain to carry off filthy water."

Of course, this Victorian-era reticence wasn't just an army thing. In a meticulous scale drawing of the crew's quarters of the ironclad USS *Monitor* that appears in the *Battles and Leaders* series, there is nothing to indicate where these men answered nature's call. They had to go somewhere, and "over the side" just wouldn't do; the *Monitor*'s famous fight with the *Merri-*

mack (CSS *Virginia*) lasted for hours, and nobody on board either vessel was about to risk a pit stop on deck while enemy cannonballs were bouncing off the metal-plated hull. But on board the *Kitty Hawk,* the bathroom experience is too integral a part of ship's life to ignore.

A sign on the stainless-steel door reads "Officers' Head." Bathrooms, like most of the living spaces on this ship, are restricted by rank. (So is the SEAL berth. The sign "Officers' Country" is prominently posted at the entry.)

The bathroom, like most spaces on board is "unfinished"; that is, the walls expose bundles of wires, pipes running in all directions, valves, meters, levers, handles, and arrows. The bottom line, however, is steel. It's what the floors, walls, and ceilings are made of. This bathroom has three toilet stalls and three shower stalls. The piping that services these fixtures seems complicated, but many bear black stenciled words that explain everything: "Salt Water In" and "Waste Water Out."

The only privacy I've enjoyed on ship is inside the toilet stall and the shower stall. Except for the common areas of my berth (which space is shared with dozens of others), the bathroom, at the moment, isn't being shared with anyone. I draw the shower curtain and put my face into the stream of water for about ten minutes.

Just then I hear a voice from the next stall.

"You with the media?"

"Yes, Sir." (He must've seen my identity badge hanging on the hook outside the shower.)

"Well, welcome aboard!" The voice seemed hearty and friendly for this hour of the morning.

"Thanks."

"By the way," the voice quickly added, "it's best not to take too long in the shower. We have to distill every drop we get, so try to conserve as much as possible. And hey, have a nice day."

He turned off his shower (which lasted less than a minute), I heard a towel whip around, and he was gone. Time elapsed from shower to dry to out: about three minutes. The officer who had gently admonished me—who he was, I never learned—was, of course, correct to do so. Where the hell did I think I was? At home with my multihead steam shower, heated towel rack, and cheap access to the ever-ready aquifer?

One by one, I am meeting my media colleagues. The first is Paul, a forty-something American who has been living in Madrid for twenty years. He's a photojournalist from Reuters and, because photography is what he loves, has probably never had to "work" a day in his career. I know *bubkes* about photography, and Paul's array of cameras, lenses, cases, flashes, and whatnot strikes me much as the sight of White men's matches and mirrors must have struck the first Indians who saw them. Paul has just returned from several weeks of taking pictures on the West Bank and Gaza.

"Pretty rough over there?" I asked.

Paul smiled and, for a moment, seemed lost in a thought. "I discovered long ago," he finally replied with a sigh, "that my duty in life is to bear witness to events, not judge them." *like Bernard Shaw in late 1980*

On paper, the words look pompous, but as expressed by Paul, they weren't. His look and his tone had a sense of helplessness and a hint of sadness. There weren't any bon mots to this, so I just shook his hand and smiled.

Paul introduces me to Mark, one of the few guys aboard older than I am. Tall, with a gray crew cut, he is also a photojournalist, working for Gannett newspapers and *Navy Times* newspaper. Mark is also different from every journalist on the boat in two other respects. First, he's a Navy veteran from the 1970s with sea time on the aircraft carrier USS *John F. Kennedy*. As far as I'm concerned, this makes him a genius; I can't even find the men's room without asking directions. Second, unlike most others on board, Mark is voluble. But this only adds to his glitter. In the first few minutes of conversation, he proves that he knows both the text and the subtext of Navy life.

"You know what the sailors call this boat?" Mark smirks.

"No."

"The Shitty Kitty."

"Really?"

"Sure, look around," he replies. "This boat's old. Old pipes, too many coats of paint, too many welds and rewelds. She's been around too long. Lots of sailors don't like her. She's a pain in the ass to clean and too damned expensive to run. That's why she's going to be mothballed in '06."

"What do you suppose they do with an old aircraft carrier?" I ask.

"Why?" he asks. "You in the market?"

Mark's a wiseass but affable. He's got my number. I'm the "new guy in town," the one who just last night fell off the turnip truck.

Standing patiently behind me is James, the face of the British Sky Television News crew that's on board. And in the tradition of television correspondents everywhere, it's a handsome face, cherubic, and blue-eyed, with a shock of blond hair that frequently requires his hand to brush it away. He is a gentleman whose sense of professional courtesy comes easy, an honest expression of a kind heart.

"We've been here for a few days now," he said. "If there's anything you need—directions, what-have-you—please don't hesitate to ask."

I smile and ask, "Where can I get something to eat?"

0615
Wardroom II

I'm on a roll this morning. It turns out that where I get my food is only a few frames past the head—which means that I know how to get there.

The wardroom is for officers only, and the media have been given a seagoing equivalent of a key to the city (except as already noted). This means that we have access to the wardrooms and the officers' heads and may walk through the blue-tiled corridors that are reserved for the higher ranks. I acknowledge everybody I pass, and all the kids say things like "Good morning, Sir," or "Are you finding everything you need, Sir?" It all makes me feel like I'm fifty years old, going on ninety. But damn if I don't relish the respect.

The wardroom is a hybrid of push-tray cafeteria and sit-down restaurant. A long, narrow p-way presents a cafeteria rail for sliding trays and various hot foods behind steaming glass counters. The white-uniformed kitchen crew stands behind the counters and doles out whatever you want. This morning it's eggs, potatoes, cold cereal, bacon, sausage, and waffles. It looks good, although I can't have much of it: half disqualified for diabetics and the other half for people struggling to keep some semblance of kosher. Fortunately, there is another p-way that is lined with beverage machines, including diet sodas, water, and, most important, coffee. This p-way leads to a nook with all the edibles that people with odd diets would want: a salad bar, whole-wheat bread, fruits and nuts, and cold cereals. What is especially interesting is that every beverage and most entrées are labeled with the number of calories they contain. And these aren't the tiny labels on the sides of food packaging; these are plaques with big letters that even middle-aged guys with bifocals can read.

What don't appear on plaques are the dining rules. Those have to be learned by observation which fortunately doesn't take long. The cues are few but will mark the diner as fit or unfit company, and thankfully (unlike my son's fraternity handshake) most can be intuited from simple notions of courtesy. One first asks permission to join those who are already seated; permission never seems to be refused, but it's an important gateway courtesy, the first cue that one is familiar with the rules. Once seated, don't intervene in conversations already under way unless asked. The pace of dining is more measured and better mannered than I've observed elsewhere. Napkins are placed in laps, food is consumed slowly and neatly, drinks aren't slurped, and voices aren't raised. When leaving to refill a beverage, one offers to refill those of others. When leaving the table permanently, one thanks one's fellow diners for the company and then excuses oneself.

Blue and khaki uniforms encircle the round tables; an occasional table is encircled by only green flight suits. These are pilots, and another dining cue becomes apparent: The pilots eat by themselves. No rule mandates this, of course, nor would a nonpilot be asked to leave or be made to feel uncomfortable if he sat down at a pilot's table. However, all things being equal—and in the wardroom they are usually equal—the pilots are simply left alone. I'm too damn blurry-eyed to think this morning, but it may express the unit cohesion that I've written about in the context of other wars. I make a mental note to follow this up.

In the meantime, I've located a promising table. Seated are two officers, who immediately introduce themselves after I request permission to join them. One man looks to be in his mid-thirties, is balding, wears black-framed glasses, and has a highly intelligent affect. The other is tall and pale with deep-set eyes. Both have soft hands.

"Raul L. Barrientos," one of the men says, offering his hand. "And this is my colleague, Steve Pollack." Pollack looks cautious but manages a "Welcome aboard." The two men give me a moment to sit and adjust my napkin, stir my coffee, and slice my wheat bread before asking me the routine questions: how I find life on the ship, what I think of the Navy, where I am from, what I do, and so forth. But I soon realize that these inquiries don't simply reflect the ennui of bored conversationalists. They are intended to vet me—for attitudes about the Navy, about the world these men and women inhabit, a world to which many of the officers are deeply committed. As in most conversations, interviews are reciprocal.

Each man wears a gold badge depicting two crossed sabers joined at the intersection by a gold oval with an oak leaf frieze. This is the badge of dental officers, and both men are doctors of dentistry. Lt. Cdr. Steven Pollack, Lieutenant Barrientos, and sixteen sailors together provide dental services to as many as fifty-five hundred men and women. They tell me that just about everything described in a dental textbook will eventually show up in their offices. "We're very busy," Dr. Barrientos says, "and on a ship there's nowhere to hide when the phone rings at 4:00 A.M." They don't do implants or braces; sailors needing those go elsewhere. But these men were eloquent about one simple fact of life: A serious toothache is enough to ground pilots and degrade the efficiency of any sailor unlucky enough to have one. And for obvious reasons, the usual treatments for dental pain—various synthetic or natural narcotics—are just as bad or worse than the ailment when it comes to maintaining the alertness necessary to perform most jobs on a warship. (I'm later told that during the 1991 Gulf War dental problems were a leading cause of medical evacuations.)

I was very curious about their experience in treating newly enlisted sailors aboard the *Kitty Hawk*. Dentition is one of the more obvious clues to social class. The poor can least afford dentistry; among those who can afford it, it is the first medical necessity cut in tough economic times. Still wondering about last night's experience on the sponson, I give in to an old prejudice about military service. "I'll bet a lot of these guys you see have never been to a dentist before," I remark.

Dr. Barrientos thinks for a moment before replying. "I wouldn't say that's true. When I first started years ago there was a larger percentage of people coming aboard with pretty bad teeth and not much dental hygiene. But even then it was a small percentage. In the years since, that number's gone down a lot."

"Why do you suppose?"

"For starters, I don't see these kids when they first show up. A lot of dental problems get fixed during their basic training. But there's still been a huge improvement over the last fifteen years. I don't know if it's because dental care has gotten more accessible in the country or if these kids are just more aware of how they look, and make it a priority not to have black spaces in their smiles."

1000
Engineering Training Room

Twenty embeds have gathered in this room to receive what the Navy calls "chemical, biological and radiological defense training." What this means is learning how to don a protective suit, put on a gas mask, and use self-injected drugs in the event of exposure. In my opinion, it is but one step above placing my head between my legs and kissing my ass good-bye. However, if we do get hit by a chemical or biological warfare (CBW) weapon, my opinion is likely to change.

The sailor instructing us is DC2 (SW) Donald Morgan of engineering's R-division. He is a compact, bespectacled young man, a concisely spoken twenty-something, who, like other sailors I've met here, handles himself with the aplomb of a fifty-year-old. And it is just my luck to be selected as the mannequin for modeling the suit.

This suit consists of a heavy, charcoal-lined dark green woodland camo jacket and trousers, fish shoes, gloves, gas mask, and the bag of drugs. The gas mask goes on first, then the trousers and the jacket, and finally the shoes, which are actually flat pieces of black rubber (vaguely resembling the outline of a fish) that are pulled over the foot and secured with thick black laces. The canvas drug bag that will be issued to each person in the event of a CBW attack (but is meanwhile kept locked up) contains atropine and diazepam (Valium).

Inside the protective suit, the temperature quickly zooms to triple digits. Movement is slow and, for pudgy, untrained, out-of-shape geezers like me, unsustainable for long—in my case, I would guess a few yards. But we are advised not to think about moving very much because perspired water will eventually have to be replaced, and trying to drink through these suits is a chore. We will be issued three canteens of water that connect via a special tube into the gas mask. We will also be given chemical detection strips that indicate not only the presence of toxins but also what kind they are. At every step, we are assured that the odds of this ship getting hit are practically nil.

Nevertheless, after years of Saddam's cat-and-mouse games with UN weapons inspectors, this drill and all it portends tell me that, mistaken our government may be about the tyrant's cache of poisons, but insincere it is not. The entire crew is walking around with bagged CBW gear strapped to their waists.

The Blue Rainbow

March 11
0001
Enlisted Mess

*H*UNGRY. But what remains of the salad bar in wardroom II is unappetizing. The ice in the glass bowl has melted and the lettuce floats. But Mark tells me about "midrats"—the combination supper-breakfast offered those sailors ending and those starting work between 2300 and 0100. And so I'm off to the enlisted mess.

I take my place at the end of a long line. The media are given officer privileges, so I could cut to the head of the line, but I wouldn't dare. I'm content with the "Yes, Sirs" and the "May I help you, Sir?" and won't push an unearned privilege any further. Besides, it's discourteous.

The differences between the enlisted mess and the officers' ward room are many but mostly atmospheric. The officers eat on blue linen, their flatware is fancier, their plates are cleared by white-coated attendants, and the large, round tables have real chairs. By contrast, the sailors eat on long metal picnic benches, there are no tablecloths, and they clear their own trays. Perhaps the biggest difference is the decibel level. The wardroom reminds me of lunch in the Red Room at Boston's Union Club. It's quiet, and the faint sound of ice tinkling in glasses can be heard above the murmured conversation.

But the enlisted mess has a large TV bracketed to the ceiling, and the volume is blasting. It needs to be, because this room is filled with life lived loudly. The sailors talk, high-five seldom-seen companions, and trade jokes, shoptalk, scuttlebutt, and the NBA scores du jour. It is the talk of the young:

— 94 —

sports, ports, the daily buzz, boyfriends, girlfriends, and just friends. My messmates politely welcome me but quickly resume talking to one another. Sitting at my table are two White men, a Black woman, two Asian men, and one Hispanic man.

The first thing I notice is myself taking notice. Why do I care what color these kids are? As I look at my fellow diners, it's apparent that they don't seem to care. The two Asians are sitting at opposite ends of the table and don't seem to know each other. One, a kid who looks about nineteen years old, is talking and laughing with the Black woman. One White guy apparently bunks with the Hispanic, and both are watching the basketball game on television. The other White guy is complaining about something to the other Asian, who looks skeptical. I look around the mess room and see this same deracinated and "de-ethnic" dispersion at *every* table. While there are cliques—groups of friends grabbing contiguous spots on a bench—they, too, seem racially and ethnically interspersed. It is as if some great and wise hand has snatched a flock of souls from the air and scattered them about the room, randomly as to race but knowingly as to temperament, sense of humor, and love of basketball.

I feel a little ashamed at being in such wonder. How different it is from, say, Harvard. During my undergraduate years in the mid-1970s, self-segregation by race and ethnicity—most notably at meals—was already pervasive. I remembered, too, that I observed the same self-segregation just a few years ago at my Twenty-fifth reunion. Indeed, today, when I take the occasional lunch at the Science Center or on the few occasions when I sneak through the dining area at Memorial Hall (for a look-see at the newly mounted regimental flag of the Twentieth Massachusetts), I've witnessed the same phenomenon. It's not invariable, of course, but common enough to be noticed.

But it's not common here. The Navy can order the integration of work crews and of berths. They can issue any damned order they want. But they cannot control the company one keeps at meals. Am I witnessing a fluke? I intentionally linger over my salad and then get up and fetch another. Meanwhile, sailors come and go, but the pattern of no pattern persists. Here in this place, nobody seems especially conscious of their own "heritage" (one of many civilian euphemisms) or of that of their messmates.

Is it this way throughout the ship? I leave the bow mess room and walk to the aft mess, which is just a few frames past wardroom II. I take a seat beneath the TV and scan the faces. Many are upturned toward the tube;

many are chatting; a few stare at their food. Yet it is the same story—racial, ethnic, and gender randomness.

Now I make a point of eavesdropping on conversations. In the otherwise dopey chatter of something-teens and twenty-somethings, I make a second discovery—genuineness. The talk is light and funny or intense and whining or loquacious or terse or competitive or the occasional punctuations of just listening ("uh-huh," "sure," "right"), but in all events, it lacks the formalism, the walking-on-eggshells effect of excessive sensitivity typical of exchanges between groups unaccustomed to exchanging anything. After raising three teenagers, I know a relaxed kid when I see one. And these kids, grumbling or content, seem relaxed, at least in each other's company.

I hadn't expected this. I always assumed that the military's much-touted success with affirmative action was defined not by genuine positives but by the absence of negatives. A person's race or gender would *not* impede enlistment, would *not* be an obstacle to promotion, and would *not* interfere with one's happiness in uniform. But analyzing racial, ethnic, or gender equality simply through an absence of negatives implies that these differences are equivalent to some infirmity, like the occasional news item about a handicapped person who *nevertheless* wins a footrace.

0130
Enlisted Smoking Sponson

I am now alive to this issue and want to understand it better. I have come to the living library of naval life, the smoking sponson, where a forty-five-minute cigar permits a real swim in the collective stream of consciousness of the enlisted world. As I walk through the hangar deck, things I had looked at without seeing suddenly became the most telling sights on the *Kitty Hawk*: Integration was everywhere. Engine mechanics crawling over jet cylinders, avionics specialists with their heads buried deep into the open panels of aircraft, G-3 ordnance squads moving dollies stacked with munitions, sailors sorting packages, camo-clad Navy cops walking their beat, groups in jogging shorts walking to the exercise room, and other sailors on break and just palling around were guys, girls, and every color in the human rainbow, and it was as natural and unthinking as drawing a breath.

And on the sponson, bathed in the soft red of the smoking lamp, it was the same story. If the Navy doesn't tell sailors with whom they must eat, it sure doesn't tell them with whom they may smoke. On the sponson, people don't have to talk with one another, and some do squeeze into a corner or lean over the rail, preferring their own company. But most don't. Most circulate, visit with friends, and talk shop or talk trash.

Sailors come and go, light their smokes, linger for a few minutes, have another if they have the time, or just flick their butts over the side and return to the artificial daylight of the ship. I chat with some about themselves, about what they do or what I do, and about what they hear or what I hear. I'm looking to understand the diversity around me, but not at the cost of strained conversation or embarrassment.

Standing next to me is a young man with an unlit cigarette in his mouth, patting himself down in search of a match.

"I got it," I said, and lit his smoke.

"Thanks."

"So where you from," I asked.

"Near Corinth, Mississippi." He had a drawl to match.

"Just a few miles down river from Shiloh," I said with a smile. "I've been to Corinth." He smiled and took another drag.

"So what do you think of the Navy?" I asked. Next to "where are you from?" this was the second most asked question on the sponson.

"So-so. I can take it or leave it."

"What's your job?"

"Engines. I work on the F-14."

A moment silence passed and then the opening.

"So what do *you* think of the Navy?" he finally asked.

"It's different," I said with a hint of ambivalence. "Boy, is it different." Fly cast.

"How so?" He asked, apparently intrigued. Fish rising.

"I've never seen so many different kinds of folks in one place. It's amazing," I volunteered.

"Takes some getting used to, huh?" he asked.

"You can say that again," I said. Now it was time to set the hook. "If I know Corinth," I said, "it couldn't have been too easy on you." This was dishonest of me. I had only driven through Corinth once, retracing Gen. Beauregard's line of retreat following the Battle of Shiloh.

He flicked his cigarette over the side and drew another. I lit it, and he grew thoughtful. Hook set.

"I had my share of problems with it at first," he confessed. "I made it through training OK, but I kept my distance. I knew I'd be with Blacks; there were some in my high school, but I kept my distance there, too. As far as Asians went, I'm not sure I ever met any before enlisting. I always figured, given their say, that people will stay with their own. I always did."

"So what happened here?"

"Same stuff at first. Then one day, a couple of weeks into it, we've got a big piece of an engine on chains, and somebody screwed up, and one of the chains slipped, and the damn thing nearly came down on my arm. But this Black dude standing next to me pulled me back and probably kept my arm from being crushed. Or worse."

"So he may have saved your life?" I asked, thinking that now I had "gotten" his story.

"No, no, it wasn't that," he smiled. "*That* just broke the ice. It was what happened afterwards."

"What happened?"

"*He spent the next few months teaching me my job.* And now we're shipmates."

He flicked his cigarette over the side and returned to the hangar. And the only one hooked was me.

Later, I look up some lines from Daniel Defoe's *The True-Born Englishman*:

> Thus from a mixture of all kinds began,
> That Het'rogeneous Thing, *An Englishman*:
> In eager Rapes, and furious Lust begot,
> Betwixt a Painted *Britton* and a *Scot*:
> Whose gend'ring Offspring quickly learnt to bow,
> And yoke their Heifers to the *Roman* Plough:
> From Whence a Mongrel half-bred Race there came,
> With neither Name nor Nation, Speech or Fame.
> In whose hot Veins Mixtures quickly ran,
> Infus'd betwixt a *Saxon* and a *Dane*.
> While their Rank Daughters, to their Parents just,
> Receiv'd all Nations with Promiscuous Lust.
> This Nauseous Brood directly did contain
> The well-extracted Blood of *Englishmen*. . . .

c. 0300
Wardroom II
Sailor's Phone

I've decided to file a report about diversity on the *Kitty Hawk* while the thoughts still swim in my coffee-soaked brain. Besides, a smoke on the sponson does wonders for my radio voice. The best public voices are all stained with coffee and tobacco. It's not healthy but does wonders for the baritone. Many people could vouch for this, but many, like the legendary Edward R. Murrow, are dead, and some of them from lung cancer.

As I'm sitting in wardroom II's television room, playing with my script and waiting for the sailor phone to clear, a chaplain opens the door and sticks his head in. (It is the one rank instantly recognizable even to dummies; his bluejump suit has a gold cross on his collar.)

"Hello, Chaplain," I said.

"How are you?" he replied, maybe a bit surprised to find me ensconced with a laptop in the otherwise empty room. "You look busy."

"Filing a radio report," I shrugged. Then an idea occurred to me. "Chaplain," I asked, "is there any conflict between religions on this boat?"

"All the time," he immediately replied.

"Really?" I was disappointed. His answer ran counter to my thesis.

"Oh, sure," he continued matter-of-factly, "lots of religious conflicts on board—but they're all over scheduling the use of the chapel!" He smiled, and I leaned back in the couch and began to laugh.

I had my ending.

The notes say that I'm allowed 30 seconds for this report, but I can't do it in less than 45 seconds, so screw it. Forty-five seconds long it will be, and even at 45 seconds, it's only a fraction of what needs to be said. Soon the sailor phone clears and I talk slowly and loudly:

> The looming war with Iraq and the use of United States aircraft carriers to project American power remains controversial with many Americans. Opinions about the desirability of war divide many, not only on shore but on this ship as well. But there is an aspect to life on the *Kitty Hawk* that divides no one: The Navy has succeeded where civilian life has failed in abolishing the color line. A glance at the mess hall tells the story. White, black, yellow, and brown dine together as groups of friends, not races. Every hue on earth will be found scattered in every rank throughout this ship. In talking off the record

with many sailors about shipboard issues, the question of affirmative action never arose—perhaps because it doesn't have to. Life aboard this ship can be hard, but the work and the dangers are equally shared. When I asked the chaplain if there were any religious conflicts on board, he replied, "Yes, but only scheduling conflicts about using the chapel." The American military may be bringing hope to some Iraqis; but it can also bring hope to many Americans who despair over the prospects of our multicultural society.

I also had an idea for my first interview.

God on the *Kitty Hawk*: The Ship's Chaplain

. . . for sailors are almost all believers; but their notions and opinions are unfixed and at loose ends. They say,—"God won't be hard upon the poor fellow," and seldom get beyond the common phrase which seems to imply that their sufferings and hard treatment here will excuse them hereafter,—"To work hard, live hard, die hard, and go to hell after all, would be hard indeed!"

—Richard Henry Dana Jr.
MONDAY, NOVEMBER 19, 1834
Two Years Before the Mast

1400
Office of Chaplain Gary Carr

AT MY REQUEST, Brook De Walt arranged a meeting for me with Chaplain Gary Carr, one of the four chaplains serving aboard the *Kitty Hawk*. My interest here is strictly academic. I have spent the past two years reading hundreds of Civil War eulogies for soldiers and sailors, period sermons about the meaning of that war, countless secondary sources about martyrdom from the time of Socrates, the Maccabees, Jesus, Flavius Josephus, the early Christian martyrs, and John Foxe's *Acts and Monuments*. In America during the mid-nineteenth century, practically all public discourse was couched in biblical language, metaphors, allusions, or outright invocations; when war came, the language of sacrifice, martyrdom, and blood imagery fills both written and spoken discourse. Scholars have posited various theories about "why that generation fought," including peer pressure, social class, coercion, shame, ideological motives, "small group cohesion," and religious values. I believe that, given the prevalence of religious imagery and ideas in virtually all aspects of American life during the first half of the nineteenth century, too little attention has been paid to the influence of religious ideas on combat motivation.

But today I don't care about mid-nineteenth-century America. What I want to know is about the influence of religion in today's Navy.

More ladders up, down, and crossways. Since I already know that I'm going to get lost, I start very early and arrive a little early. The chaplains' area is a suite of three main spaces: a large room with a small, receptionist-served sitting area, which faces the private offices of the chaplains; the chapel itself; and the chaplains' library, a space crowded with stacks of books, videos, and music recordings. However, the library's major draw seems to be a large-screen television. Like every other open space on this boat, it is crowded with sailors. Except for the blaring TV, however, this room has its own etiquette that starts with a curious and, in spite of the television, a very personal silence. Unlike the mess hall, the sponsons, the hangar deck, or any other space on board, here, no one talks. They watch television, but they don't watch television. I take a seat among them and discover that some sleep, look at personal mail, or just stare away into some far-off, unknowable place of mind, which is probably the only space aboard where a sailor can really be alone.

When I rise to meet Chaplain Carr, I am surprised to discover that he is the same man who the night before had stuck his head in the wardroom and answered my tactless question with more grace than it deserved. (Now, he either didn't remember or pretended not to remember.) A full commander, the chaplain stood slightly shorter than average, a bit stocky, a mustached man with a round, open face and the personal style of a natural gentleman. He was soft-spoken yet penetrating in conversation without dominating or—forgive the word—preachy. He is a man whose own radar works overtime to map the emotional contours of whomever he's with, to locate both the jagged edge and the smooth spot.

"Chaplain," I said, wishing to dispense with one very special open item, "is there some sort of discretionary chaplain's fund I could contribute to? I would like to make a small donation."

He seemed surprised. "Well, we don't really have a fund per se, but it's very kind of you to offer."

"No," I replied, "the kindness would be all yours. Before I left the States, my rabbi entrusted me with a *shliach mitzvah*—if a traveler is bound to perform a good deed both on his arrival and return, God may provide an extra measure of protection for his journey."

"I've never heard of that before," he said, genuinely surprised. He immediately asked his receptionist to come in. I handed her the ten-dollar bill the rabbi had given me.

"What a beautiful practice," Carr said. I think he meant it.

The rabbi had asked me to make the donation, but I now realized that, intended or not, another purpose had been served by my offer. Chaplain Carr, an ordained Methodist minister with twenty-six years of naval service, proved to be "safe." (Of course, he was always safe, except in the mind of an overly sensitive Jew unaccustomed to dealing with Gentile clerics.) I wasn't roasted by him, so I found it easier to warm up. We then spoke generally about how the Navy accommodates religious practice.

"The Navy recognizes over two hundred religious denominations," he began.

"Does the roster include a chaplain for each denomination?"

He smiled, unsure whether I was genuinely incredulous or just joking. I wasn't certain myself.

"No, but chaplains are cross-trained in one another's rituals and traditions. On the *Kitty Hawk* now are three chaplains besides myself—Pastor Roman, who is with the Assembly of God; Father Cunya, a Roman Catholic priest; and Chaplain O'Halloran, who is Evangelical Episcopal. We also have lay leaders on board. One of our ship's doctors conducts Shabbat services for Jewish sailors, and also on Fridays, afternoon prayer for Muslims is led by our Muslim lay leader. There are now three imams in the Navy."

"How do you identify a sailor's religion?"

"Purely self-identified by enlistees," he replied. "Obviously, nobody is forced to practice any particular faith or any faith at all. But we do have one interesting practice, and from all that I gather, the sailors find it helpful."

"What's that?"

"The evening prayer. It's on the mike at 2200 every night."

I sat back in my chair. *So that's what I heard over the intercom the past two nights.* I thought I had heard the words "evening prayer" but probably screened it out from disbelief. Was such a thing possible on public property other than "In God We Trust" on coins and currency? Most of these sailors had gone through the public schools, where professing a belief in any deity was as welcome as chest pain in a sixty-year-old. The Navy's stock, already very high in my book, rose even higher.

"Of course, it's completely nonsectarian," he added.

Yeah, but it's *something,* I thought.

Chaplain Carr said that his twenty-six years included service during the 1989 Panamanian invasion and the first Gulf War.

"So you've had experience dealing with the effects of combat on sailors?" I ask.

"And pilots," he added.

"What do you do when somebody comes in with combat fatigue?"

"For us, pastoral care is really the mitigation of stress," he replied. "Of course, that's true for combat and noncombat situations. But dealing with combat stress requires a special approach. The chaplains operate as a team no matter what particular differences there are on matters of religious doctrine or ritual. We also work closely with the ship's doctors and the ship's psychologist. Dealing with combat stress today is really a collaborative effort among several departments."

What Chaplain Carr calls combat stress has had many names in many wars. Eric T. Dean Jr., in *Shook over Hell: Post-Traumatic Stress, Vietnam, and the Civil War*, observes that what is now called posttraumatic stress syndrome (PTSD) "is only the most recent incarnation of psychological problems that earlier American veterans experienced under the rubric of combat fatigue, shell shock, or in the Civil War era, melancholia, nostalgia and irritable heart."

The different terms used in the past to describe this disorder are easily matched to the military tactics and technology of particular wars, as well as prevailing social attitudes. During the Civil War, there were no scientifically established diagnostic categories for depression ("nostalgia" or "melancholia") or related anxieties ("irritable heart"), and doctors had little patience for soldiers showing symptoms that today might be considered as PTSD. The typical attitude was expressed by Roberts Bartholow, a Federal surgeon who had spent years in the prewar army and who stayed with the Union after the attack on Fort Sumter. In 1863 he wrote *A Manual of Instructions for Enlisting and Discharging Soldiers.* In combining practical advice and a summary of War Department regulations (the subtitle said it all: *With Special Reference to the Medical Examination of Recruits, and the Detection of Disqualifying and Feigned Diseases*), Dr. Bartholow devoted several chapters to advising surgeons on how to smoke out malingerers, the common term for men thought to be feigning illness in order to secure a discharge, beat work details, or evade combat. Among other behaviors that Bartholow thought to be dodges could be found among men who

> decline to fix the locality of their pains, who content themselves with the assertion that they suffer "all over," and who spend their time in bed or in lounging about the wards, and can with difficulty be induced to take exercise in the open air. They oppose a passive resistance to all the measures for relief proposed for their benefit, are dull, listless, and apparently absorbed in the contemplation of their sufferings.[1]

Bartholow described these men as "a class of malingerers" and he advised stealth to detect their fraud. He urged physicians to covertly watch them for "the inconsistencies of the patient observed when he supposes himself free from *espionnage* [*sic*]."

World War I was characterized by fixed trenches (at least on the Western Front) in which the long interludes between battles were filled with constant artillery exchanges, sometimes including chemical weapons. That generation understood combat stress in terms of "shell shock," since unremitting exposure to these relentless barrages appeared to cause the disorder. But by World War II, the dominance of mechanized warfare produced rapidly mov-

---

1. In an interesting sidelight to Dr. Bartholow's description, a recent edition of the *Merck Manual* includes the following description under "symptoms and signs" of posttraumatic stress disorder: "Most patients, furthermore, complain of a numbing of their responsiveness to people, objects, and events, in the world around them. They lose interest in their usual pursuits, feel emotionally dead and unreal, and experience detachment and estrangement from others." It looks like Bartholow's "malingering" and contemporary PTSD are quite similar. What a difference a theory makes!

ing armies whose fluid fronts could shift hundreds of miles in brief periods of time; moreover, war was now largely liberated from the ancient constraints of season and climate. This meant that active operations were ongoing every day of the year. Logically perhaps, combat stress was now understood as "combat fatigue." (However, among some, the Civil War view survived well into the twentieth century. In 1943, Gen. George S. Patton visited a military hospital, slapped a soldier who had been admitted for combat fatigue, and accused him of cowardice. Afterward, Gen. Dwight D. Eisenhower reprimanded Patton and forced him to apologize publicly to the offended soldier and the hospital staff. Whatever prejudice the old guard expressed against combat fatigue probably ended with this episode.)

In 1980, in the wake of the Vietnam War, the American Psychiatric Association officially admitted PTSD into the canon of psychiatric illness. However, PTSD, like its predecessor diagnostic categories, was also time-bound in its conception through its linkage to the specific conditions of Vietnam. Eric Dean states that

> the Vietnam veteran has come to serve in the United States as a psychological crucible for the entire country's doubts and misgivings about the Vietnam War, and about war in general. Consequently, America's continuing agony, grief and obsession with Vietnam is largely explained by the perception that Vietnam veterans incurred harm that was catastrophic, tragic, persistent, and completely out of proportion to any good that the war accomplished or might have accomplished.

PTSD was thus originally rooted in the political judgment that tended to cast veterans as victims. However, in the generation since PTSD was formally recognized, its etiology has grown. The *Merck Manual*'s summary includes stressors such as fires, explosions, airplane crashes, floods, earthquakes, and tornadoes, as well as combat and POW situations.

Chaplain Carr's career corresponded almost exactly with the unfolding of this enlightenment in military mental health. And there was nothing in his approach that suggested that he viewed PTSD as something other than a treatable psychological problem, which, if dealt with early ("if possible, 24 to 72 hours after the experience," he said), would allow the subject to move on with his or her life.

"So if you're dealing with someone you believe has combat stress, what do you do?" I asked.

The chaplain laid out the approach with a good lawyer's precision.

"I make an evaluation based on four things. First, I look at their proximity to the action. How close physically were they to the experience? Am I dealing with a pilot who dropped ordnance on a target or one of the G3 crew who placed that ordnance on the flight deck? Second, I look to duration. How long were they exposed? Was it a POW situation lasting months, or was it something that somebody experienced only for a moment? Third is intensity. What exactly did they see? Was it a quick look at death or destruction, or was it someone's agony in dying? Finally, I look at precondition. Is there anything unique about that individual that leaves him or her especially vulnerable to what they experienced? Lots of things go into the mix here. A person's feelings and fears about death, their religious and cultural background, and any issues of guilt and personal responsibility they might have. There are probably as many factors here as there are people on board this ship."

One question that most civilians would like to ask those who are asked to take human life at their country's call is "How does it feel to kill someone?" Most people understand the pure tactlessness of the question and never ask. When I was a young boy, I did ask my father, a battle-scarred World War II veteran of the Pacific War. I was met by a glaring silence, followed by an admonition that smoldered with feelings I had never witnessed before. "*Never, ever, ever* ask a man that question!" he said in a quiet voice that nonetheless seemed to shake the walls.

"How do you deal with those who may have guilty feelings about taking life?" I asked, still smarting from my father's reaction some forty years earlier.

Chaplain Carr became thoughtful, although it was not because he was searching for a reply. I guessed that he was recollecting some private pain associated with his mission.

"What we don't do is judge," he finally said. "The first thing is to communicate that what they're feeling is a completely normal reaction to an abnormal event. We emphasize that during war, the responsibility for taking life is a corporate responsibility. And every person on ship, from the bakers to the boiler operators, shares in that responsibility, because without sailors to operate the ship, check the weather, and staff the hospitals, no one could fulfill any combat assignment. While somebody may drop a bomb or fire a missile, that person is really at the end of a long line of command that starts with the president of the United States."

"But in telling a sailor that everyone's responsible, isn't that like saying that no one is responsible?" I wondered.

"Not really, because any understanding of that 'long line of command' has to include the Congress who votes in support of military action and the American people who elect both them and the president. In other words, anyone who personalizes guilt needs to understand that what they are asked to do here is to carry out the policy of the government, not execute a private vendetta. We remind our people that the government is not some emperor but acts through a majority of the American people (which includes their own friends and family) who act through the chain of command. So policies may be mistaken, but they are deliberated in a democratic way and agreed to after debate and a vote. The point is that a sailor who pushes a button is no guiltier of taking a life than every other civilian or uniformed person who supports them."

The chaplain had raised an important issue, perhaps the key issue with the Bush-Rumsfeld policy of preemptive war against states harboring terrorists or developing weapons of mass destruction. Democracies may win wars and may even win them handily, but they get into them only after a lot of kicking and shouting, with debates, speeches, votes, editorials, opinion polls, protest marches, dueling talking heads, arguments around water coolers and living rooms, teach-ins, seminars, full-page newspaper advertisements, and press conferences with Hollywood celebrities and members of the UN Security Council. By the time all of that plays out, one way or another, there either is—as there currently is for action against Iraq—or is not a domestic consensus in favor of military action. After that kind of a process, it would be difficult to deny the chaplain's corporate responsibility thesis. It also fulfills one of the objectives of the Nuremberg trials of Nazi war criminals after World War II. That trial not only fixed personal responsibility (having been ordered to commit war crimes was not a defense) but also sought to impose responsibility on Germany as a nation for what had happened. The perspective urged by Chaplain Carr is arguably based on this premise.

Anyway, I suppose if a sailor doesn't want to push a button, he has other options—the Navy no longer hangs sailors who jump ship.

But one thing troubled me as I considered the chaplain's role in all of this. My recent studies included secondary works that persuasively documented the declining power and prestige of American clergymen during the course of the nineteenth century. And there wasn't much that had happened in the twentieth century to reverse that trend.

"Chaplain," I wondered, "in the civilian world when somebody has a stressor, the first call they're likely to make is to a shrink, not necessarily their local minister."

He smiled. "Of course. And the Navy has psychiatrists and psychologists. In fact, we have a first-rate ship's psychologist right here on the *Kitty Hawk*—Dr. Jennifer Johnson." (I scribbled her name down and made a note to arrange an interview.) "But," he continued, "we like to think we have many things, but we know there is one thing that we have that is really unique in the Navy."

"And that is?"

"Absolute confidentiality. The admiral himself couldn't make me reveal what I'm told while counseling a sailor."

Law school had familiarized me with the priest-penitent privilege as an exception to discovery, but it wasn't the only exception (there is the doctor-patient privilege, for example); I didn't quite understand why that made chaplains unique. Unfortunately, this question occurred *esprit de l'escalier*.

c. 1500
The Chapel

Chaplain Carr gave me a tour of the chapel, which was located only a few steps from his office. It is a large, well-lit room with movable chairs and a podium at the front. There were prayer books stacked on small tables against the walls and wooden cabinets where different faiths stored ritual items. But what caught my immediate attention was the art on the wall, for a ship of war is a singularly artless place. There hung a huge backlit mural of colored glass depicting the *Kitty Hawk* at sea protected from above by two large hands, presumably belonging to God. It was not anything that one would find at a synagogue—at least a traditional *shul*—but it had a powerful effect on me, a reminder that the sea was a large place, like the universe, and that the *Kitty Hawk* was tiny, just like the earth, and that whatever divided us paled by comparison to what did (or should) unify us: that whoever we were, as passengers aboard this vessel, our fates were all in the same tight weave—and all under the watchful eye of the Divine.

I wondered how relevant this place really was. After all, the diminished role of clerics over the last two centuries only reflected the increased secularization of the Western world in general.

"How important is this place to the sailors here?" I asked. My tone probably suggested a subtext of "does anyone really care?"

Just before he could reply, several sailors tentatively entered the room, unsure if their presence was an intrusion.

"Many of these kids," the chaplain said, "come to the Navy to transform. They arrive with a faint faith, and many leave with a much stronger faith. What I do is bring in God on the job."

Boys and Girls on the *Kitty Hawk*

> *In this country [England] it is thought well to kill an admiral from time to time to encourage the others.*
>
> —*Candide*, by Voltaire

March 12
1230
SEAL Berth

DISASTER! Returned from the head this morning and discovered that my camera had, in the Navy's words, "grown legs and walked away." It was a brand-new Canon PS-230 digital camera, about the size of a pack of cigarettes, and it took great pictures. On the way to my rack last night, I was too damn tired to futz with my locker, so I just stuffed it behind a wall space, thinking it was secure. It serves me right for thinking that, after forty-eight hours, I knew better than a good thief where to hide things on this boat. Besides, I was beginning to aggrandize the Navy and all of its sailors. There is nothing like a brush with depravity to restore one's faith in complete cynicism.

On the other hand, this may represent a reporting opportunity. It's lemons into lemonade, and all that. Getting ripped off is part of living anywhere. I decide to go through the system. I'll report the theft and see what there is to be learned. I have no hope of recovering the camera—the last time I was robbed, a $100 cell phone was taken in an office of forty people who probably made, on average, about $200,000 per year. Go figure.

The evening before I had eaten supper with Lt. Andrea Schreiber, whose nickname is the Sheriff. She runs ship security for the *Kitty Hawk*, which probably means that no matter how smart she seems—and she seemed as sharp as a razor—she's probably a lot smarter. I have scheduled an interview with her for tomorrow, but it looks like I'll have to talk to her today.

1250
Walking through the Hangar Deck

The captain has just been on the 1MC to announce an approaching sandstorm. A sandstorm? I thought that was something that happened only to the French Foreign Legion. The ship will be battened-down, vents will be secured, hatches and hangar doors closed—in fact, similar measures to those taken in the face of an impending chemical or biological weapons attack. It's not supposed to hit until very late tonight, but still—a sandstorm? We're in the middle of the Persian Gulf!

1316
CV-63 Security Patrol Office

I'm facing Boson's Mate 3 and Security Patrolman Holloway, who is sitting on the other side of an old gray metal desk and completing a form called a voluntary statement. In spite of the title "patrol*man*," BM3 Holloway is really a she, a young twenty-something, rosy-cheeked girl with strawberry blonde hair who is wearing a regulation blue jumpsuit and who has just now instantly (and for her sake, I hope temporarily) assumed the grave mien of an investigating police officer. It must be doubly hard in this case because I'm convinced that when she looks at me, she's thinking that the jerk sitting across from her was too damned lazy to lock up his expensive camera at night, too damned stupid if he thought he was going to outwit the veteran thieves on this boat, and as a member of the media, he's probably a liar and a scoundrel to boot. Whatever she's thinking, she's very new at this, because every slot on the form provokes a "how-do-I?" question to the security officer standing behind a nearby counter that functions like the night desk at a precinct house. Sailors come and go, forms are given and returned, and questions are answered, all relating to ship security. It's a busy place.

"How do you like the Navy?" I ask BM3 Holloway.

"And Sir, what hour of the day did you first notice the camera missing?" she replied.

"About 1100," I answered, then added, "So how long have you been in the Navy?"

"Was anything else besides the camera taken?"

"A battery and a 16-bit flash card." I waited and smiled while she clicked off details of the theft on her computer keyboard. I was about to ask her another question, but I finally got the message that this wasn't the smoking sponson, that BM3 Holloway had a job to do, and that there was an extreme outside possibility (given the age difference, very outside and very extreme) that I was perhaps violating some hitherto unsuspected code of gender etiquette on a vessel where women numbered only 15 percent (just over eight-hundred) of the fifty-five hundred sailors aboard.

I must have observed something like this on the sponson (yet without noting it) because as I sat with Boson Holloway, a few smoking lamp-lit images from the sponson came to mind. There the atmosphere was relaxed with laughter and the easy trash talk of young people on break. But perhaps that did not include all of the young people. How the men and women related to one another now struck me as slightly askew; the camaraderie between the men was absent between men and women; the women didn't really circulate as the guys did; many smoked alone or stuck to one group and remained smoking with them. The men did not showboat for the women, and the women did not flirt with the men. It had the feel of a middle school prom where the kids are too polite and too concerned about faux pas because their well-scrubbed ears were still full of a parent's advice urging boys who were not yet men to behave as if they were.

After the word processor had finished, Security Patrolman Holloway asked me to review the voluntary statement and then sign it. There was also an oath. I raised my right hand and swore that the statement "is true and complete to the best of knowledge," which indeed it was, with the single exception that I had omitted any acknowledgement that I was a dummy for having left the camera out in the first place.

I thanked BM3 Holloway for her help and wished her well. But she did not reply.

c. 1500
SEAL Berth

I take my seat at one of the four computers and log on to check my E-mail. Sitting next to me is Mark Faram, photojournalist and Navy wiseman extraordinaire. He's just returned from the flight deck and is now reviewing his amazing handiwork, dramatic pictures of launches, recoveries, and the people who make them happen: jets at the moment of rotation, the collective drama of launch crews, the vaporing trails of catapults discharging their winged trusts, helmeted heads of flight deck workers silhouetted against the sky. In his work, he must borrow time that doesn't exist and freeze fluid actions that can't really be frozen. He must do it in his mind's eye long enough to recognize a picture, intuitively understand its significance, and then record it.

"Hey, Mark, is it me, or do the men and women on this ship act weird toward each other?" I asked.

"Well, you know what they call the *Kitty Hawk*, don't you?" he asked.

"Shitty Kitty?"

"Besides that."

"No."

"Well, you and I are old enough to remember who Gavin McCloud is, right?" he asked. I knew I was being set up for something funny. I searched my brain, but it didn't take long.

"Didn't he play the captain of . . . *The Love Boat*?" I asked, immediately breaking into a smile.

Faram smiled. "Are you online yet?" he asked.

"No. Slow as molasses today."

"Well, when you are," he said, "go to a search engine, type in *Kunkle*—with two *K*s—then *Kitty Hawk*. You might find some answers there."

The Love Boat was a 1970s television show about *The Princess*, a cruise ship where each week a crew of regulars, which included the stock shipboard characters of captain, ship's doctor, purser, and so forth, interacted with passengers who had boarded, it always seemed, to find love, or one another, or a galactic truth. Like all of these shows, nobody had politics, religion, or terminal illness; nobody dropped dead from a cardiac infarction or had schizophrenia or lupus. It was a seagoing utopia that might be missing the existential Anguish of Abraham, but in return, the characters had each other. And each other person was evaluated not on the basis of being a Jew who controlled the banks, international finance, and the media, or an Arab wrapped in explosives, or a gun-grabbing liberal, or a corrupt union boss, a poverty pimp, a Catholic, a crooked Enron executive, a Socialist, a neo-con, a hateful boss, someone from France, or a Serb. No, it was love—finding it, getting it, keeping it.

Soon I was looking at an article from *Stars and Stripes* dated February 14, 2003, titled "Kunkle is relieved as commander of USS *Kitty Hawk* Battle Group." A few excerpts:

> The USS *Kitty Hawk* Battle Group commander, Rear Adm. Steven Kunkle, was relieved of command Thursday, accused of an "inappropriate relationship" with a female officer. . . . [a spokesman said]. "Vice Admiral Willard [Kunkle's superior] took action as a result of his loss in confidence in Rear Admiral Kunkle's ability to shape morale, good order and discipline in his assigned forces as evidenced by his part in this inappropriate relationship" [a spokesman said].

What were the effects on overall morale of the admiral's alleged philandering? Interpreting official releases requires something of the old Kremlinologist's skill, but a few paragraphs later, the article offered several possible clues. First, the spokesman wouldn't identify the lady in question, "although," he said, "I can tell you that she is not in Rear Adm. Kunkle's chain of command." Translation: By *shtupping* somebody outside the flag staff, Kunkle probably increased the number of people who knew about the affair. And finally, a key disclosure: "[The spokesman said] an individual notified the chain of command of what the spokesman termed 'credible concerns about a possible inappropriate relationship.'" Translation: Some underling dropped a dime on Kunkle. It could have been a grudge, but my own twenty-six-year tour of duty in the securities industry (a high-pressure business that breeds philanderers) suggests two factors that typically motivate the dime-dropper—jealousy (of one or more of the partners) or job favoritism that doesn't favor the dime-dropper. Either way, affairs stink for morale.

As I was about to leave the Net, one other ostensibly unrelated news story caught my eye—unrelated and absolutely on point. It quoted a woman who had served on board the *Kitty Hawk*. Describing her first weeks on ship, she remembered, "When I got there, no one would talk to me. They were afraid to look at me. They were convinced if they said 'boo' I would scream sexual harassment." Although this story predated the Kunkle episode, something told me that with dime-droppers afoot, both men and women naturally become more cautious. After all, informality could be misinterpreted, and as the Navy puts it, discovery in these cases is a "career ender."

Maybe BM3 Holloway was simply in a bad mood, or maybe my breath was bad. But that wouldn't explain the tension I sensed out on the sponson. Perhaps the heat was on.

1645
The Brig

If an aircraft carrier is a small city, then it must have a jail. The *Kitty Hawk* has a jail—in naval parlance, a brig—and it's reportedly well used. When I supped with Lieutenant Schreiber last night, I asked for a tour of the brig, and she promised one today. There was only one condition: The brig would have to be empty of inmates. For a variety of understandable reasons, the Navy forbids media free-for-alls in its inhabited jails. Unusually (and luckily for me), no one is currently in the pokey.

Like most civilians, my only prior acquaintance with brigs is from Holly-wood movies. What are the elements of a Hollywood brig? It's always located in the bowels of the ship, wherever those are—or actually were, since Hollywood brigs show up only in films about navies from the days of wooden hulls and canvas sails. Such navies had no electric power, of course, so the brig was always dark; the only source of light was usually an oil lamp hung from a beam just outside the bars, and it rocked to and fro with the motion of the ship. There was always a wooden bucket present that served some unknown function. Was it for sanitary purposes? Perhaps for food or water? It's never clear, but using such a bucket for either purpose seems distasteful. Punishment rations were always moldy bread and dirty water.

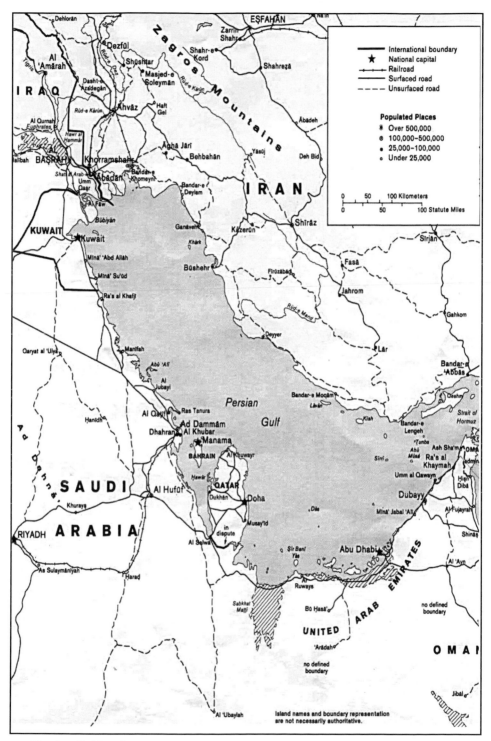

Persian Gulf region

Prior to Operation Iraqi Freedom, in November 2002, flight deck crewmembers conduct an aircraft barricade rigging exercise. Two hydraulically operated stanchions support nylon straps which form a net across the deck to stop aircraft making an emergency landing, when landing gear has failed or sustained damage *(courtesy of the U.S. Navy)*.

Seagoing art adorns certain departments of the ship, in this case that of the Marine gunners.

Miller on board the USS *Kitty Hawk* in plane handler gear

Kneeling in front of Phoenix missiles, ordnancemen help promote Talk Radio News Service, the author's sponsor.

An aerial view of USS *Kitty Hawk* (CV-63) en route to the 5th Fleet area of operations in support of Operation Enduring Freedom *(courtesy of the U.S. Navy)*.

Kitty Hawk (CV 63), the Navy's only forward-deployed carrier, at high-speed. Commissioned on 29 April 1961, the carrier became the oldest ship in the Navy on 30 September 1998. During Operation Iraqi Freedom, it hosted more than forty national and international media representatives simultaneously, the most by any ship in U.S. naval history *(courtesy of the U.S. Navy)*.

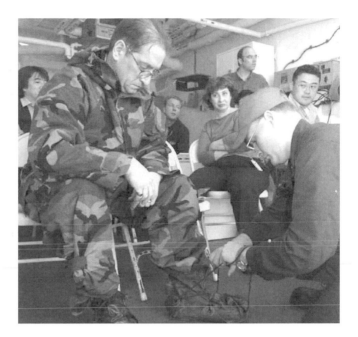

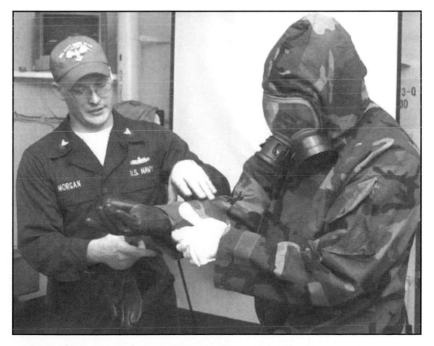

In these photographs (above), the author's colleagues look on as Petty Officer Donald Morgan outfits him with a CBW (chemical-biological weapons) protective suit.

Weapons line *Kitty Hawk*'s hangar bay on 22 March 2003 (*U.S. Navy photograph by Journalist 1ˢᵗ Class Dwayne S. Smith*).

The business end (shrouded) of a Phoenix missile, which is used exclusively on hte F-14A/B/C Tomcat aircraft. Its length is 13 feet and it weighes 1,000 pounds.

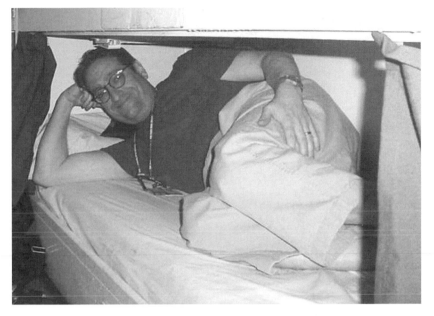

Miller demonstrating the close quarters and tight bunking arrangements that the majority of the carrier's enlisted men and women must share.

who's arguing!

Xiaoming Hu, correspondent for Xinhua News Agency in China.

Petty Officer Michael Bailey. The eternal sailor—smart and lucky—and willing to rent his camera.

Lt. j.g. Jeb Colt after a mission during "Shock and Awe." Colt seemed older to the author here than he did earlier in the afternoon.

Dr. Eric Elster, during a rare moment of relaxation for this seagoing RAMBAM.

A thoughtful warrior, Lt. Bill Blacker

With arms upraised, the aircraft handling officer spots F/A-18 Hornets (CVW-5) for launch in these photographs.

(Above) Steam from the previous launch still rises. Catapults thrust a 48,000-pound aircraft 300 feet, from zero to 165 miles per hour in 2 seconds.

An S-3B Viking armed with conventional bombs prepares for launch.

A member of the catapult crew kneels to attach the aircraft's towing bridle to the catapult, preparing an F/A-18 Hornet for launch.

The aircraft handling officer signals for launch. Note the rescue helicopter in the background.

Arresting gear crew watch as an F-14 Tomcat of CVW-5 lands on board *Kitty Hawk*.

An aircraft handling officer and a member of Carrier Air Wing Five (CVW-5) monitor the "ouija board," which indicates the spot of every aircraft on the flight deck at all times.

Aviation Warfare Systems Operator 2nd Class Matthew Wittman checks the oil level of an SH-60F Seahawk tail rotor gearbox while on the flight deck. This is one of the helicopter anti-submarine squadron's pre-flight checks while undergoing an extensive five-month maintenance period in Yokosuka, Japan. *(U.S. Navy photo by Photographer's Mate 3rd Class Jason R. Williams).*

Kitty Hawk (top), with Carrier Air Wing Five embarked, and sistership *Constellation* (CV 64), with Carrier Air Wing Two embarked, underway in the Arabian Gulf on 13 April 2003. *Constellation* was decommissioned in August 2003 *(U.S. Navy photograph by Photographer's Mate 3rd Class Adam Gomez).*

On 6 May 2003, tugs assist *Kitty Hawk* in the ship's return to Yokosuka, Japan from her deployment to the Arabian Gulf *(U.S. Navy photograph by Photographer's Mate 1st Class David A. Levy).*

Seagoing art from the sailors who move the bombs and missiles between decks: "Chapter 63" refers to the ship's hull number, CV 63.

Rear Adm. James D. Kelly, Commander of Carrier Group 5, leads master chief petty officers, senior chief pettyofficers, chief petty officers and chief petty officer selectees on a run past the USS *Kitty Hawk (U.S. Navy photo by Chief Journalist (SW) Rick Chernitzer)* .

After Operation Iraqi Freedom, *Kitty Hawk* entered drydock in Yokosuka for repairs and upgrades that would extend the ship's life for another five years *(courtesy of the U.S. Navy)*.

The Hollywood brig was cramped, and the wooden ship's creaking was loudest there, which, coupled with the loneliness of solitary confinement (I've rarely seen more than one inmate in a Hollywood brig), amplified the sense of confinement and hence punishment. But the brig was not without its pluses. It was safe, at least relative to what the audience knew *could* have been the punishment—hanging from the yardarm, keelhauling, walking the plank, running a gauntlet, or having stripes publicly laid on with a cat-o'-nine-tails.

The *Kitty Hawk*'s brig is tucked into a corner of the hangar deck; there's some stairs, a series of buzzer-opened doors, and, of course, an escort. Once inside, chief jailer MA1 Brandon Denison from El Paso, Texas, conducts the tour. I recognize him from the smoking sponson. He is a tall, neatly attired man (late twenties?) with bloused trousers and a very professional air. He introduces me to two colleagues, ABE2 Christopher Peabody from Lancaster, California, and MA2SW Gregory Schlumpf from Carollton, Texas. Three things are clear from the outset: First, like all the sailors I've met here, these guys are intensely proud of what they do, and regard their function as indispensable to the ship's mission; second, they talk, move, and act in the kind of natural synchronization found among good friends who spend lots of time in each other's company; third, working down here isn't just a job, or an adventure—it's a parallel universe.

"We could be at war right now," Mr. Denison tells me, "and working here, I'd never know it. Down here we're sort of cut off from the world upstairs."

The brig is really a long, narrow steel hallway with three barred cells lining one side. It holds up to eleven inmates. Unlike Hollywood's dark and dank brig, here it is very light and dry. It isn't as cramped as movie brigs, which is not to say that it's spacious. But each cell does have a normal bed and mattress (as distinct from the berthing racks), a chair, and a Bible. Cells are also monitored by camera from television screens in a small anteroom, which is the jailers' office. The three men who staff this facility are in a sense prisoners themselves, surrounded by the same steel walls and present almost as many hours. The only difference is where they sleep. Of course, Hollywood brigs depict few jailers (I recall only burly first mates walking around with jangling keys on a huge metal ring) and nothing at all of the quiet hours—and it is very quiet in this brig—devoted to simply monitoring the inmates.

To my surprise, however, Hollywood didn't get everything wrong.

"Prisoners can be sentenced to three days' bread and water," Mr. Denison replied to a question.

"Is that common?" I ask.

"Common enough. Food's important on a boat. Bread and water slows people down, gives them a chance to cool off," he said.

"I notice you have a Bible in each cell. Are they read?"

"Well, no one is forced to read them, and we don't care if they do or they don't," he replies. "But they are there, and you'd be amazed at how many of the guys do read them. That's also like the bread and water. It gives them a chance to think about things."

"Any visitors permitted?" I ask.

"None purely social," he said. "Of course, their commanders can visit them, and so can the chaplains. This isn't really a prison; it's for short-timers. When we get somebody likely to go to prison, we only hold them here short-time until they can be taken off the boat."

"So what's the profile of your average inmate?"

"All types, really, but mostly fights and repeated insubordination. People sometimes get carried away on a ship which has been at sea too long. But," Mr. Denison added significantly, "this sometimes doesn't show up until we dock and sailors go off on liberty. *Then* and right after they get back on board, we see the problems."

"How long have you been in the Navy?"

"Six years."

"Have you noticed any changes in behavior since then? I mean, are you handling more inmates, fewer inmates, or have you seen changes in inmates?" I wasn't entirely sure what I was driving at—maybe testing the declinist thesis, that things are always getting worse.

"I've been in six years," Denison replied, "and I'd have to say in general that things have gotten better—especially because they're taking seriously the Liberty Risk program."

Exactly what this program had to with the brig wasn't clear, and it remained murky until the ship's top-ranking lawyer explained it to me later. But I was familiar with the name, Liberty Risk program. It had turned up on the Internet during my Kunkle quest. Essentially, it tries to spot troublemakers before they make trouble; if they've already made trouble, it attempts to limit them in ways that might prevent more serious trouble. (What's limited—or eliminated completely—is off-ship liberty, the source of so much trouble in the Navy. The program is founded on one of William Shake-speare's more memorable trite-but-truisms: "What's past is prologue.")

The program recognizes that not all trouble is equal; the three classes of limitations reflect this. The first and most lenient category is Class Alpha. Alphas can't drink alcohol and are required to return to ship at 1830 for muster. The second category, Class Bravo, requires that sailors can leave the ship only when escorted by an E-5 or above. They also have to return to the ship by 1830 for muster. Sailors in the third category, Class Charley, aren't allowed off the ship at all. As a parent of two current and one former teen-ager, I both understand and applaud this program. In my household, it's called being "grounded."

However, unlike my own teenagers' occasional indiscretions, out-of-con-trol sailors roaming around foreign ports have serious implications for national security. Indeed, the Navy justifies the program almost exclusively on national security grounds. As one of the Navy's lawyers phrases it, "There are two recognized purposes behind a lawful liberty risk program: (1) The essential protection of the foreign relations of the United States, and (2) international legal hold restriction." The statement goes on to advise commanders that the program should be "limited to cases involving a seri-ous breach of the peace or flagrant discredit to the Navy." In spite of legal guidelines (for Constitutional reasons, such a preemptive program cannot apply to sailors while in U.S. ports), what contributes to the program's suc-cess is the relative lack of legal procedure. The Liberty Risk program is run not by lawyers but by the chief petty officers, the people with their ears clos-est to the deck. Liberty Risk is not classified as a judicial proceeding but rather as an administrative proceeding, a technicality perhaps, but one that avoids the process being subjected to the formalities of the Uniform Code of Military Justice. The chiefs can take a good, hard look at troublemakers and know how to differentiate between nonrecurring adolescent binges and socially inappropriate or criminal behavior that is likely to be repeated.

Is there anything easier to understand than the pent-up energies of fifty-five hundred mostly postadolescents who are corralled at sea for months and suddenly debarked in a pleasure port whose chief industries are separating thirsty, horny, and cash-rich sailors from their money? As one Navy journal-ist explained it:

> When Sailors trade their controlled shipboard environment for the free-wheel-ing, ready-for-anything liberty world, they are thinking of fun, not hazards.

Add booze and late nights to the situation, and you have all the ingredients for trouble, whether it's getting beat up in a fight or falling off a pier and drowning.

And that's just the small stuff. A "standing head" (the nickname for a newspaper headline that is always true) could easily be "U.S. Sailor Accused of Rape in [pick one: Japan, South Korea, Okinawa, etc.]." These headlines are invariably followed by protests, threats of base closings, and restrictions on U.S. military personnel in the host country, as local politicians capitalize on citizen outrage directed against the lust-crazed foreigners. (It is a universal trope of history that all foreigners of every time and place are lust-crazed.)

But the *Kitty Hawk* has its own very recent history. In September of 2002 (only six months before Kunkle was sacked), the *Kitty Hawk*'s captain, Thomas A. Henj, was relieved of command over what the Navy described as a "loss of confidence in the captain's ability to lead his crew." These included a range of problems, some of which could have been taken from the movie *The Caine Mutiny*—while in the port of Singapore, the *Kitty Hawk* hit a buoy and damaged one of her screws—but also a few problems no one ever laid at the doorstep of Capt. Queeg or his crew. One twenty-three-year-old sailor was arrested in the *Kitty Hawk*'s home port of Yokosuka, Japan, on suspicion of armed robbery and assault. Three days earlier, another *Kitty Hawk* sailor had been busted trying to smuggle a kilo of marijuana through the Narita Airport near Tokyo. Moreover, Japanese police arrested four other sailors in two separate robberies. In short, the twelve months preceding the day Kunkle was canned was very much an *annus horribilis* for the USS *Kitty Hawk*.

Every man is a novel. Not all tales are well told, but all are fascinating, and the jailers are more interesting than the jail. I asked Mr. Denison why he enlisted. "My father was in the Army," he replied, "so naturally I chose the Navy." There was a look in his eye when he said this that implied some gigantic struggle, perhaps not yet entirely resolved; it is the same struggle by which sons have separated from their fathers since the beginning of time. But now this younger Mr. Denison is a father. He has been married for one year and has a nine-year-old stepson. He spoke affectionately of the boy, and I wondered: If his son ever enlists, what branch of the service will he choose?

One of the jailers first told me that he was from Dayton, Ohio.[2] But as I

---

2. Out of respect for this sailor's privacy, I have changed the names of the towns.

was about to leave, he approached me privately and asked that I cross out Dayton and write instead Cincinnati. "More family there," he helpfully explained, but with a pained expression. Heaven only knows what personal issues suddenly moved him to change homes on the spot.

On the way back, I stop at the enlisted sponson for a smoke. I speak with four young men, all friends, all shipmates, and all from New York City. They had enlisted right after the attack on the Twin Towers, based on some sort of agreement between them, an "if you do it, I'll do it" kind of thing. So they all did it. One saw the towers come down; all were still angry about it. They were here because, as one said, perhaps quoting a long-forgotten movie, "It's time for payback."

I couldn't agree more. But what I think doesn't matter, and I've been remiss in not asking more sailors about how they feel about this maybe war. I promise myself to do better.

The Ship's Doctor

1900
Wardroom II

AT SUPPER, *b'shert*—Jewish shorthand for fated relationships—proves once again to be an active force in the universe. I choose a table at random, ask permission to sit, and find myself next to Eric Elster, the man Chaplain Carr said was the boat's lay Jewish leader. He is the ship's surgeon, in title as well as function. (It seems that all physicians on a boat are called surgeons, whether or not they wield a scalpel.) But Dr. Elster is a real-time sawbones.

Dr. Elster is in his forties, with a bodybuilder's arms and torso (I later learn that he is a devoted iron-pumper) and the striking red hair that I generally expect to see at a Boston Celtics game—on the scalps of Celtics. He asked me where I was from.

"Originally, a suburb of Cleveland," I replied.

"Do you mean Shaker Heights?" he smirked.

We both laughed and immediately fell into a few rounds of Jewish geography. This struck me as odd, given that, as we spoke, the *Kitty Hawk* was plowing her way through a corner of the northern Persian Gulf bordered by Kuwait, Iraq, and Iran.

In civilian life, the dreaded hospital can usually be kept in a comfortable and deniable time frame. To civilians, smoking, overeating, drinking to excess, or overworking typically will kill only others, especially those who tactlessly appear in the newspaper obituaries that are read with the morning coffee. But things on an aircraft carrier are different. Here the blood-red tiled floor of the medical area is located amidships and spans the width of the mess deck. Its p-ways are filled with the chemical smells that pervade hospital and mortuary alike; lined up against its walls stand the suffering, waiting-to-be-seen, and through its hallways scurry busy professionals, whose hospital greens represent dawn to some and dusk to others. Go on the *Kitty Hawk* where you will, but you must go through this area to get almost anywhere.

One of those green-garbed professionals is Dr. Elster, one of six physicians on board. His world is bounded by those blood-red tiles on which sit six operating rooms and triage areas, an emergency room, a pharmacy, and a 65-bed hospital. Dentists Barrientos and Pollak have their offices here; tenants also include an optometrist, ship's psychologist Dr. Johnson, and the corpsmen (nurses), the mainstays of medical care here as elsewhere. What differentiates these men and women from their civilian counterparts isn't so much what they do but what they might have to do. During routine patrols in times of peace, the medical needs of thousands of crew members include everything a group practice of family doctors is likely to see, especially among a large, postadolescent patient population (venereal disease, pregnancy, mood swings, the flu, acne, job-related injuries), as well as the occasional odd case. Dr. Elster tells me that once, on request, he actually reversed a sailor's long-ago vasectomy.

But repairing the human wreckage caused by war requires skill of a different sort. Unlike, say, Massachusetts General Hospital, the *Kitty Hawk* doesn't boast a thick directory listing hundreds of staff doctors with almost as many specialties; sailors burned, shot, blown up, gassed, irradiated, and infected can't be fobbed off to some other physician in the east wing, and there is no go-to guy in case a sailor walks in with his severed hand in a bag. There's only Dr. Elster and his colleagues. Eventually, the patient might get evacuated, but for a long time, the go-to guys that matter are all *Kitty Hawk* doctors. Consequently, they must be prepared, on a first aid basis if nothing else, to treat every person shredded by combat. In short, among the oft-marveled medical facilities on an aircraft carrier are doctors who must be versed in many specialties, the simultaneous mastery of which would seem to defy human intellectual capacity.

(The extent to which popular conception has gotten this feature of naval medicine wrong is portrayed in the movie *The Bedford Incident.* Type A *ne plus ultra* personality and warship captain Richard Widmark denounces

Martin Balsam, the ship's doctor and a naval reservist with twenty years' experience. "Well, I have to wonder why after all these years you quit civilian life and went back on active duty," Widmark mocks him. "Your wives, divorces—three, weren't there?—your practice. Rough going everywhere, so you decided to nip back here for awhile.")

Lost in these thoughts, I find myself listening to a man also dining with us. He is more solid than portly, a bull of a man but on the order of Ferdinand rather than ferocious. I noticed the cross on his lapel and his name tag. It was Javier Roman, the pastor from the Assembly of God that Chaplain Carr had mentioned. Just at that moment, something about his story caught my ear.

"Eighteen-year-old Marine, mind you, *18 years old!* So he comes asking for my advice about marrying the woman. 'Tell me something about her,' I want to know. The kid says, 'Well, Chappy, I love her and she loves me. What else matters?' 'OK,' I said to him, 'how old is she?' 'Forty-five,' he answers. 'Where'd you meet her?' 'Well, Chappy, when I got off the boat at Yokosuka, it was, like, there she was, waiting for me. It was like fate.' 'OK,' I said, 'how long ago was that?' 'Two weeks,' the kid answers. 'And does she have any children?' I asked. 'Oh, yeah, Chappy,' he says, 'I think she's got four kids.' Then, like he was figuring it out for the first time, he says to me, 'I guess she must've been married before.' 'And how old is her oldest child?' I asked. 'I met him," this Marine tells me. 'He's a real nice guy. I think he said he was 25.'"

Chaplain Roman could barely contain his laughter to finish the tale. "I grab this Marine by the collar and say, 'I'm going to take a guess here, homey—you've never known a woman before her, have you, son?' He says, 'How'd you know that, Chappy?' 'And here's another guess—whatever money you walked off the ship with is gone now, right, son?' Well, this Marine is starting to get a little edgy. 'But I *love* her, Chappy, I *love* her!' So I take him aside, put my arm around his shoulder, and tell him, 'Look, son. You're an eighteen-year-old kid who the minute you say, "I do" winds up as the father of four children, one of whom is already seven years older than you are. I've been in this racket a long time, and let me tell you, these dockyard birds flock to the fence just waiting for somebody like you.' 'But Chappy, I *love*—'"

"Well, I couldn't take it anymore," Chaplain Roman concluded, "so I put my hand across this Marine's mouth just to shut him up, and I finally said to him, 'Look, kid, you ain't in *love* with her. You're in *lust* with her. There's a big difference. And when you've figured it out, we can have another talk about marriage."

I was introduced to the chaplain a moment later and, a moment after that, was invited by him and Dr. Elster to climb the stack to Deck 11 for a cigar. They didn't know that I smoked, but a man of the cloth who tells a good story and a *chevreiman* like Elster both deserve a really good cigar, so I fetched three R&Js.

Chaplain Gary Carr is a man whose love of his God flows through his brain; Chaplain Javier Roman has the same love but it flows through his heart. Chaplain Carr reasons with minds, but Chaplain Roman touches hearts in the language of hearts.

A passage from *Pirke Avos* comes to mind:

> Rabbi Yochanan ben Zakkai said to his five disciples: Go out and discern which is the good path to which a man should cling.
> Rabbi Eliezer says: A good eye.
> Rabbi Yehoshua says: A good friend.
> Rabbi Yose says: A good neighbor.
> Rabbi Shimon says: One who considers the outcome of a deed.
> Rabbi Elazar ben Aruch says: A good heart.
> Rabbi Yochanan ben Zakkai then said to them: I prefer the words of Elazar ben Aruch to your words, because your words are included in his words.

2330
The SEAL Berth

No sandstorm tonight. I'm disappointed. It looks like the captain was mistaken.

March 13
0330

It looks like the captain was right.

One half hour ago, I left the sponson after a good-night smoke. On the hangar deck, I was shocked at suddenly being enveloped by a thick brown mist that had filled this gigantic space. At first I thought it was dust up from the deck or equipment cleaning or that my glasses had misted over, as indeed they had; they were coated with fine particles of Kuwaiti dust. I wiped them clean, but it made no difference at all; the air in the hangar deck looked as brown as before. In fact, unbeknownst to me, things were worse on the sponson but had been obscured by darkness and the red smoking lamp. But it did explain one mystery. Tonight's crop of smokers had seemed an especially unhealthy lot, filling the muggy night air with a cacophony of hacking, coughing, and wheezing.

I hadn't thought *sandstorm* because there were no whistling winds, blowing dunes, or people wrapping cloths around their mouths so they could breathe. But as the captain's earlier announcement made plain, sandstorms were serious business. It threatened the *Kitty Hawk*'s mission, perhaps worse, in a sense, than an enemy attack. It was, after all, an act of God, and clouds of fine dust blown from empty deserts can spread over an area far larger than enemy bombs or bullets could. This same dust that had found its way onto my glasses also gets into jet engines, sensitive avionics, motors of every description, service equipment, and the ship's HVAC system. As I look at air that I can suddenly see, a chilling thought occurs. The captain knew well in advance that this storm was coming, and he took every precaution against it. But these particles could just as easily be weaponized spores of anthrax or, worse, much smaller molecules of poison gas.

The *Kitty Hawk*'s answer to sandstorms is a pound of prevention and thousands of gallons of cure. Not only are hatches and ventilation systems sealed in advance but also the apertures of jet engines and exterior panels for avionics are closed, and cockpit bubbles are lowered. Sensitive machinery is similarly secured, and mechanical repairs are deferred until after the storm passes. The cure consists of water, lots of water. As I walk through the hangar deck, it and everything in it are being hosed down. I am told that the same thing is happening on the flight deck. Nevertheless, this gargantuan space, illuminated by the occluded suns of the overhead lighting, retains an other-worldly aspect.

But it doesn't remain other-worldly for very long. I pause midway through the hangar deck and quickly return to sea-level as I watch a swarm of G3 red shirts stack the white, pencil-thin AMRAAMs (Advanced, Medium Range, Air-to-Air Missile) in the space where mail is usually distributed. These kids push and pull four AMRAAMs to the dolly, while a chief directs what is actually a carefully choreographed set of motions. The missile is 12 feet long but only 7 inches in diameter and, like so many of these tech weapons, has an improbable lethality relative to its appearance. Like most radar-guided munitions, it has wings—spanning 21 inches—and (in the Navy's words) its own "inertial reference unit and microcomputer system [which] makes the missile less dependent on the aircraft fire control system [which] enables the pilot to aim and fire several missiles at multiple targets." The AMRAAM is carried by the *Kitty Hawk*'s F/A-18 Hornets and weighs only 335 pounds, although it travels at what the Navy will describe only as "supersonic" speed. This missile carries a small, blast-fragmentation warhead—not a lot of explosive is required to knock an enemy jet out of the sky—and it's a safe bet that the cost of one of these is a fraction of a fraction of the cost of the planes it's designed to down. That makes it cost-efficient in a Harvard Business School sort of way.

As I stretch out in my rack, I read up on the AMRAAM in *All Hands*. The missile is made by Raytheon, which is headquartered in Lexington, Massachusetts, the next town over from Concord and not too far from the Harvard Business School itself. In fact, of the eight missiles reportedly carried on the *Kitty Hawk*, seven are made by Raytheon. What an odd thought! The upcoming annual town meetings for Lexington and Concord both feature sanctimonious anti-war resolutions; the local town papers are filled with thundering "And now I take my stand" letters from self-appointed Martin Luthers denouncing the hypocrisy and venality of the Bush Antichrist, some claiming to speak for Jesus, or Emerson, or Gandhi, or some other long-dead cat's paw for the living, while just down the road sits . . . Raytheon!

But they'll never say *bubkes* about Raytheon, unless it is to whine about layoffs.

0615
Wardroom II

Couldn't sleep and couldn't care less. As war approaches, life on this ship is like a river in springtime. The waters grow higher, move faster, and roar louder with each passing day. And there's no staying dry on a warship. We're all in it, up to our necks.

I had breakfast with Hu Xiaoming, a correspondent from the Washington bureau of Xinhua News Agency. Xinhua is the largest news agency in Red

China and is owned by the state. Should I still refer to it as "Red" China? Or are they now only a semicentralized run-of-the-mill dictatorship, boasting a mixture of free markets and female infanticide? If they're something more (and worse), I wonder why the DoD approved this guy to embed on a U.S. naval vessel in time of war? But I won't worry about that now. Whatever I think, none of this James Jesus Angleton moment of mine will output through the impenetrable barrier of my phony smile. At any rate, if he chooses me to learn something secret about this boat, he's a lousy spy and ought to be recalled.

Besides, my prejudices aside, Hu seems like a splendid fellow. He's in his mid-thirties and his mastery of English seems terrible. But he exudes a genuine warmth that trumps the language barrier and also likes to laugh—although what (or whom) he's laughing at is always a question. Overall, he is ambitious but needs a guide.

"Stories," he declared. "Idea to write?" he asked.

"All over the ship," I replied. "Everywhere you look there's a story."

Later while I was killing time watching TV news in wardroom II, he approached me.

"Where stories? I have trouble. Editors big pain," he said, pleading.

"What are you doing tomorrow at 1300?" I asked.

Hu shrugged.

"Then meet me at the office of Dr. Jennifer Johnson," I offered. "She's the ship's shrink. I guarantee you that there'll be something to write about—assuming the war doesn't start between now and then."

Hu wrote something down and gave me a quizzical look.

"What a shrink?" he asked.

Opinion and War

1200
Wardroom II

TODAY I BEGAN my quest to figure out what the crew of the *Kitty Hawk* thinks about the prospect of war. Of course, I don't expect anyone to be carrying a placard pro or con about the matter. It's more than just the fact that the U.S. Constitution gives the civilian branches of government exclusive control of war, as well as of warriors; it's also true (and almost of equal importance) that two centuries of constitutional government have resulted in a culture of caution among the military. In challenging civil authorities, there have been no military victories, only Benedict Arnolds, George B. McClellans, Douglas MacArthurs, and hosts of junior officers whose gaffes, slurs, vents, and public mutterings have resulted in ignominious retreat, followed by early retirement.

But sailors do have opinions. Since I'm not here to publicly humiliate anyone, prove my personal asininity by playing "gotcha," or ferret out traitors, anonymous letter writers, or those in league with the opposition political party, some people prove willing to discuss their views—as long as they're not made to feel like a trick to a media whore.

One such person is Cdr. Bill Jackson, a good fellow and frequent lunch and dinner mate. A reserved, self-confident man of about fifty, Cdr. Jackson seems taller than the mess chairs allow; he towers over the table and must lean forward on his elbows to eat. How he negotiates the narrow p-ways and short hatches on this vessel is proof of some undiscovered law of physics.

I cautiously slouch toward the topic of war. But it's all for naught. The table is no sooner cleared than he raises the issue himself.

"I've been hearing a lot from my sister," he suddenly says. "She's ex-military and she's been driving me crazy lately with her E-mails about the war."

"Pro or con?" I ask.

"Heavens, she's very much against it," he says with a gentle smile. "She's been getting more and more worked up about it, and just recently she told me that I ought to resign from the Navy. You know," he added, "we've been at sea so long, and being based in Japan, I'm not sure anybody on ship realizes how crazy the debate back home has become about this thing. My sister's emotion is like a barometer."

A moment of silence passed, and he asked me how I felt about the war.

"I'm for it," I replied, "but I'll allow your sister a point. Americans make lousy colonialists."

"Yeah, well, I also have my doubts about it," he said. "Winning will be the easy part. I don't think the Iraqis have a clue about what's in store for them. But where I have trouble is what comes after the war when we're stuck in Iraq. If we're burdened with running the country afterward, I don't know if I'd be prepared to call that a victory."

1300
Ship's Security Office
Interview with Lt. Andrea Schreiber

Regular cops wear uniforms in part to mark their authority to the civilians they protect. But on the *Kitty Hawk*, where everybody already wears a uniform, the cops must wear a different uniform—woodland camo. This uniform serves the same purpose as those in civilian law enforcement. On a city street, if somebody imperiously demands, "Move on," they're just as likely to be told "Screw you" as they are to be obeyed—unless the speaker is dressed like a cop. It's no different on this boat.

No other Navy job (except perhaps that of the ship's captain) is as recognizable to Americans as Navy cops (in movies, the ubiquitous Shore Patrol). After all, embedded in the stereotype of the Navy is the imagined sailor, sensually deprived by too many months at sea or in the service and thus prone to drunkenness, sexual license, and violent behavior. Has there ever been a Hollywood movie about the Navy that didn't include the Shore Patrol busting up fights, throwing sailors in the brig, and declaring all kinds of bars and brothels off limits? Just think of Frank Sinatra's Maggio in *From Here to Eternity*, Jack Nicholson in *The Last Detail*, or the barroom scenes from *The Sand Pebbles*.[1]

Lieutenant Schreiber and her cops have two jobs: law enforcement and force protection. The first job is easier to comprehend if not to perform. Keeping the *Kitty Hawk* afloat means not only keeping its sailors on the straight and narrow (e.g., sober and obedient to regulations) but also keeping good order and discipline. *Kitty* cops patrol the hangar deck, cordoning off areas where sensitive or dangerous operations are under way; they keep order in the often long lines to the smoking sponson, protect the mail, patrol the officers' p-ways and prevent lower ranks from unauthorized access, inspect the ship for messiness and clutter that could be dangerous in an emergency, and, in one of the most curious security operations I've witnessed, stand guard, shotgun at the ready, when the onboard ATM machines are serviced. (Where would a would-be robber hide?) Perhaps most important, just like their civilian counterparts, *Kitty* cops intend simply to be seen and, by the simple fact of ubiquity, deter wrongdoing and encourage good behavior.

What never shows up in movies but has occasionally dominated recent newspaper headlines is the second function of Lieutenant Schreiber's group: force protection. When the USS *Cole* was rammed by an explosive-laden motorboat and seventeen American sailors died, force protection was suddenly news. It wasn't the first time, of course. The hit on Khobar Towers and the 1983 suicide bombing of the Marine barracks in Beirut also testify to the importance of force protection. For the Navy, the relative military

---

1. There is a subtext to this image of the sailor. For most of Western history, when few traveled more than 20 miles from the place they were born, the sailor was a conspicuously free character. He traveled the world and visited mysterious, pagan places about which many hometown folks knew little. As a result, the sailor was a figure not only of mystery but also of danger—who could say what influence these faraway places had on his character? Or, since he lived in a world imagined to be less constrained than that of the village he left behind, his character was perhaps more animal, less governed by impulse control and conventional morals. The sailor as drunken, thieving, violent, and sexually promiscuous served to reassure landlubbers that their own world was preferable, while at the same time appealing to their fantasies or fears of life elsewhere.

powerlessness of radical Islam, coupled with their medieval fanaticism, guarantees that one important battleground in the war against terror will be the immediate perimeters around ships in ports and at sea, the harbors into which they sail, and the piers at which they dock. And so Lieutenant Schreiber's duties include what she describes as "waterside security." For security reasons, I don't press her for the many details that she wouldn't offer.

Lt. Andrea Schreiber's office is home to several woodland camo–clad NCOs sitting behind gray metal desks and reviewing papers or staring into computer monitors. Besides being dressed alike, these men share one other attribute: They're big. Not fat, but big as in fullback big. I long ago learned not to separate jocks from brains, but even assuming these guys are joint Harvard–MIT doctoral fellows, I still wouldn't want to cross them, even if I were packing heat and had the drop.

But what a contrast Lieutenant Schreiber is! Diminutive, fine-boned, fair-skinned, with blond hair worn up—camo uniform notwithstanding, she moves with grace in one of the most graceless spaces on this boat. Like every other office on board, this place is cluttered with—with what? Life, I suppose. People coming and going, bringing with them their papers and headaches, questions to be answered or benignly neglected, and then there are the papers that come without the people, the forms, the memos, the software, the updates, the patches, plugs, orders, and advisories. And in a corner of this essay in monochrome gray steel, white papers, and bland fluorescence is the desk belonging to the *Kitty Hawk*'s chief of security, Lieutenant Andrea Schreiber.

They call her the Sheriff, and based on comments overheard on the sponson as well as the praise heaped high from fellow officers, she has a formidable and—for those contemplating wrongdoing—terrifying war face. But as we make small talk in advance of this interview, that face is nowhere present. I wonder where it has gone.

This woman, who could easily pass as being in her late twenties, has been in the Navy for more than 20 years. A Texan since grade school, like several of the officers I've met here, she knocked around some before joining up. She was a legal secretary in Corpus Christi and spent two years in college. Then she entered the Navy and spent her early years as a hull maintenance technician. I don't say anything, but it is even harder to imagine her as a metal bender than it is as the Sheriff. But she liked it, and the reasons add up.

"It gave me a worthwhile feeling," she said, "something I didn't experience before the Navy."

"Better than taking heat from a bunch of lawyers about your typing?" I asked.

She laughed. "Yes, you could say that."

"Hull technician—are there many women in that line of work?" I asked.

She smiled gently, but I sensed it was a smile she had worn before. "Oh, it didn't matter," she replied in a soft voice. The voice remained soft, but she looked at me with a penetrating gaze. "I've never felt that being female required me to be meek. You know, courtesy goes a long, long way."

(Later I looked up the word *courtesy* in the OED and found in its first definition: "Courteous behavior; courtly elegance and politeness of manners; graceful politeness or considerateness in intercourse with others." I began to understand where the war face was.)

"Did you have to deal with male stereotypes of women?" I asked.

"We're in a closed environment here. This is a perfect place to discount stereotypes," she replied.

I asked her if that closed environment might work both ways, à la *Love Boat*. To her credit, she didn't flinch.

"Look, anytime you put young men and women together, stuff is going to happen," she said somewhat resignedly. "But I'm not sure that it's really those kinds of relationships that are the issue."

My ears perked up. "How so?" I asked.

"More common is how men and women relate to each other on the job. Remember that, on this boat, you've got men and women doing the same jobs. It's not like the Army, where you have specific jobs, say, combat positions, where women aren't allowed. The Navy has ranks. People get to tell other people what to do. I think the biggest issue with men and women on this boat deals with those men who haven't worked for a woman before and have problems with that."

"Authority issues?"

"Yes."

"What about your function and authority?" I asked. "Security is something many people associate with men."

She laughed, and I sensed the return of the survivalist's courtesy.

"Oh, for all of us here, it's just a job and we want to do it well."

I try another approach. "Overall, is the Navy a positive experience for women?"

Her reply at first struck me as a nonanswer. "I think everybody should do at least one tour in the military," she replied.

"Why?"

She paused and reflected. "You must start at the beginning," she said slowly. "You must teach girls to have strength of character. Only boys are supposed to have adventures. But what about girls? Shouldn't they be able to go out and experience the world?"

A good question, I thought.

"You know," she finally said, "I can't imagine staying in one place and doing the same job for forty years."

1500
Enlisted Smoking Sponson

It's a pleasant afternoon on the sponson. The sun shines, jets launch and land, helicopters swoop in the distance, and faraway ships appear and then disappear as they and the *Kitty Hawk*'s paths diverge. By now, I've grown used to the roar of jet engines; when the sound overwhelms me, I just clench the cigar in my teeth while both index fingers join the wadding already in my ears. The blasts last only a moment and then don't repeat for another eight minutes.

I'm approached by Smitty, a thirty-something Black man, male-model handsome, whom I met earlier at a PAO briefing. He's a Marine photographer, wears a neat desert camo uniform, and likes his cigarettes. We make small talk, and I finally ask the question.

"So what do you think about the war? Should we be doing this?"

Smitty smiled, flicked his butt over the rail, and lit another.

"Man, did you know that the Defense Department was looking for a name for this operation?" he asked.

"No," I replied.

"I'll tell you how that went. Somebody actually said to Rumsfeld, 'I think we oughta' call it Operation Iraqi Liberation.' So Rumsfeld agrees, and just as he's about to sign off on it, somebody comes along and says, 'Hey, if we call it that, the acronym will be OIL. Is that the message we want to send?' So they rename it Operation Iraqi Freedom."

"C'mon, Smitty," I said, "you're putting me on!"

"Well, maybe a little," he replied more seriously.

"Do you believe this is only about the oil?" I asked.

"No, not *only* about the oil," he said. "I don't doubt that they've got other problems. But hey, if you're going to tell me that it's *not* about the oil, then I've got a bridge in New York I can sell you."

I asked Smitty what most sailors thought about the war.

"Hey, we've got over five thousand guys on this ship, and no way is there going to be an opinion poll, so forget that. But use some common sense. These kids are drawn from every part of America, every group, class, and race. If America's divided, it's a safe bet that the crew's going to be divided. It probably isn't any more complicated than that."

"What about differences of opinion based on race? For example, do Blacks and Whites on board look at the war differently?" I asked.

"My man," Smitty replied in earnest, "whether they wear a uniform or not, Black people are always going to be more suspicious of authority. And if authority says, 'It's not about the oil, it's about WMDs,' then, hey, I think a lot of them are going to say, 'OK, show me.' But a lot of Whites will say, 'OK, if you say it, I believe you.' It's just a question of the starting presumption, man. There's a lot of history there."

Indeed.

"But I'll tell you this," Smitty added, his eyes looking off toward the horizon. "I'd give anything to be in Kuwait right now, ready to step off with the boys."

1730
Wardroom II

Over the past few days, I've noticed an increasing number of officers stopping in to watch the news on the TV in wardroom II. Television programming alternates every hour between Fox News, MSNBC, CNN, and Armed Forces broadcasting. Other channels include movie reruns, a 24/7 live-cam of the flight deck, and a separate channel that displays a compass showing in real time the *Kitty Hawk*'s heading, speed, and exact longitude and latitude. But lately I've noticed that the officers are watching only the news. Everybody senses that something is up, way, way up, and what used to be the white noise of talking heads, rumors, and true-for-the-day headlines have now become topics of wardroom conversation.

Increased interest in war news is evident only with the officers in the wardroom. In the enlisted messes, where I stop several times a day for a soda pop, a seat, and some eavesdropping, the contingent war doesn't even draw contingent interest. The mess televisions are still not tuning in to news channels. It's either sports, rock concerts, or news about sports or rock concerts. At first, I saw this as evidence that the crew was either indifferent or ignorant about current events. But no, I forced myself to remember that at 18 and 20, I didn't care much about current events either. Jiggle was far more interesting.

Tonight in wardroom II, I met another officer, Mr. Reid. A tall, courtly African American, he strikes me as the embodiment of the sailor-scholar. It's a treat to listen to him as he articulates the same way I aspire to write when I'm in academic mode. His words are clear, concise, and deliberate; his erudition is ubiquitous yet appropriate, and his remarks reference philosophers, historians, and, much to my delight, none other than Jacques Barzun.

"What's the last Barzun book that you've read?" I ask.

"*Simple and Direct*," Reid replied.

"Me, too!" I said. "I keep a copy on my desk. Whenever I get carried away, I go back to it. Barzun has saved me from myself more times than I can count."

Mr. Reid smiled and leaned back into the sofa. "The Navy is something of a paradox," he calmly observed. "The work is hard and constant, yet we have time to read. It's my pastime. I studied philosophy in college."

We paused for a moment to watch some TV talking head argue for an attack on Iraq.

"What's your philosophy about *that*?" I asked, referring to the war.

"Let's just say that I'm not exactly gung ho about the prospect. I've listened carefully and read even more. The rationale—or should I say rationales—is a moving target. Policy should have clarity."

"How so?"

"We need a reason to go to war besides feeling good about going to war. What is our reason here? Do they have WMDs? Are we going in simply to replace a bad, very bad leader? Is there an Arab-Israeli component to this? Is there an economic component? I mean oil, of course. Not that we're going in just for oil. Nobody is that crude. But there are oil-related concerns."

He slipped that one by.

"Such as?" I asked.

"Well, consider this," he replied. "Iraq has the second largest oil reserve in the world. If they come under US influence, wouldn't that potentially offset Saudi influence? Wouldn't it potentially bring Russia into line? I mean they're also sitting with massive reserves. Doesn't it give the United States a new chip in the oil game?"

He paused, perhaps to consider my reaction to all of this. But my reaction was, for the purposes of this conversation, my own business.

"Don't get me wrong," he quickly added. "There's nothing wrong with securing oil reserves as a foreign policy objective. Lots of American jobs depend upon it. But all I ask is that the administration level with the American people. Let's just call things for what they are and then allow the public to form its conclusions."

Mr. Reid had raised some powerful issues, several of which were trenchant enough to penetrate the fog of ideology that frequently (in my own case, for example) prevented a candid assessment of why this war might be necessary. I had become so incensed at seeing hard-left placards bearing slogans such as "No Blood for Oil" that I reflexively tended to discount to zero any economic motivations for the war. But this was naïve on my part. There was an Arab-Israeli component to this, and many believed, me included, that the sacking of Saddam might just bring about another "Oslo moment" in a new Middle East peace process. And many of the business publications I subscribe to, starting with the sainted *Wall Street Journal*, had reported on the impact that this maybe-war might have on both oil and its politics.

1830
Media Room

At the briefing tonight, a few of my colleagues finally figured out that when they agreed to embed, they also implicitly agreed to swap the big news picture for the little news picture. Lieutenant De Walt is catching hell from several reporters. He is accused of not providing enough information about everything from the ship's operations to the larger strategic picture. What's fueling this is the television news. TV reception on board is poor but not poor enough to prevent my colleagues from learning that their colleagues stationed at the Pentagon, the White House, Qatar, Camp Doha, and else-where seem to be reporting much more news much earlier than they are. Moreover, it seems that the PAO on the USS *Lincoln* has decided to brief and release certain matters that the *Kitty Hawk* PAO claims shouldn't be released, at least according to his interpretation of the rules.

If true, it is a wholly foreseeable consequence of the embed rule that gives local commanders discretion as to what news can or cannot be released. Some problems with this policy, such as a lack of news-rule uniformity between different commands, were probably anticipated but ignored in the greater interest of permitting the guy on the ground to authorize release of news based on the reality on the ground. But there's another consequence to this policy that is more serious and more interesting, and anyone with even a rudimentary knowledge of American military history probably should have anticipated local commanders' use of media contacts to boost the pro-file of themselves, their units, their ships, or the funding prospects for any of the foregoing in the next federal budget cycle.

Access in exchange for favorable press coverage—now there's a news flash! Shortly after his appointment to lead what would become the Army of the Potomac, Gen. George B. McClellan had reporters filling two omni-buses invited to his Washington headquarters. General McClellan strode into the parlor where the newsmen were waiting, in the words of one histo-rian, "his face mottled with dust and perspiration from a long ride up the Banks of the Potomac." He looked every inch the fighting general and, mindful of his audience, spoke like every inch the publicist. He described the press "in flattering terms of the newspaper profession," before reminding everyone present that he had worked with reporters before and "had found no reason to regret having made their acquaintance." The press was satisfied with this interview. In his classic study *The North Reports the Civil War*, J. Cutler Andrews described the result:

> Within the next few days extensive accounts of McClellan's meeting with the press were published in newspapers throughout the country. They included detailed descriptions of the General's personal appearance, one of which referred to him as a close-built, compact man, reminding one of Napoleon. This characterization caught the popular fancy, and thereafter the youthful General was commonly referred to in the press as the "young Napoleon."

But General McClellan was with the Army. The Navy, then and now, has its own set of headaches for reporters. Reporting from a warship at war is often incompatible with insta-know. After all, the vessel's precise location is a permanent secret; its steel frame and constant movement impair satellite telephones, sailor phones, and Internet access, when these modes of communication are not already impaired by River City status. However, in principle at least, it was ever thus. James M. Perry in *A Bohemian Brigade* characterizes naval journalism during the Civil War:

> For editors, North and South, covering fighting on land was a lot easier than covering fighting on water. Reporters on land could use the telegraph; they could jump on railroad cars and ride to their newsrooms; they could even use the mail. Reporters afloat had none of those newsgathering advantages. And so most newspapers simply finessed the idea of creating specialists to write about naval warfare.

2315
Media Room

One half hour ago, a breathless Brook De Walt came down to the SEAL berth and told us to assemble in the media room at 2315 for a "breaking story." A crew of eight Iraqi fishermen had radioed May Day and was rescued by a detachment from the USS *Gary*, a Navy guided-missile frigate. The *Gary* belongs to the 15th Squadron, commanded by a chap named Commodore Mahon, and is part of Carrier Group V, the *Kitty Hawk*'s battle group. The commodore would be available for an interview.

Brook De Walt is excited. We're excited. As we wait for the press conference to begin, we talk among ourselves and stretch thin the few known facts to cover amazing possibilities. Someone suggests that the fishing boat story itself might be fishy. Perhaps it's only a legend to allow defecting Iraqi scientists to escape the country. Somebody else wonders if the boat might have contained weapons of mass destruction, or perhaps it was loaded with explosives and headed our way.

The buzz was silenced by the entrance of Cdr. Mike Brown and a compact man in a khaki uniform, of average height, with ruddy face, brown hair combed back, and a hawk's eye. Brown introduced him as Capt. Mahon, but it was De Walt who first took center stage.

"I want to let you know," Lt. De Walt announced, "that this story is being made available first to the media embeds on the *Kitty Hawk*. No one else has it, and this is Commodore Mahon's first press conference. And you guys should feel free to release this story whenever you want." (I'm guessing my colleagues were right about *a* conspiracy behind this story, but wrong about *the* conspiracy—this is a conspiracy to get them off of the PAO's back.)

The commodore (whose actual rank is that of captain), like many of the officers I've met here, seemed accustomed to public speaking but not to media who were recording, filming, or taking notes of every word he said. It is here that the concision of mil-speak, a language with a style something like Joe Friday's "Just the facts, ma'am" is very helpful, a safe harbor.

Arms folded behind him and voice clear, Capt. Mahon told his story. "At 1750 the guided missile frigate USS *Gary* responded to a call from Capt. Mohammed, who reported that his vessel was taking on water and sinking. By 2200, the Iraqi vessel was boarded and eight fishermen were saved. Two of these men were rescued from the water. They are reported in good health, and once their status is confirmed, they will be returned to Iraq."

"Can you tell us if any weapons or chemical weapons of any kind were found?" a reporter asks.

"None that we know of," Capt. Mahon replied.

"What happened to the ship?"

"It sunk."

"What can you tell us about the Iraqi fishermen?"

"So far, they appear to be who they say they are."

A moment of silence passed. Remarkably, the reporters had run out of questions. It was as if Brook De Walt, having earlier shouted, "Incoming!" now appeared mistaken—the whistling had stopped, but there was no explosion. And indeed, there wasn't much to this story. Had it not been for prospect of war, which hangs over the Gulf waters like a heavy, snarling thundercloud, this story would have been a virtual nonevent (except for the Iraqi sailors). It took the naval experience of Mark Faram, sailor (retired) to bring out those details that gave the story what little color it had.

"What were the weather conditions at the time?" Faram asked Mahon.

"The seas were at least four feet and the winds were 25 to 30 knots," he replied.

"Was the Iraqi vessel boarded?"

"Yes."

"Were the boarders armed?"

"Yes."

"Had this vessel been under observation previous to receiving the distress signal?"

"Oh, yes," Mahon replied, somewhat more at ease now. He probably sensed in Mark's questions the presence of a man with naval experience. "One of our missions in the Gulf is to spot and track vessels in the area. Capt. Mohammed's boat had been on our screens for some time."

"Could you describe the Iraqi vessel?" Faram asked.

"She was about 30 feet, and in very poor shape—which is not unusual for fishing craft in this region," Mahon observed. "Also, she had no life boats. That is also not unusual."

"And has the *Gary* ever been involved in rescue-at-sea actions before?"

"Oh, yes," Mahon replied, "this isn't our first time."

Faram had broken the ice. Most reporters on board, like me, had no naval experience that would help them conjure up the mental images that must precede a good question. (The most effective naval journalist during the Civil War was probably the *New York Herald*'s Bradley Sillick Osbun; not surprisingly, Osbun's prior service afloat was extensive and included duty on a canal boat, a transatlantic sailing ship, a South Seas whaler, duty with an international coast guard suppressing pirates in the China Sea, and a naval filibustering expedition to Argentina.) Now with Faram's assistance, the reporters were determined to make lemonade from a lemon, if no other reason than to get the home office off *their* backs.

"Tell me," another reporter now asked, "we've heard reports that scores of Iraqi vessels are leaving their harbors for the open seas. Was Capt. Mohammed's boat one of these, and does this exodus represent a threat to Coalition naval vessels?"

Everyone's ears seemed to perk up for Mahon's answer. After all, the *Kitty Hawk* was a Coalition vessel.

"I don't know why the Iraqi vessel left port," Mahon replied. "But I do know that in our experience, whenever tensions rise in an area, privately owned craft will frequently leave their ports for the open sea. There's nothing sinister about this. Mostly, they're just fishing boats or small commercial craft trying to protect themselves."

The Q&A continued like this for another few minutes. Most of the reporters simply wanted to leave to rush down to their computers and E-mail the news to impatient editors. But Lt. De Walt wanted to make sure that everyone understood the importance of this story, its context, and its place in the Milky Way. He seems to operate on an assumption—how correct it is I cannot say—that reporters are like pillows and assume the shape of the last person sitting on them. And Lieutenant De Walt intended to be the last person.

"I think the *Gary*'s response shows the goodwill of the Coalition forces toward the Iraqi people," De Walt almost shouted as the reporters dispersed. "I also think it shows one of the important roles played by support ships in a carrier battle group."

Good points all, but by then the room had practically cleared.

March 14
0315
Wardroom II, Sailor's Phone

It's time to file another prerecorded report. Two telephone numbers to call: Talk Radio News Service in Washington and American Urban Networks in Pittsburgh. I'm going to hold off on my story about how African Americans feel about the war. Although I've had three good conversations with Black sailors, I'm still at least three cigars away from generalizing. However, on the topic of how sailors feel about the maybe-war, I'm at least three cigars late. I file the following report:

> Day after day, the sailors of the USS *Kitty Hawk* go about their business of supporting flight operations that are enforcing the no-fly zone in Iraq. To the casual observer, things appear routine. But spend a few minutes on the sponsons, which are the large outdoor platforms below the flight deck, and a different picture emerges. It is here that the sailors, men and women, come to smoke a cigarette during breaks and take a moment to relax from the otherwise deadly earnest business of maintaining this gigantic warship. And it is here that one senses the mounting tension of the looming war. As they do in America, opinions on board vary about the war. Four sailors from New York City, who enlisted right after 9/11, look forward to settling scores with one of America's historic enemies. But Bob, another sailor, has his doubts. "I think we'll win this thing," he says, "but I'm not too sure about what happens next." However, while the airwaves heat up in America with debate about the war, the prevailing sentiment here is one of fatalism and acceptance. "If it comes, it comes," says another sailor. "I don't worry too much about it. Can't worry too much and still expect to keep my head." As the *Kitty Hawk* patrols

the warm waters of the northern Persian Gulf, this is perhaps the soundest advice of all.

I have to meet the ship's psychologist, Dr. Jennifer Johnson, at 1300 today. I must also do my laundry. Of the two, which is the most important? Tonight, I cannot say.

0930
Media Room, Morning Briefing

Three new journalists arrived on the *Kitty Hawk* today: Jay, a newspaper man from Taiwan, and two television reporters from Abu Dhabi News. Once somebody mentioned my name, Jay made a beeline to me and introduced himself. He had met Ellen Ratner at the Diplomat Hotel in Bahrain and brought greetings, but this was only a cover, a code, for a far more insidious message: "And she also wanted me to tell you," Jay continued, himself completely puzzled at what it all meant, "that the eyes of The Cottage are upon you and something about words equaling awards."

That manipulative shrew! The Cottage was a family compound on the shores of the once-Technicolor Lake Erie, where Ellen, I, and a dozen other cousins had spent the first thirteen or so summers of our lives. The Cottage was also a metonymy for our extended family, as in, "I'm circulating all of your reports to the family, so remember, we're watching you!" The bit about words equaling awards was Ellen's belief that with two of Talk Radio News Service's reporters on the ground in Kuwait and one at sea, there might be some industry recognition for her efforts. But to win a reporting award, one must first file reports. Talk radio, like cable news, is a 24/7 medium, and it has an insatiable appetite for reports. Ellen believed that if enough reports were thrown at the wall, some might stick long enough to be recognized, and recognition meant enhanced value for Talk Radio News Service, and enhanced value for that meant more money for Ellen, and so on. In short, Cousin Ellen had just been transformed from dear Cousin Ellen into a pushy, demanding, manipulative editor, akin to Walter Matthau in *The Front Page*.

I met my two colleagues from Abu Dhabi News Service. They are a TV crew consisting of a cameraman and a correspondent. The cameraman is a burly fellow in jeans and a t-shirt who seems half-asleep and speaks so little

English that even swapping names proved impossible. But the correspondent is a different sort, a short, dapper man with a whiff of cologne, impeccably dressed in a blue blazer, creased gray wool trousers, and a starched-collared shirt, altogether ready for an outing at the country club rather than service on a warship. His name was Abdullah al-Saafin, and he was Abu Dhabi's Washington-based TV correspondent.

In a group setting, he was reserved, cold, and almost unapproachable. Was he overcompensating for being a Muslim on a ship whose purpose might result in the deaths of other Muslims? I couldn't be sure. But one on one he is different. Talkative, almost loquacious, he tells a fascinating story in flawless English. Born a Palestinian, he received his doctorate in Middle Eastern studies in Britain and for several years worked for the BBC. Among the many languages he spoke was Hebrew.

"Really?" I asked, genuinely surprised. "Why Hebrew?"

"I want to understand Israeli books, newspapers, and broadcasts," he replied matter-of-factly.

I was struck by his use of the present tense of the verb *want*.

"Why?" I asked, laying some bait. "What can you read in *Ma'ariv* and *Ha'aretz* that you can't find in the *London Times* or the *New York Times?*"

He smiled and shook his head.

"One shouldn't be naïve," he replied. "If there is to be any kind of a future in the Middle East, we had better start speaking one another's language."

I admired Abdullah's reply. But I could not forget the circumstances that brought us together, nor the fact that the next voice I hear could belong to President Bush, telling me that we're now at war with Iraq, which in turn is launching chemicals at us (including this ship), as well as Kuwait, Saudi Arabia, and Israel; that Iraqi saboteurs had detonated bombs in Boston, New York, Washington, and London; or that toxins or other bugs have been released into the water supplies of Chicago, Tel Aviv, or Houston. Crowds of Arabs might even be cheering this on the streets of Gaza, Amman, and Cairo.

I looked at Abdullah and wondered which of the two of us was being naïve.

CHAPTER

13

Couch of the *Kitty Hawk*: The Ship's Shrink

Adjustment Disorder: Diagnostic Criteria

A. The development of emotional or behavioral symptoms in response to an identifiable stressor(s) occurring within 3 months of the onset of the stressor(s).
B. These symptoms or behaviors are clinically significant as evidenced by either of the following:

   1. marked distress that is in excess of what would be expected from exposure to the stressor
   2. significant impairment in social or occupational (academic) functioning

Adjustment Disorder Subtypes are selected according to the predominant symptoms:

- *with Depressed Mood*
- *with Anxiety*
- *with Mixed Anxiety and Depressed Mood*
- *with Disturbance of Conduct*
- *with Mixed Disturbance of Emotions and Conduct.*

—From the *Diagnostic and Statistical Manual*, fourth edition

1300
Office of Dr. Jennifer Johnson

DR. *JENNIFER JOHNSON* is a thirty-something PhD in Psychology (University of South Carolina) with light brown, shoulder-length hair, the skin tone of a girl, and a broad, open face, which, even at rest, conveys kindness and earnestness and, an asset in any business, beauty. It is also the face of a big sister, best friend, gal pal, or perhaps something even more important on a ship whose population is 85 percent male, that is, distinctly maternal. It is a face that invites conversation.

Hu has joined me in Dr. Johnson's small, steel office, whose floor, shelves, desk, and walls are cluttered with books, pamphlets, memos, and stacks of papers. In spite of the ubiquitous, cold, inescapable fluorescence that illuminates every corner of this ship, there is something warm about Dr. Johnson's office. It might have been the sense of privacy, on a vessel where privacy does not exist.

"What was your dissertation about?" I began. She seemed slightly surprised by my opener.

"Mostly it dealt with the link between adult intimacy and the experience of intimacy in childhood and adolescence," she replied. "I spent quite a bit of time doing clinical work with teens and young adults."

As an academic matter, such training would seem ideal for the demographics of the *Kitty Hawk*.

"Why did you opt to be a therapist rather than practice, say, behavioral science with lab rats and labyrinths or design tests for ETS at Princeton?" I asked.

She paused for a moment, probably in the interests of concision. Answers to this sort of question only come in two varieties: insufferably long or intriguingly short.

"Oh, I think I'm a novelist at heart," she replied. "I like hearing stories. I also like helping people. The two can go together, don't you think?"

I didn't answer but wore my usual phony smile as I scribbled down notes. When I looked up again, Dr. Johnson seemed more serious. "Therapy only becomes possible where you can let go from the responsibility for curing," she added.

"Can't save the world, eh?" I stupidly asked, not at first grasping her fascinating reply.

"No," she smiled, "but you can try to be there for it."

I thought about Dr. Johnson's last two responses. They had a quality that was both distant yet loving. Perhaps this is a necessary mask for those whose job it is to sit and listen.

My next question must have struck her as logical.

"I know that every shrink has a shrink that they talk to," I said. "On a ship at sea, who does Dr. Johnson talk to?"

"It's an issue," she acknowledged. "Dealing with countertransference is always a professional challenge. But I maintain E-mail relationships with doctors on shore, and I also have several friends on board."

"And where do you get most of your cases?"

She explained that most patients show up from one of three sources. "The chiefs of the boat," she said, "are the closest we have to parent figures. Many of them are very sensitive to the emotional health of their sailors. The rest are self-referrals. Every sailor on board knows that I'm here, and the door is always open. Also, some are referred by the chaplains."

I remembered something that Chaplain Carr had mentioned—confidentiality. In civilian life, usually enshrined by statute, therapists enjoy the benefits of the doctor-patient privilege. Essentially, barring evidence of a crime or the intent to commit a crime what is said in the doctor's office stays there. It is difficult to imagine therapists winning the trust and confidence of their patients without it.

I decided to put a hot-button question directly to Dr. Johnson: "Suppose a sailor comes in and tells you that he or she has had a recent homosexual encounter or, more specifically, that they believe they are gay. Are you prohibited from disclosing that?"

Dr. Johnson leaned backward and sighed. "No," she answered slowly, "I am duty bound to disclose it. And not just matters of sexual orientation. I also have to disclose any impairment resulting from substance abuse. In fact," she added, "the Navy requires me to disclose any issue that comes up in this room that might impact fitness."

"Don't some of your patients ever feel betrayed?" I asked.

"They shouldn't," she replied. She reached into her file and handed me a form.

As I scanned it, she explained that before counseling any patient, she asks that they read and sign this form. No one, she explained, could have any doubts about what the limits of confidentiality were in her office.

The relevant parts of the form read:

LIMITS OF CONFIDENTIALITY

Mental health providers are bound by code of ethics to insure your confidentiality. However, unlike lawyers or chaplains, we do have limits to what we can keep confidential (which is also true of our civilian counterparts). The general guideline in reporting your information to those with a "need to know" is that any information disclosed about violations of (or the intent to violate) the UCMJ [Uniform Code of Military Justice] or civil laws may be disclosed. In these situations, we will make every attempt to either obtain your permission or inform you of what we will report.

Some of the more common situations where we may have to disclose your information include:

- —Any risk of homicidal behavior
- —Evidence of spouse, child, elder or handicapped abuse
- —Clinical chart reviews by accreditation inspectors or by other therapists/hospital administrators
- —Your written or signed approval to release the information to whoever you designate.

If you have any concerns about our limits of confidentiality, please discuss them with your mental health provider.

The lawyer's eye immediately rests on the words "violations of (or the intent to violate) the UCMJ." This disclosure document notes that both civilian and military therapists share limits on what can be kept confidential; this is certainly true for both in the case, say, of a homicide. But the UCMJ is different from its civilian criminal legal counterparts in that it prohibits a variety of activities that may not be prohibited in civilian codes or, if prohibited, may not be enforced. Homosexuality is one such activity that the military deals with through its "don't ask, don't tell" policy. Dr. Johnson explains that she is quite clear with her patients that to tell her about it is to "tell" under that policy.

"If they come in here and tell me they're gay," she adds, "it's because they want me to know. And if they want me to know, it's because they want out."

I'm suddenly gripped by an abstraction. What is gay? If a sailor confesses to uncertainty about orientation or has had fantasies, is that a "telling"? After all, there must be some percentage of young men and women aboard whose personalities may not have, in the Freudian sense, completely integrated. Entire spectrums of identities may still be under construction.

But Dr. Johnson is quite clear that fantasies—and not just about sex—don't qualify as a "telling." "Thinking or fantasizing or being unsure about sexual orientation doesn't force me to disclose anything," she declares. "People think about a lot of things that they just don't do. I've had many sailors express fantasies about jumping off the boat and most never do it."

It was here that I became dissatisfied with the interview—not her answers but rather my questions. I was veering into the margins of Navy life and not exploring its day-to-day center. As a political issue, gays in the military might appeal to the editorialists at the *New York Times*, but my guess was that, to a majority of sailors, it meant less because it wasn't part of the woof and warp of daily life on a steel island. What I won't guess about is what would happen to shipboard morale if a tiny clique of black robed mandarins or DoD appointees succeeded in forcing a homosexualist agenda in the Navy. In the old days, one might say, "Let the voters decide," but these days, the only thing the loyal opposition despises more than Republicans are the voters.

So I changed the subject. I was right to do so, because when I asked what percentage of her time she spent counseling gays, she laughed and told me that because the chaplains did have absolute confidentiality, anyone in need of serious counseling about sexual orientation went to them. "So what kind of mental health problems do you see most often?" I asked.

"Adjustment disorder. It's recognized by the *DSM IV*," she explained. "It's often temporary but it can be terribly painful. I usually see it with kids who are at sea, sharing living quarters or coping with the lack of privacy for the first time. Consider the realities of shipboard life. They share racks, showers, and toilets with one hundred-fifty other people; liberty may be restricted for lengthy periods of time; the hours are long, and the work they do might be necessary but may also seem meaningless or repetitive. Remember also that the *Kitty Hawk* is based in Japan. Many of these kids are absent from the States for months or even years."

She also explained that adjustment disorder can present at any age. On a ship in foreign waters, sailors are far away from children being born or family sickness and deaths. Often, the sailor can't be there for the occasion. Grieving (although bereavement is excepted from the formal definition of adjustment disorder), anxiety, fear, and uncertainty all constitute stressors that might trigger the disorder. But sudden stressors aren't the only cause. "The problem is that the sailor experiences a lack of control," Dr. Johnson explained, "or at any rate, the illusion of control over these life situations. It's these situations that can wear down mental health, not immediately but slowly."

"The symptoms of adjustment disorder can mimic depression. Irregularities in eating and sleeping and mood swings are a part of it. Sadness, anxiety, and bursts of anger can also show up. Most patients are self-aware that something's up; the chiefs almost always notice these things."

"How do you treat it?" I asked.

"It depends on the symptoms and other factors. If depression or mood swings are predominant, we'll prescribe Zoloft or other psychoactive medicine," she replied.

"Do you deal with major depression on the boat, I mean, people who are severely or chronically depressed?"

"No, we can't, here," she said. "If I suspect a serious bipolar disorder, I'll refer them out for further diagnosis and treatment. You must understand that the Navy's concept of fitness is usually in the interests of both the sailor and the service. In case you haven't noticed, an aircraft carrier is a very dangerous place to work. If a sailor is having difficulty focusing on his job or is a risk to himself or his shipmates, he shouldn't be on this ship."

"You know, Dr. Johnson, I have to ask a question that keeps the civilian population in perpetual wonder about sailors at sea for long periods of time," I began. "With so many young men and women on board, some of whom might still be in grip of raging hormones, where does all their sexual energy go?"

She laughed at my logorrheic prudishness. "Well, I do manage a number of anger management classes! But seriously, we do run well-attended groups for anger and stress management, although I don't want to attribute sexual frustration as the main cause for them. Believe it or not," she added, "people don't talk a lot about sexual frustration per se. Perhaps some of it appears as anger and complaints."

"How does anger show up on a boat?"

She nodded and smiled. "Complaints," she replied. "Sailors feel that they are yelled at for no reason. Or that they are assigned an unfair amount of work. Or that their chief or some officer has it in for them."

Returning from the interview, my civilian self somehow felt violated by the Navy's policy of ratting out patients who might have sought treatment in good faith for substance abuse or serious emotional problems. But walking through the mess decks, I now had second thoughts. The stacks of Phoenix missiles and 2,000-pound bombs seemed to be growing higher by the day as the probable war approached. And standing by these stockpiles, loading and unloading ordnance, or simply keeping watch were the ubiquitous red-shirted kids from G3. In the name of preserving a civilian convention, did I really want to protect their right to get drunk, stoned, have a tantrum, or decide, fuse in hand, that "today is the day"? I don't think so.

Perhaps one of the first casualties of war is preciousness.

1430
Wardroom II, Dining Room

The dining room is almost empty, so Hu and I sit at a table to review our notes from the interview with Dr. Johnson. In one sense, I am Hu's seeing-eye dog, because I can translate for him. Not from English to Chinese—I don't speak a word of the latter. Instead, I translate from the fast English of spoken discourse to the slow English of "I no get what she say about that" of later reviews. Why would the Chi-Coms/Chi-Caps (capitalists) send a spy on a Yankee boat who doesn't speak any English?

Spy or not, he's an excellent companion.

Sabbath at Sea

1800
The Chapel
Shabbat Service on Board the *Kitty Hawk*

*T*ONIGHT *I ATTENDED Shabbat* services on the ship. About five or six men showed up, not enough for a minyan (a minimum of 10 are required), but any number greater than one is enough to break the loneliness of this otherwise isolated Jew. Besides, God can ignore numbers. Rabbi Chalafta ben Dosa of Kfar Chanania once asked how we know that the Divine Presence may be found even if someone is alone. Because, he answered, it is written in the Torah, "In every place where I will cause My Name to be mentioned, I will come to you and bless you." *Kedusha*, or holiness, now fills this chapel. That the Holy Name has been invoked by other faiths in this same space only tells me that G-d is used to visiting this place.

The few men attending include another of Dr. Elster's colleagues, Dr. Seigel; the rest are enlisted personnel, several of whom work on the flight deck. The service itself is conducted in Hebrew and English, with Elster leading the prayer and also selecting an occasional hymn. We lack harmony, several voices are off-key, and some stumble through the words, but it is beautiful.

At the conclusion of the liturgical service, Eric spoke a few words. "This may be the last *Shabbat* service we will hold on this ship," he began, "before we find ourselves at war. If and when war does come, none of us can know where we'll be or what we'll be doing. All we know for sure is that everyone in this room and every sailor on this ship will be at risk. The pilots we send into the sky, men and women we respect and some we call friends, are sure to be flying into harm's way. Tonight, while we pray that war does not come, I think we must also pray that if it does come, G-d will spare our friends, protect this ship, our country, and provide guidance to our leaders."

He then reopened the siddur (prayer book), and together we recited a prayer for soldiers and sailors.

Tonight, the soldiers and sailors we prayed for were us.

2200
Wardroom II

I feel sad. I don't like spending Shabbat away from Alyson and the kids. This weekend is doubly hard because it's my sister's fiftieth birthday. I was a bit misty-eyed during services. I self-diagnose: low-grade adjustment disorder.

March 15
0200
Wardroom II, the Sailor Phone

It is story-filing time again, and the living is, well, increasingly uneasy. I've noticed that as the prospects of war draw nigh, more and more officers fill the TV room. I've also noticed that while some channels offer movies, over the last few days, fewer officers watch them. Now the news is on whenever reception is possible. But the enlisted persons still seem to be ignoring war news, at least based on the sports channels preferred in the mess halls. After my time on the sponsons, however, I have come to believe that it's not because of willful ignorance or a lack of interest in current affairs on their part. Instead, it has a quality of fatalism about it. If there is a common consciousness shared by these young people, it is that the war will come if it comes; if it doesn't come, it won't; if it comes, the captain will tell them that it's here, and then they'll fight it as ordered, hopefully make quick work of it, go home, and be thankful that they're going home. As I write these words, these ideas might suggest thought chains that are stupidly tautological. But in the world that is this boat, the world that is actually felt and lived, the thoughts are neither stupid nor circular. These thoughts help sailors survive from moment to moment. It is wise thinking.

I finally connect with the Talk Radio News Service recorder. Today's piece condenses my chat with Dr. Johnson into something snippy and sage and just as forgettable. It's a good thing that people aren't at all as depicted in news reports.

Providing medical care for over five thousand crew members of the USS *Kitty Hawk* requires as many specialists as any good community hospital. On board are doctors, dentists, oral surgeons, opticians, and pharmacists. Surgeries are performed, cavities filled, and lenses are ground for glasses. But there is another specialist afloat that deals with the all-important issue of mental health—the ship psychologist.

Dr. Jennifer Johnson holds a PhD in psychology from the University of South Carolina. Her tour aboard the USS *Kitty Hawk* began in June, and from her tiny office on the ship's medical deck, her door is open to any sailor who feels the need for counseling. But the nature of that counseling is not quite the stuff of your average suburban shrink. In helping her clientele, she must walk a fine line between Navy requirements and the doctor-patient confidentiality that most civilians have come to expect from mental health professionals. The cold reality is that for crew members whose job requires servicing fighter jets, handling millions of gallons of fuel oil, and deadly explosive ordnance, there is no margin for error. If a crew member has a substance abuse problem, if they admit to possessing drugs and alcohol or a weapon or any violation of Naval regulations, Dr. Johnson is obligated to inform the commanding officer. "I cannot conceal issues that affect a sailor's fitness to perform," she says. "Too many lives depend upon it."

Most of Dr. Johnson's cases fall into the category of adjustment disorder, an emotional impairment recognized by the *DSM IV,* the bible of the mental health care industry. Why this is so is not hard to understand—life on ship, with its lack of privacy, its hard work, its remoteness from so much that is familiar to civilians, requires a personal flexibility that does not come easily to everyone. One controversial issue that occasionally arises falls under the "don't ask, don't tell" policy of excluding homosexuals. "Simply having gay fantasies is not a sufficient basis to report a patient," she says. But where the patient is avowedly gay, it is a matter that she must disclose.

From an ethical standpoint, Dr. Johnson resolves her sometimes delicate position through some disclosure of her own. "Before I counsel a patient," she says, "I tell them what the ground rules are. If they choose to continue talking after that, they do it with full knowledge of my responsibilities."

Indeed, she has a form acknowledging this that all new patients are required to sign. "After the disclosure," she says, "most patients who want to talk about their sexual orientation want me to know in order to separate from the Navy."

Dr. Johnson may tread a fine line sometimes. But then life isn't easy for anyone aboard the USS *Kitty Hawk*.

After my spiel, I look at the script and feel embarrassed.

As if life was easy for anybody anywhere.

0730
Wardroom II, Breakfast

Moldy bread. Heavens, I thought that was something confined to the days of the wooden navy. At the same time, I notice for the first time that the bread's plastic wrapping is covered in Arabic script. I ask one of the ward attendants about this. *The ship must have its own bakery!*

"Yeah, we get our stuff wherever we're in port," he replied.

"With all this talk of terrorism," I wondered, "does it make you nervous buying the ship's food from Arabs? I mean, how do you know it's not poisoned or something?"

"Well, Sir," he said, voice dropping to a whisper. "Just between us here, how would you know the difference?"

I thought better of the quality of meals than he did.

On the other hand, it's only a matter of weeks before I'll be eating Chinese food whenever I want.

The Ship's Captain

1400
Captain's Quarters
Interview with Captain Thomas A. Parker, Commanding Officer

THE ENTIRE MEDIA tramped up ladders and through p-ways to the long-awaited interview with Capt. Thomas A. Parker, commander of the *Kitty Hawk.* Trudging along with the rest, I wondered to what a Navy captain might be compared. Not merely one holding the rank of captain, but the rank joined with the function of commanding a vessel. Literature and movies are full of captains, and the better known are usually depicted as somewhat demented. The greatest of all imaginary captains was Herman Melville's Capt. Ahab of the *Pequod* (monomaniac), then Capt. Bligh of the HMS *Bounty* (sadist), followed by Capt. Queeg of the USS *Caine* (paranoid); there are Capt. Findlander of the USS *Bedford* (authoritarian) and Lt. Collins, commanding officer of the USS *San Pablo,* a postmodern captain who is emotionally overwrought and conflicted between serving a democracy and imperialism and who, at one point in the film, contemplates suicide. The captains described by Richard Henry Dana Jr. are less constructed because his description flowed from his experience with real men under whom he served during his two long years at sea. "Whatever the captain does is right, ipso facto," he observed,

> and any opposition to it is wrong, on board ship; and every officer and man know this when he signs the ship's articles. It is part of the contract. . . . To be

sure, all power is in the captain, and the officers hold their authority only during his will; and the men are liable to be called upon for any service.

Of course, I understood that the imaginary captains probably bore as much verisimilitude to real sea captains as Gordon Gecho (*Wall Street*) did to real investment bankers or Dr. Szell (*Marathon Man*) did to real dentists. But a country like the United States, born in a revolution against monarchy, rent by civil war against federal authority, and peopled by the perpetually dissatisfied who still see monarchs, tyrants, and despots inhabiting the White House or walking the corridors of the Capitol, is bound to have a neurosis about authority. The sea captain becomes the inkblot in which writers of many persuasions see their own fears and obsessions.

For my part, I thought that a Navy captain was no more or less than a seagoing CEO. In part, this was because in the corporate world, naval metaphors are pervasive. "Welcome aboard," new hires are told; "we must all row/pull/stroke in the same direction," many a CEO has proclaimed; corporate books are supposed to be "shipshape," and CEOs themselves are often referred to as "captains," employees as "the crew," and the company as "the ship"; good CEOs keep their companies on "an even keel" while poor ones "steer off course" and occasionally "sink the company." One could argue an even closer analogy between captains and CEOs, and posted throughout the *Kitty Hawk* are organization charts with the photographs, names, and titles of the various department heads, reminiscent of dozens of such charts I've seen throughout my years in the securities industry.

Thus I went into this meeting with Captain Parker assuming that the only difference between him and, say, the chief executive officer of Widget Corporation was that one wore gold buttons on his blue suit and the other did not.

Certainly the captain's quarters, in its spaciousness and fine appointments, bore resemblance to many an executive suite. They were the most elegant rooms I'd seen on this ship (although I did not see Admiral Moffit's quarters). Today's media—perhaps fifteen reporters—are escorted down blue-tiled p-ways and through doors with brass portholes into a bright, spacious conference room with real windows overlooking the sea, much as one would expect from a stateroom on a luxury ship. The floor is covered with real blue carpet, and the furniture is made of real wood; some pieces, like the Windsor-style chairs around the conference table, even pretend to style. An easy chair has been placed at one end of the room, and both the British and South Korean television news crews are focusing their cameras and adjusting the light levels around it.

"Rise for the captain!" an aid suddenly announces, and everyone in the room stands. I am not disappointed, because the khaki-clad man who enters looks every inch the captain. He is a tall, square-faced man with short, graying sandy hair and a gray mustache, gold-rimmed spectacles, ruddy skin, and a very deliberate manner. As he takes his seat and surveys the room, allowing the cameras to focus and lights to adjust, I observe that his deliberate manner is really a product of something else—control. He is, first of all, self-controlled for, without being told what is what, he sits in stony silence, purposely not moving or talking until after the reporters have finished with their gear; there will be no nervous chatter from him. Second, his serious mien seems to invite everyone present to control themselves. This is a man in whose company I would think twice before using profanity or telling an off-color joke. It is not that Capt. Parker is humorless—quite the contrary. Every morning on the 1MC his good-natured Georgian drawl describes weather conditions, the ship's daily agenda, and especially his Hard Charger of the Day award (given to a sailor who shows special initiative on the job), and almost always his remarks will draw a smile from his crew. What Capt. Parker really is, is focused—in a world of channel surfers, he is the anti–attention-deficit disorder, a man of priorities, a man on whose shoulders are perched the lives of many thousands, their feet always dangling in the business at hand. In short, he is a man about whom it can safely be said: The main thing is to remember that the main thing is the main thing.

Yet Capt. Parker would never express such a sentiment. He doesn't have to, for he is its avatar.

Before the Multi-Culti-cult changed things, Capt. Parker's background would have been considered, simply put, American. Fifty years old, he was born to a Catholic family in Savannah, Georgia, one of seven children. His father was a career Marine officer, and the captain attended parochial school until the eighth grade and afterward the local public high school. In a published interview, Capt. Parker, an Eagle Scout, credited the Boy Scouts with having been "a major influence on my upbringing." Religion was also a major influence in his life, what he once called the "Catholic experience." What he meant by this can't be judged in a public press conference; more pressing issues matter. But the product of these influences now sits before me, a man whose four gold bars and star on his epaulets arrived not through a stock market windfall or inherited wealth (at least not a monetary inheritance) but through discipline and a career path that had not yet collided with the Peter Principle.

After graduating from high school, he attended the Virginia Military Institute and then to Aviation Officer Training Candidate School in Pensacola. In 1976 he was commissioned an ensign and checked out to fly the E-2C Hawkeye.

Flying the Hawkeye perhaps augured something of Captain Parker's future. The Hawkeye is described by the Navy as an "all-weather, carrier-based tactical warning and control system aircraft" whose missions include "surface surveillance coordination, strike and interceptor control, search and rescue guidance and communications relay." In short, the Hawkeye is a thinking man's aircraft, intended to allow other thinking men to better manage a conflict. And Captain Parker's career is, if nothing else, a combination of hands-on flying and combat experience with lots of time spent studying bigger pictures. He's logged more than thirty-five hundred hours in the Hawkeye and made six hundred fifty arrested landings (!), but he's also earned a master's degree in international studies from Old Dominion University. In the 1980s, he was involved in freeing Grenada and capturing the *Achille Lauro* hijackers; in 1990, on the eve of Desert Storm, he was appointed executive officer of a combat flight group aboard the USS *Theodore Roosevelt*. But shortly afterward, he was awarded a Federal Executive Fellowship and spent a year with the RAND Corporation in Santa Monica.

The combination of action and academics served him well. After his stint with RAND, Captain Parker became the operations officer aboard the USS *America* and was involved in the Balkans campaign (1995); he then served as the tactical aircraft analyst in the Secretary of the Navy's Office of Program Appraisal. Having done his office time, his next berth was as executive officer of the USS *Belleau Wood* (1998), an aircraft carrier for attack helicopters; one year later, he became its captain, during which time he was awarded the Marjorie Sterritt Trophy as the best ship in the Pacific fleet. One year after that, he became captain of the USS *Essex*, another helicopter carrier, and then, following his earlier pattern of alternating think jobs with action duty, he spent several years at the U.S. Space Command in Colorado Springs and the legendary facility at Cheyenne Mountain.

All of that was on one side of the ledger; on the other side was the fact that his pilot nickname was Turbo. It must have been a moniker from a long-ago but not misspent youth or some well-concealable side to his personality because try as I might to imagine it, the man in the easy chair sure didn't look like a Turbo to me.

He didn't look nervous either. He must've known that the scoop-deprived reporters standing, sitting, and crouching before him were a greater danger to his career than any of his six hundred fifty arrested landings. Some of my colleagues had muttered their resentment that the media on other boats had gotten better stories; others were frustrated with the lousy ship-to-shore communications. But all were under pressure from their editors for more of everything. Add to this the delicate international situation—Bush, Blair, and Aznar are meeting this weekend in the Azores to jaw their next move (which means that appeasement, hypothetically, still has a chance), and meanwhile the diplomatic jockeying among France, Germany, Russia, and the United States continues—and it's pretty clear that one foolish word from Capt. Parker, whether actually uttered or not, in or out of context, will be beamed worldwide to the millions of political carnivores whose appetites cry out for a foolish word.

In short, if the captain is too bellicose or too pacific, if he provides too many details about upcoming operations or the wrong ones, or if he confuses the role of captain with that of a TV talking head, he may find himself standing in a long and distinguished line of early retirees, along with George B. McClellan and Douglas MacArthur and, more recently, Adm. Kunkle and Capt. Henj (albeit the last two for other reasons).

But the interview begins with a question from Capt. Parker. He asks the Japanese reporters how they would say the *Kitty Hawk*'s nickname, "Battle Cat," in Japanese. A little banter follows, and with the reporters' help, the right translation is found. The *Kitty Hawk* is based in Yokosuka, to which it will return when this Iraqi business concludes. The captain's opener struck me as a smart way to begin.

The first question is an invitation to disaster. A reporter wants to know what aspects of this maybe war with Iraq will be different from Gulf War I. The question is dangerous because it's open-ended. It could invite a discussion of specific tactics, strategy, and politics better left fluttering in the thin air of platitudes. But Parker cuts it off at the pass. "I cannot discuss tactics," he says, and then ascends to that thinner air. "What I can say is that there

has been a revolution in military affairs in the ten years since the last war."
He adds thoughtfully, "And procedures will reflect that revolution."

The next question comes from Mark Faram and, as I would expect, it's
informed. Faram has picked up grumbling that the boat is undermanned,
that work shifts are short, with people having to perform multiple jobs. "Is
this true?" he asks.

Maybe it's true, and maybe it isn't, but Capt. Parker has no intention of
being tomorrow's headline ("Not Enough Men To Fight This War, *Kitty
Hawk*'s Captain Complains"), so he's firm in his dog-bites-man reply. "This
ship is manned very, very well," he says. "There are no glaring shortages."
But there is one moment of absolute earnestness, and the captain echoes
words that I've heard from sponson to ward room. "We are America's 911
telephone number," he says. "When world emergencies happen, the *Kitty
Hawk* gets the call. Our force levels have to be adequate."

Now it's my turn. Earlier, I had managed to see a few moments of an
Ari Fleischer press conference and heard several reporters raise questions of
morale: Rumored invasion dates have come and gone; meanwhile, troops sit
in the desert and sailors float on the sea with no end in sight. How long can
the troops keep "their fighting edge" with this kind of uncertainty? I wondered how the hell Ari Fleischer would know. The man who would know
was sitting just a few feet from me, so I asked the question.

Once again, the dog bit the man. He explained that the *Kitty Hawk*, as
the country's only permanently forward-deployed aircraft carrier, is always
under way and always on duty. "A lot of the crew is feeling that they just
want to get things over. But they're here for as long as it takes. In the past,
they've spent six months without taking a break. The truth is that once on
deployment, they're always ready, war or no war. Crew morale is good," he
concluded.

Capt. Parker moved through the next series of questions, complimenting
the media at every turn. He was impressed with the embed program and
impressed with us. "We're not trying to roll you; we're not trying to steer
you," he declared. "It's a crapshoot from our standpoint, but in the end,
we think it will be good for everybody. People are delighted that you're
here. So far, I've gotten no feedback of a negative nature." Then he became
serious and for good reason, since dead reporters are always bad press. "Just
remember now," he said in earnest, "be careful. An aircraft carrier is a very
dangerous environment." When asked about his greatest challenges as com-

manding officer (always an invitation to self-inflate), he complimented his department heads and emphasized the ship-as-team concept. When asked about the threat of Iraqi chemical or other attack, much to the delight of every reporter present, he sounded confident. "We keep an eye on the Iraqi Navy. But neither terrorism nor the Iraqi Navy frightens me at the moment. It's very difficult to sneak up on us."

He's also confident about mines ("We're prepared for that eventuality"), and, of great concern, he's confident about dealing with a chemical weapons attack. He explains that gas clouds show up on radar and that the ship can quickly move through them or steer clear of toxic bursts altogether. Besides, the ship has procedures that can seal the *Kitty Hawk* from the outside environment in a matter of minutes. Someone asks about how reliable precision-guided weapons really are, the question's subtext being, "How do you really feel about all the innocent civilians you're going to kill when you drop these bombs?" It's an Oprah question, and it's loaded. How does anybody feel about killing innocents? But Capt. Parker takes it in stride. "I don't spend a lot of time worrying about that," he says, "because our training, our technology, and our air crews are the best in the world."

Kendra Helmer, a thirty-something reporter with *Stars and Stripes*, then asked the best question of the afternoon, the only one that came close to discomfiting the captain. She had heard considerable griping from the sailors that somebody had reduced the number of smoking sponsons; moreover, the smoking area had also been reduced on the sponsons that remained. How would Capt. Parker address those complaints?

I had also heard these things but lacked the presence of mind (or *chutzpah*) to put it directly to the captain. And following Kendra's question, the room fell silent. Great issues of policy, strategy, weapons, and seamanship were forgotten while Capt. Parker was finally served a question that, while it would end no one's career nor provide fodder to an enemy nor damage any national interest, was nevertheless a cherry bomb in a teacup. As he struggled for an answer, Kendra kept talking. She said that according to the scuttlebutt the new restrictions had been ordered because Admiral Moffit's quarters were near the sponson, and he didn't enjoy the smoke.

Then, for the first time during the press conference and perhaps for the first time in his life, Capt. Parker had a Chauncey Gardiner (*Being There*) moment. He was briefly at a loss for words, shifted about in his chair, and finally answered, "Well, as we say in the Navy, a grumbling sailor is a happy sailor."

I thought about the captain's reply for a long time but could make no sense of it. On the other hand, it wasn't any less nonsensical than most of the postmodernist drivel one hears in and around Harvard Yard.

c. 1500
Captain's Quarters
Abu Dhabi Television's Interview with Captain Parker

The press conference is over, and most of the media have left. But Abdullah al-Saafin from Abu Dhabi Television is setting up for a separate interview with Capt. Parker, and I decide to stick around. Abdullah's audience isn't exactly the same as the readership of *Stars and Stripes*. Who knows what will be asked or answered?

During this setup, I asked the captain a question of my own: "Did I hear you say that you attended VMI, Sir?"

"Yes," he answered. "Are you familiar with it?"

"Not any recent graduates," I replied, "but I am familiar with a few of your older alums."

Capt. Parker nodded his head and beckoned for names. There were a slew of them that I wanted to mention, but I could remember only three.

"Let's see: Stonewall Jackson, William Mahone, and Robert Rodes," I answered with a smile. All three were prominent Confederate generals.

"Stonewall!" the captain exclaimed with a grin. "He's my hero!"

Then Abdullah takes a seat across from Capt. Parker while his cameraman is positioned between them. Abdullah nods toward his cameraman, and the interview begins.

"Capt. Parker," Abdullah asks, "your ship is based in Japan, where the people are welcoming and your force is wanted. Here in the Middle East, the people are hostile to you. What can you say to them about your presence here?"

Without missing a beat, the captain answers, and he is blunt: "Our business is to follow our orders as given. If we are ordered here, then this is what we will do." He pauses and then speaks directly to the camera.

> I hope that the civilians understand that we are here to encourage Saddam Hussein to comply with UN resolutions, and if he does not, to liberate the

Iraqi people. I would hope the local population understands that we're not here for the Iraqis' oil. We're here to eliminate a cancer from the Middle East. The end will be better for everyone.

Abdullah launches his next question: "What is the *Kitty Hawk*'s purpose in being in this region?" His words sound neutral in print, but his tone is hostile and suspicious. Like TV people everywhere, Abdullah is playing the role of tribune to his audience and not straight journalism. But Capt. Parker's answer, while friendly in tone, remains blunt in its message: "We're here to support the policy of President Bush," he replies, "and our purpose here is to support the president's goal in the disarmament of Iraq. The real issue is Saddam Hussein. He must meet his obligations."

Abdullah is allowed one more question. It's not clear who has limited him to only one more question, but it's a wise move. His tone is becoming increasingly hostile, and there's no point in prolonging this interview. There's something Abdullah wants that he's not getting from the captain. He rephrases for a third time what is essentially the same question: "Could you tell me what is the *exact* role of the *Kitty Hawk* in being here?"

Capt. Parker now assumes the attitude of a man who has an aircraft carrier waiting to be commanded. He flashes a quick smile then answers: "We carry aircraft that deliver precision ordnance."

End of interview.

c. 1800
Wardroom II

At dinner tonight, I listen to an officer I don't know describe how Capt. Parker is well liked by his sailors in a way his predecessor was not. "He talks on the 1MC every day," he said. "With the other guy, days would go by, and we'd never hear from him. Capt. Parker's voice is popular, especially now. One of my chiefs said that he got the feeling that the captain actually *worries* about *him*."

Is a Navy ship captain like a CEO? I can now answer that question: no. Perhaps in management terms, there are some similarities, but the differences are so vast as to make comparisons superficial. At the end of the work day in corporate America, the CEO returns home to Dover or Beacon Hill, which, measured by social and economic distance, is light-years away from where the employees sleep. But a captain's separate quarters are just rooms in a house he shares with the lowest ranked sailor on the ship. In the corporate world, employees can be fired, injured, killed on the job, or taken ill, and the CEO is essentially protected by a web of insurers—the government's safety net for those unemployed, workers' comp for those injured on the shop floor, health insurance for those who get sick. As long as somebody else pays, the CEO skates away. But as Capt. Henj discovered, a ship's captain is liable for everything his sailors do, on or off the ship. He is accountable for injuries, discharges, arrests, suicides, accidents, crimes, property damage, and drug use, no matter who pays. In short, he is always accountable—in peace and war, awake or asleep, on or off the bridge—for human life whose numbers include the many thousands under his direct command and many times this number of civilians or enemy combatants in his area of operations.

And no doubt this is why novelists prefer sea captains to make their points about God and Man, Good and Evil, the Universe, or the Human Condition—because slapped on the sea captain's shoulders is the sum of every life aboard and the destinies of a good many ashore. The responsibility is as inescapable for him as a sailor's tattoo, bearing the word "Jesus" or "Mother" or "God."

Of this, a corporate CEO would have no idea.

2000
Enlisted Smoking Sponson

Success! I obtained another camera, Navy-style, I suppose. On the sponson, I found myself standing next to a young man who was peering through a videocam no larger than a pack of cigarettes.

"Pretty neat," I said.

"Only 499 bucks," he said proudly. "It takes stills, too."

"Yeah?"

"Yeah," he replied. "Let me show you." He took the camera through its paces; so much packed in such a little space. It was the damnedest thing I'd ever seen. Then a thought occurred.

"You wouldn't have an extra camera for rent, would you?" I asked.

He looked me over very carefully.

"Fifty bucks if I can use it until I leave," I added hopefully.

His eyes were fastened to the media credentials around my neck. This sailor was young, but he wasn't stupid.

"So what organization you with?" he asked.

"Talk Radio News Service."

"Never heard of it."

"Well, talk radio is really big in the States," I explained.

"You mean, like Rush Limbaugh?" he asked, eyes a little wider.

"Yeah, but we don't carry Rush Limbaugh. He has his own network."

"Cool," he replied. A moment passed. "I'll tell you what," he offered. "You look trustworthy. I've got a Sony Mavica. It's neat. The pics go right on a floppy. All you do is put the floppy in your computer and, bam, you're done."

I reached into my pocket and pulled out two twenties and a ten-dollar bill. "Here's the money up front. I'm down in the SEAL berth."

"Michael Bailey," he said and offered his hand. He seemed impressed that I'd fork over money without even asking his name.

Bailey was a nineteen-year-old OS3 from Florida who worked in Strike Operations, or Strike-Ops for short. The Navy defines this critical department as "responsible for planning, scheduling, and coordinating [of] ship and air wing operations," which includes "strike and weapons employment organization [and] the development of conventional and special warfare plans, including the overall coordination of weapons employment and the execution of strike operations." Translation: Strike-Ops knows the where that will get hit by what and by whom and when. If war comes, it will be Bailey and his colleagues who'll be inside the frontal lobes of the *Kitty Hawk*'s attack plans. What he knew is something that the Iraqis and not a few reporters would give their eyeteeth to know.

But he wasn't on the sponson to talk about any of that.

"I shouldn't be here, you know," he said to me in a quiet voice. He was staring off into the distance somewhere and spoke so quietly that at first, I wasn't sure he was talking to me.

"How so?"

"When I was a kid, I had a rare blood disease. It was so rare that only four other people had it when I did. You know how many are alive today?"

"Just you, I'm guessing," I replied, taking a chance.

Bailey smiled and winked. "You bet, Mr. Miller. Just me," he said.

"Is it something that has to be managed?" I asked.

"No. It went into remission when I was still a kid. It never came back. The docs don't know what happened or why it happened." He put a cigarette between his lips. But before he struck a match, I had my lighter out.

"Screw 'em," I said. "If they knew what they think they know, you'd be dead now."

"Hey, Sir, that's a cool thought."

I looked him right in the eye. He was only a few months younger than my own son.

"Very cool," I replied.

March 16
1145
The Hangar Deck

I filed my "God is my copilot" story with Talk Radio News this morning. A near-useless sat phone means that all my reports are filed by telephone into a tape recorder. While the sailor phone blinks on and off, depending on River City status, the ship's course, and pop goes the weasel, 30 percent efficiency beats 0 percent efficiency every time. Besides, unreliable communications means that I'm not tethered to a live broadcast schedule. Since my world is now damn close to 24/7, I can file when I want.

Today's broadcast is 301 words and takes me one minute and thirty seconds to read:

> As a wise man once said, somewhere in every person's soul, it's always 4:00 in the morning. It's the alone time where a man or a woman takes stock of their life and concentrates on the bigger questions. Perhaps nowhere are those questions more pressing at this time than among the fighter pilots aboard the United States Naval aircraft carrier, the USS *Kitty Hawk*. Many of the pilots are married, and many have children. Four A.M. can be a very difficult time indeed, for those who are asked to fly directly into the jaws of death.
>
> So what do the pilots think about in the quiet hours? Spirituality, says one, is a large part of it. On a warship in time of war, the planes are busy 24/7, making formal church, synagogue, or mosque worship impossible. But that does not mean that the pilots have abandoned a belief in a Higher Power.
>
> Interestingly, says one, God becomes their copilot only after the immediate danger has passed. One pilot describes a recent near-catastrophe in the air

when a critical piece of the wing malfunctioned. "During the whole time we were up there, it was all about how to deal with it," he says. "It was only after I had landed that I discovered my knees were knocking. I knew then that I owed my survival to God." Many of the pilots—enough to be called a fair sample—have said that, in one form or another, they all offer prayers and ask God to, in the words of one, "keep watch over me." A thorough knowledge of procedure, flying skill, and good self-confidence may help land the plane safely. While the pilots may provide the skill, most look far beyond the rule-book for the spiritual strength needed to go on.

Later on, I review this report and am embarrassed. I pretend it's the year 2103 and a historian is listening to century-old recordings of talk radio broadcasts, trying to learn something about this maybe war. What would the historian learn? That pilots facing the prospect of death think about spiritual matters? That's one hell of a news flash. No Bancroft Prize in tackling that one. Or perhaps that the reporter found it necessary to include the formulaic phrase "church, synagogue, or mosque," when, as a statistical matter, a mere sprinkling of Jews and even fewer (if any) Muslims pilot fighter jets. If the historian could prove that that formula was widespread despite the shortage of numbers, there might be a research paper or a book chapter in it. Somebody writing about fighter pilots might use it for color. That's it! My reports are purely anecdotal, a bit of color, the flame in the flambé, maybe even tasting good but otherwise calorie-free.

How this interview on which my report was based came about is more interesting. After a lonely cigar on the khaki sponson, I decided to wander around the hangar deck. As I ducked to avoid getting my skull halved by the leading edge of an F-14 Tomcat's wing, I literally bumped into Lt. Bill Blacker, who was also ducking the same wing at the same time. We both emerged on the trailing edge. But that was the place he wanted to be. He immediately turned around and stood to observe an airframe crew working on the wing.

"Yours?" I asked.

"No," he replied, "I fly something else. I just want to watch these guys work on the wing."

Lieutenant Blacker stands about six feet tall and, like every other pilot I've seen here, is a trim man. His eyes and hair are only slightly browner than his khaki flight suit, which he always wears. Like most pilots I've met on this boat, his eyes, even at rest, are always intensely focused on something. Bill Blacker is a quiet man, but it is a reserve of contemplation and not standoffishness. He has probably spent more ward room time with the media than any other pilot, although not for publicity reasons. Bill just seems to enjoy the off-duty congeniality of reporters, perhaps because it diverts him from his own job pressures.

I wonder if he realizes that, for reporters, all "off duty" really means is that the disk recorder is switched off and they're not taking notes. But it doesn't mean that they're not working. The ebb and flow of casual conversation is not just informative; although not for attribution, it may be one of the most useful sources of information: ideas for future stories, corroborating current stories, and earning goodwill from potential sources on stories not yet conceived. I won't criticize because it's a mentality I know all too well. During my twenty-five years in the investment business, it was my mentality. Every contact made was potentially part of next year's bonus pool.

"What am I looking at here?" I ask Bill.

"These guys are checking the aileron. It's lowered by a set of gears, and it's something that you definitely want to make sure is working before taking off." He was carefully studying the mechanisms' assemblies, which the aviation structural mechanics had partially exposed. I wasn't clear if he wanted to talk, so I just shut up and stood there.

"I had a problem with this recently," Bill finally said.

"What happened?"

"I was flying, and I sensed this very slight vibration from the wing. At first I wasn't sure it amounted to anything, but it got worse as we started our return leg."

It was apparent that just by retelling the story, "it" was getting worse again.

"What did you do?" I asked.

He looked at me with a smile and nodded his head. "There's probably two answers to that," he replied, "what I did when I was up there and what I did after I landed. Up there, it was like being numb to everything except procedures. I don't know how I felt because I wasn't really *feeling* anything, I was *thinking*—about checklists, emergency procedures, and different in-flight things to try to get a handle on the situation. When you're up there, it's all about how to deal with it."

"And after you landed?"

"My knees were knocking! And that really surprised me." Now he was smiling broadly, as if he was experiencing once again the relief of having made a safe landing.

"Do you ever get spiritual about these risks?" I wondered, half expecting a nonanswer. Religion is a topic I study but rarely discuss.

"Definitely," he replied without embarrassment. "But it comes later, after the landing. Then I felt the sense that I wasn't just lucky, that I owed my survival to God."

Who knows what a future historian might conclude from all of this? Maybe that the society waging this maybe war wasn't quite as secular as the old microfilms of the *New York Times* editorial pages wished that it was.

CHAPTER 16

A Christian Sabbath

1900
Forecastle
All Hands Gospel Praise Service

I WENT TO THE Gospel service tonight. It was an amazing experience. I've never attended a Christian service before, save a wedding or two in liberal, Protestant churches, which, like those of Reform Judaism, rarely invoke God's name. But that wasn't true here. The name of God is loudly and joyously proclaimed with every utterance, in prayer, in song, in clapping, shouting, testifying, and finally in the sermon. *Kedushah* fills this room, and prayer, like a messenger-bearing bird, soars to heights simply unattainable through any other experience. It is a literature without words, with a beginning and a middle that lift toward the crescendo, peak with great sweat and power before resolving, spent, exhausted, yet fulfilled by the end. Emotions are swept up and carried aloft, willing passengers, even those belonging to an old Hebrew like me. But it doesn't matter, because Christ or no Christ, what's happening here is also done in the name of the Father, and the Father is something I do believe in, as in the *Aveinu, Malkanu* ("Our Father, Our King") prayer that Jews recited each *Yom HaKippurim.*

The room in which this service was held is itself a fascinating place. It houses the anchor chains of the *Kitty Hawk.* Two of these lie parallel across the deck, creating a useful rectangle between them some 30 feet wide and 80 feet long. The anchor chain ultimately stretches more than 1,000 feet in length and is composed of links weighing 360 pounds each. If the chain is almost inconceivably long and strong, it must be, for the anchor at its end weighs 30 tons. (The *Kitty Hawk* has two such anchors.)

Unexpectedly (to me), the worshipers are not solely African American. There are a fair number of white and Hispanic faces, including a white member of the gospel choir. On the far side of the far anchor chain was a small ensemble, including an organist, a drummer, and someone to spin records of background music. On the far side of the near anchor chain stood the media, which tonight, consisted mostly of my Japanese colleagues and Hu, whom I persuaded to attend. Eventually, though, I decide to sit with the other parishioners.

Before the service, I am introduced to Lt. Dee Etheridge, a tall, 40-something, mustached Black man from Decatur, Georgia. Rarely have I received as warm and genuine a welcome to anything. Lieutenant Etheridge began the service by asking all newcomers to rise and introduce themselves to the congregation. I did so with great embarrassment, as I felt a stranger on two counts, as a Jew and as a member of the media there to report a story. But these feelings didn't last long. As each person rose and gave a name and hometown, Lieutenant Etheridge led the congregation in a round of applause and welcome.

The gospel singers harmonize complexly, sweetly, in a wholesome way that invokes the sights and sounds of a summer morning on a Vermont hillside or dusk settling across the Nantucket moors in July. As six days were necessary to construct the hillside and the moor, so this congregation works and studies six days to create the sounds that seem to lilt from their lips on Sunday. The choir practices on Wednesday and Saturday, a singles ministry meets on Tuesday, and Bible study is held Monday, Wednesday, Friday, and Saturday.

Later I file my story, one that I am genuinely proud of.

> At 1900 hours every Sunday—that's 7 P.M. to civilians—a remarkable event takes place on the forecastle deck of the United States Naval aircraft carrier USS *Kitty Hawk*: Amidst the roar of jet aircraft landing and departing on the flight deck above, the sweet spirituality of gospel singing soars, rising to figurative altitudes higher than any plane can fly. Under the management of Lt. Junior Grade Dee Etheridge, of Decatur, Georgia, an 18-year veteran of the Navy who came up through the ranks, the *Kitty Hawk*'s gospel choir suddenly transforms this ship of war into a home of all things spiritual.
>
> While the worshipers are mostly African Americans, members of all races

are found in the audience. It is easy to see why. When Lieutenant Etheridge introduces the weekly worship, his message is meant for everybody. "God is good," he declares, "and He has given us another week to be thankful for." Lieutenant Etheridge introduces new attendees who stand to the warm applause from their fellow worshipers. Tonight ten people have come for the first time, and the audience numbers about one hundred.

Then the gospel choir breaks out into song. Led by Terry Toncil, a young Black man with an especially sweet yet soaring tenor voice, the gospel choir begins singing, most fittingly in this room that houses the massive anchor chains, "There's a storm out on the ocean. . . ." This is quickly followed by that old standby "Amazing Grace" and "God Has Smiled on Me." The voices are enhanced, but not overshadowed, by an organ and drums off to the side. For a room intended to house the aircraft carrier's massive anchors, the acoustics are remarkably good.

The sermon is delivered by Pastor Javier Roman, an ordained Assembly of God minister and one of the four chaplains aboard the USS *Kitty Hawk*. His sermon is straightforward and taken from Matthew Chapter 6: The Lord's Prayer. He notes the troubled times through which this ship and crew are passing, and he emphasizes the importance of prayer and forgiveness in maintaining one's personal balance. But this is no battle prayer, and the pastor is emphatic: One should pray not only for one's own welfare, but for the welfare of one's enemies. This, he argues, is the soul of forgiveness.

The USS *Kitty Hawk* is sometimes referred to as a "steel island" in the middle of the ocean. If so, then the *Kitty Hawk*'s gospel choir is an island within this island—of peace and respite in the eye of the gathering storm.

Later it occurs to me that the Rev. Martin Luther King Jr. was not only the necessary man but was so in part because he arrived with another necessity—a minister's collar. Had he been a member of Congress, judge, lobbyist, or university president, his message wouldn't have penetrated past the franking privilege or the commencement address. The religious setting—perhaps the religious person—may be the only authentic messenger to convey the humanity of the Other. Standing before the Almighty, where everyone is paradoxically reduced in importance but heightened in significance, is one of the few places where, however briefly, differences vanish, swept away by realizations of shared mortality, sorrows, struggles, and joys; all differences submerge, much as they will in the grave.

But it was always like this in America. During the Civil War, many Whites, soldiering through the slave states, had their first face-to-face encounters with Black people and, especially, African American Christianity. Some, like the anonymous contributor to the first regimental history of the 45th Massachusetts Volunteer Infantry, were unable to surmount their racism. After attending his first Black church service, he found the singing, clapping, and shouting "ludicrous" and concluded, "It was sad to think that these poor creatures could hope to win salvation in such a manner, yet at the same time, the absurdity and comicality of the whole affair was irresistible, and showed a phase of Negro character both strange and amusing."

But not everyone felt the same. For Henry T. Johns, a quartermaster's assistant of the 49th Massachusetts Volunteer Militia serving in Louisiana, his first encounter with African-American Christianity was transforming. He entered the service believing Blacks were, "if not a happy race, [then] at least careless and lighthearted." But face-to-face contact soon changed his mind. "Observation begins to compel me to rewrite my former theories, and to set down their joyousness and happiness as a plantation lie," he wrote home in February 1863.

> I have been with them a great deal, and never before saw so much of gloom, despondency, and listlessness. I saw no banjo, heard none but solemn songs. In church, or in the street, they impress me with a great sadness. . . . I attended one of their class and prayer meetings at Carrollton, and in speaking to them, incidentally said, "The first gun fired at Fort Sumter cracked the chain of every slave in the land." I was surprised at the response. "Glory! Hallelujah!" sounded from all parts of the house. Old men cried, clapped their hands, and all gathered round me, as if I were an angel of good tidings. . . . In every prayer, blessings were invoked for our officers and soldiers, and especially for our sick. . . . Thank God, the old flag now means freedom to all under its folds.

Every group has its own *goyim*, whom they fear and loathe. For most people, personal interaction is the only antidote to "otherness."

At the All Hands Gospel Service, racism is impossible.

March 17
0400

I slept only a few hours last night, then rose at 0100. I can't sleep, I don't want to sleep, I don't care about sleep. For the first time since my 20s, sleep has become an inconvenience, a party pooper, a meddlesome authority figure standing between me and my thrills. When I arose, I made a beeline to the television set, an exercise that is now as exciting as opening the mail or waiting to get sued. CNN was reporting that President Bush's Azores meeting with Spanish Prime Minister Aznar and Tony Blair was just ending or, at least, we're just hearing about it now. It looks to me like showtime approacheth.

March 17th has been reaffirmed as the drop-dead date for both Saddam and the United Nations. As they say in Hebrew, *yemach shemot*, "may their names be erased." Rumors are strong—not ship scuttlebutt but TV-correspondent-with-sources rumors—that the president will speak to the nation sometime Monday evening, which translates into the very wee hours of local time.

To the wardroom for a hot cup of coffee, then it's out on the sponson for a smoke.

The Countdown Begins

0430
Enlisted Sponson

"*HEY, MAN,*" a sailor volunteers to me between drags on his cigarette, "I hope Bush pulls the trigger."

"Why's that?"

"Because the sooner he does, the faster we're outta here. Nothing sucks the big one like floating around just waiting and waiting and waiting. Let's just finish Saddam and go home." He was probably up all night and seemed irritated.

"Hear, hear," I reply. By now, I'm feeling as if I've earned the right to want to go home too.

As I lean against the rope rail gazing at a sky brightening by turns, it suddenly occurs to me that there is a major disconnect between the home front and the front lines. Most people here just want to pull the trigger and go home. But back home many an armchair patriot demands revenge for 9/11 and giggles when the callers on talk radio insist that our military should "just aim for the head rag" or "push a few daisy cutters over Baghdad and call it a day." (Indeed, I'll plead guilty to sometimes feeling the same.) What's striking on this ship is what's missing. There is very little evidence of bloodlust. Why is that? I've been on this ship long enough to ask the question directly.

"Since I've been on this boat," I ask a sailor a few moments later, "I haven't heard anyone yelling about getting even for 9/11 or wanting to see Saddam boiled in oil. Why is that?"

"We're professionals," he replies. "It's just business out here."

I'm not satisfied with this answer, in part because since I've been on board my own feelings of aggression against Saddam and the Islamic extremists have actually abated. I've gotten colder about it—grim necessity and all that—less emotionally involved about the enemy, and I am most definitely not a professional.

"I know it's just business," I prod, "but what do you think it is about your business that makes you so cool about this while some of us civilians are screaming for blood? I mean, for every guy marching against the war back home, there are probably four or five guys who'd like nothing better than to see Saddam swing from a lamppost."

"I don't know," the sailor replied with a shrug.

I thought that would be the end of it. But it wasn't the end of it for him, because a moment later, he turned to me with a simple question.

"Have you ever thought about what our business really is?" he asked.

"Sure. When somebody dials 911 and the phone rings in the Oval Office, Bush just forwards the call to the *Kitty*—"

"No, no, man," he gently interrupted. "Whatever you're about to say, it isn't right because there's only one word that says all you got to know about our business, at least when the action starts."

"What's that?"

"Death."

It was as if this kid pulled a string, and what had been a pile of matchsticks, bits of cloth, and thread suddenly sprang up, a fully rigged ship in a bottle. So many things about the last eight days instantly became clear to me. What this sailor meant by professionalism, and what I experienced as the serious demeanor and earnestness typical of many sailors, was actually the product of two incongruous forces that in civilian life rarely meet but over here meet daily: youth and the omnipresence of death.

This runs counter to one of our most widely held beliefs about why the young fight wars. Aside from their peak physical condition, there is also an assumption about their mental state. People believe that the young, just off the cusp of adolescence, have little experience with death and only the vaguest sense of their own mortality. They fight and take risks because death is not yet real to them. Unlike the fifty-year-old, who knows he is much closer to the end than to the beginning, the young, still somehow convinced of their own invulnerability, will take the little chances upon which big military campaigns always depend. They will take hills, damn torpedoes, go over the top, and hit the silk.

And indeed, it is the young who have done all of these things. But at least on this Navy ship, the absence of an acute consciousness of death is not among the reasons why these kids take the risks. My mind suddenly floods with a stream of images from the last ten days. They are the death cues. They are the slim, futuristic-looking missiles and bombs stacked neatly in open areas adjoining the mess halls; they are the man overboard drills and calls to general quarters, the time spent donning chembio suits, and the drills with gas masks strapped to our thighs; they are the .50-caliber machine guns bristling from the sponsons, the repeated safety warnings on the public address system and on the huge signs that dominate work spaces in the hangar deck; they are the lockers near the enlisted mess that are marked ''Armory'' and the red crosses of the triage stations throughout the ship; they are servicing aircraft whose most important passengers are explosive devices with godlike pretensions. Mortality prompts are everywhere; they startle at first, as they did me when I saw my first stack of 2,000-pound bombs. But while the eye soon grows used to it, the mind behind the eye never does.

So in a thousand subtle ways, death is all around us; its impact on behavior has been a staple of military thinkers since the beginning of organized warfare. This much is certain: The constant exposure to death cues is perpetually sobering; the bombs to be dispatched on the enemy will kill them and perhaps others who don't deserve to die; the pilots I dine with may also die. To live with death in this way breeds a constant, barely discernible fear, something like a malfunctioning appliance's low buzz that one eventually grows used to. The white noise of work, shipmates, television, and routine quickly drowns it out but never entirely stills it. If the solitude of mind deepens enough, the buzz grows louder.

Young people who confront mortality in this way become, on average, more serious in demeanor than those who manage to avoid the unpleasant inevitability of life's end. The accountability of Navy life extends far beyond having to answer to one's chief for a job poorly done; it's also the possibility of being held to account by God or oblivion or another twilight deity at the end of one's own life or of having to answer for the end of someone else's life.

In the half-light of morning, I lean over the rope rail and watch the continual shower of cigarette butts arc over my head and rain down into the sea, a thousand points of light, extinguished.

2115
SEAL Berth

Capt. Parker was on the 1MC earlier. When he addresses the crew, which is at least once a day, everyone who isn't otherwise engaged is supposed to stop and listen. Most sailors don't believe a thing until they've heard the captain say it. Now I'm getting in that habit, too. Today, Capt. Parker reacted to Bush's ultimatum to Saddam to leave Iraq within 48 hours. "I have about as much chance as being elected pope," he said, "as Saddam Hussein does of leaving Iraq in the next two days." He then asked the crew to prepare for a very busy week.

The crew likes Capt. Parker. When he signed off the 1MC, a Black crew member turned to his mate and said with a smile, "He's the man!"

March 18
0430
Enlisted Mess

Forty-eight hours. President Bush just finished his fifteen-minute speech, and Saddam has forty-eight hours to get out of town. He won't, of course. Whether he knows his Richard Wagner or not, characters like Saddam always seem to end their days with a Götterdammerung. It must be a by-product of the hardwiring inside the brains of glorified serial killers. Had Saddam Hussein been the son of a hardware store owner from Lubbock, the State of Texas would have already given him the needle after his fourth conviction for strangling and raping prostitutes. But clothe him in state sovereignty with a few European embassies, and suddenly it takes an entire army rather than a few drops of potassium chloride to finish him.

I chose to be in the enlisted mess for the president's speech. For the first time since I've been aboard, the mess TV was tuned to the news. And for the first time, too, the normal sounds of the mess were absent—no noisy conversation; no clinking of glass, utensils, and plates; no shuffling; no laughter; nothing—except the silence of tense apprehension and the voice of the president. The sailors were all gathered around the television, a hundred silent, upturned faces. Those who had to eat but couldn't see the screen chose to stand. Others simply stopped eating. Until this very moment, the talking heads and standing headlines had been just so much white noise, blending with the sound of ship's engines, the guttural roll of the catapults, and the stream of public address announcements and just as easily ignorable; however, now the noise had resolved into a single, clear sound—albeit with a Texas drawl—the voice of the commander-in-chief, essentially giving these kids a timetable many had sought vainly for months—the probable start of the war.

One kid turned to me, looked at the media credentials hanging around my neck, and said in a tone that attempted more self-reassurance than anything else, "Hey, man, like I always say—in God and the CIWS [pronounced Sea-Whiz] we trust!"

His choice of weapons system in which to place his faith, the CIWS, was revealing. The *Kitty Hawk* is protected at all times by its seaborne cherubim, the escort ships, who cast an invisible electronic net over it, the attempted penetration of which would probably disable the attack and surely annihilate the attacker; nevertheless, this sailor took his solace in the *Hawk*'s weapon of last resort: the Phalanx close-in weapons system (CIWS). And he wasn't alone. In the past few days, perhaps reflecting the growing political tensions, I have heard many sailors and officers speak confidently about the CIWS. The *Kitty Hawk* has two batteries of these guns, and their purpose is to defend the boat against the one weapon that gives pause to anyone who knows what actually kills ships in the modern age—guided missiles. It was a French-made Argentinean-launched Exocet missile that destroyed the HMS *Sheffield* during the 1982 Falklands War. Five years later, an Iraqi F-1 Mirage fired two Exocets at the USS *Stark*, a Navy frigate in the Persian Gulf, killing thirty-seven sailors. Although the *Stark* was equipped with the CIWS, it was later reported erroneously that the system was impaired before the ship left port in Bahrain. The captain of the *Stark* was relieved after the investigation.

What could be more businesslike than the destruction of a ship by a guided missile? It cost John Bull 23 million pounds in 1971 to build the HMS *Sheffield*; the Exocet that destroyed it cost the Argentines about $100,000. And it's still a bargain today. The People's Liberation Army catalog of weapons systems (accessible online with a downloadable order form) lists an Exocet knockoff, the so-called Sardine missile, for only $360,000 a copy. (The minimum order is forty units at a cost of $14.4 million—still well within the budget of any Middle Eastern coastal kleptocrat, seaside serial killer, or mad mullah.)

Against all this, as a last resort stands the CWIS. Its 20-mm cannon rounds are fired Gatling gun–style at a cyclical rate of between 1,000 and 3,000 rounds per minute. The rounds are made of tungsten and have an effective range of 6,000 yards—over three miles. It deploys in seconds and is designed to throw up a screen of dumb rounds that incoming missiles cannot evade or jam. In one sense, the CWIS beats an Exocet-type missile at its own game; 20-mm shells, even those made from tungsten, are much cheaper than guided missiles. Thus is maintained the reverse food chain of military economics: The cheaper beast will always eat the costlier beast.

Hell if I know if the CWIS actually works. I hope it does, because given the numbers, if I were Saddam, perhaps looking to launch a final jihad volley against the Crusaders and Jews and go down in the history books as a latter-day Saladin, I know what I'd do: launch every missile I owned, especially the ship killers. What better press in the Arab street for Saddam than the image of (Heaven forfend) the *Kitty Hawk* on fire in the Gulf?

They'd be cheering in the streets of Gaza.

Wardroom II
0500

Before racking out, I stopped by wardroom II. The ratio of media to officers in there was about 8 to 1. Apparently, President Bush had just finished speaking when the press horde jumped on the one officer who wasn't wise enough to flee the room. He was being grilled by the (mostly Japanese) reporters seeking reaction to the speech. I didn't recognize the officer, and for all I know he'd just escaped from the ship's brig. But for tens of millions of Japanese newspaper readers, his comments will help define Bush's speech.

There was no room on the computer table in the SEAL berth, as every reporter was online, busy clicking E-mails to their editors. The sight inspires me to file a report. Besides, I'm not tired anymore, so I walk around, stop by the sponson, sample the air, and try to eavesdrop on as many conversations relevant to the president's remarks as I can. Sometime about 0630, I file the following report:

At 4 A.M. local time, President Bush spoke directly to the men and women of the United States naval aircraft carrier USS *Kitty Hawk*. For fifteen minutes, the hangar deck mechanics working on fighter jets, kitchen crews preparing breakfast, and ordinary sailors who had remained awake to hear the president gathered around the televisions in their mess halls and wardrooms. For the next fifteen minutes, silence reigned aboard the USS *Kitty Hawk*. Even the constant low roar of this mighty ship's engines seemed to quiet in deference to the commander-in-chief.

And what they heard came, from the point of view of most sailors aboard this ship, as a great relief. No one on this vessel is anxious for war. And while few sailors doubt the military outcome of this looming conflict, many have questions about what will happen afterwards.

But for weeks, the men and women of the USS *Kitty Hawk* have asked for only one thing—certainty. What they have wanted to know is exactly when their mission will begin. The reason isn't complicated. Only by answering this question can the answer to another be found: When will we go home?

Now the president has given them their answer. Perhaps not surprisingly, the reaction of the crew of the USS *Kitty Hawk* was one of relief. In telling Saddam Hussein that he has 48 hours to leave Iraq or be deposed, the president has also given this crew the first real time line they have had in this conflict: The war may start in forty-eight hours or soon after. If U.S. planners have it right, it may be over in a matter of days. The sooner, the better for the crew of the USS *Kitty Hawk*. As one sailor said to me last night, as we looked over the calm, beautiful, moonlit, speckled waters of the Persian Gulf, "This is real pretty, but I'd rather be looking at the ice in Casco Bay." This man's home is in Portland, Maine.

Life Goes On but So Does the Countdown

Our forecastle, as usual after a liberty-day, was a scene of tumult all night long, from the drunken ones. They had just got to sleep toward morning, when they were turned up with the rest, and kept at work all day in the water, carrying hides, their heads aching so that they could hardly stand. This is a sailor's pleasure.

—Richard H. Dana Jr.
JANUARY 1836
Two Years Before the Mast

1200
Wardroom II

I THOUGHT LUNCH TODAY would be full of war and rumors of war talk. But I was mistaken. Humor dissolves tension, and there was plenty of it, mostly coming from the man they call Judge Stone.

Judge Stone is the highest ranking Navy lawyer on this ship. Just as Dr. Elster defies the stereotype of a ship's doctor, so Judge Stone embodies nothing of what a military lawyer is popularly thought to be, best summarized by the title of Lefty writer Robert Sherrill's book, *Military Justice Is to Justice as Military Music Is to Music.* Judge Stone is a balding fellow in his mid-forties, whose pronounced nose, perpetually arched eyebrows, and bright eyes look every inch the middle-aged lawyer. I've worked with Stones all of my adult life, and it's easy to imagine him wearing a $2,500 bespoke suit, cap toe shoes made by Peel, and a power tie, sitting around a mahogany conference table on the 103d floor of the World Trade Center, say, the old offices of Shearson Lehman Brothers, and all of us reviewing some trust indenture to prevent the borrower from screwing the bondholders. That work required a combination of shrewdness, imagination, and hyperintellect.

Judge Stone has all three. Somehow, the conversation turned to drug use on ship, and he regaled us with the tale of his latest and perhaps greatest bust.

"So what we did," he explained, "was give random drug tests the day before we gave everyone liberty in port. I think we tested maybe fifteen-hundred sailors."

"And the results?" I asked

"Oh, maybe sixteen confirmed positives," he replied. "But get this. Everybody knew, or thought they knew, that up until then, random drug tests were only done at four- to six-month intervals, right? So nobody's expecting the next tests any sooner. Well, everyone came back from liberty three days later, and you know what? I hit them with another test, only this time, it was everyone aboard. Everybody!"

"Right after liberty?" I asked. "Isn't everybody probably more vul—"

"Yep," he interrupted, "more vulnerable. You bet."

"How many tested positive?"

He smiled and revealed a hunter's satisfaction.

"We bagged 116 confirmed positives!"

He had every reason to be happy. On May 26, 1981, the realities of importing a drug-loose society were visited upon the Navy. An EA-6B Prowler slammed into the deck of the USS *Nimitz*; as sailors fought the fire and cleared the wreckage, a missile exploded, and fourteen sailors died. The Navy insisted that drugs didn't play a role in either the plane crash or the later explosion, but autopsies revealed that six of the dead sailors had been smoking marijuana. Flight decks that are hazardous for the sober aren't just suicidal for stoned crew members; stoners in critical positions become homi-cidal for everyone else. As a result of the *Nimitz* accident, the Navy took the pledge and adopted a zero tolerance policy regarding substance abuse. In short, the Navy handles too many big bombs that go boom to be running an Oprahfied halfway house for serial stoners, rumpots, snow sniffers, crackheads, ravers, and others in search of better living through chemistry.

"So what happened to the guys you caught?" I asked.

"Off the ship and out of the Navy," he replied.

The Judge had reason to be happy. Just before the *Nimitz* accident, a DoD survey discovered that 33.7 percent of the sailors said they had been stoned within the past thirty days. But twenty years of zero tolerance has had its effects. A 1998 survey showed that less than 2 percent of sailors admitted having been high during the prior month. However, understood in absolute numbers, it's still a problem, especially given that a single stoner in a critical position could do a lot of damage. In 2001, there were 1,339 confirmed positives (just within the surface fleet), and this number was actually expected to increase in 2002 to 1,518 positives.

I took the Judge's happiness to be as much a function of self-protection as a job well done. After all, he lives and works on this boat, has a family in Japan, seems to enjoy life, and thus is in no haste to be incinerated because some stoned moron decided to flick his Bic during a refueling. But the policy ends served by these random drug-testing sweeps is really prevention. One Navy officer involved in the program has stated, "We've increased testing not to kick more sailors out of the Navy, but to serve as a deterrent. I like to use the analogy of seeing a cop in your rearview mirror when you drive. When that happens, you don't go over the speed limit."

All of this underscores an important reality of life on a ship: Survival is a team sport. Walking through Harvard Square, I would never rat out the orange-, green-, and blue-haired punks raving in the area they call the Pit, smoking weed and playing insufferable music. (Not that the Cambridge cops would do anything.) It's purely a matter of self-interest. If these kids are determined to destroy themselves, so be it; my life or the lives of those I love aren't intimately connected with them. They're strangers.

But on ship, the sailors you've never met, will never meet, and will never even see from a distance are not strangers because everyone hangs from the same web of codependency.

It's for that reason that if I saw a sailor smoke a joint on this boat, I'd dime him out the first chance I got.

1600
Khaki Smoking Sponson

There was a moment of medium drama today. On an otherwise beautiful afternoon, what we're told is that an Iraqi naval vessel suddenly appears on the horizon. In reality, its appearance was sudden only to me. The ever-vigilant radars of the *Kitty Hawk*'s screening ships, the *Kitty Hawk* itself, manned aircraft, and who knows what other devices have probably been tracking the clunky supply ship–looking gray-painted vessel several miles off our stern.

But what I noticed first wasn't the Iraqi ship but our sailors holding powerful binoculars and wearing headphones with boom mikes that were plugged into the wall. Then I started looking at what they were looking at.

I needed more, so with the permission of an officer, I slipped under the yellow cord separating the smoking area from the ramp that encircled the stern of the ship, a ramp on which stood two sailors observing the suspect vessel. Between them was a .50-caliber machine gun, and a third sailor behind it, waiting. I stood quietly next to a lanky kid who was absorbed in his duty. He stared through his binoculars, whispered some report or other into his mike, and raised his binoculars again. I turned around and noticed that there were a number of other sailors doing precisely the same thing; some were on our ramp, and others were on ramps above us. For all of the fancy, high-tech gizmos pledged to do or die, it still comes down to a few kids with looking glasses.

"Want a look?" the sailor asked me. He offered his binoculars.

I took them and looked at the Iraqi vessel. It was painted a naval gray and had the profile of a freighter—no turret guns could be seen—but had strange, greenish panels amidships. Or were these a distortion of sun and sea? I couldn't tell.

"What is it?" I asked.

"Iraqi," the sailor replied.

"Any reason to worry?"

He smirked. "Yo, dude," he replied. "The bitch so much as farts and she's surface ash."

Fart was perhaps a better metaphor than this kid knew. The leadership was concerned with a chemical attack, and it was possible that a boat similar to this gray, nondescript vessel would, by missile, mortar, or act of self-destruction, produce a deadly cloud of sarin, VX, or who knows what else. Because light travels faster than sound, as I looked through the binoculars, I half expected to see a puff of smoke followed by the sound of a rocket launch or a chemical-tipped artillery shell being fired at us.

Although I've never heard of chemical warfare at sea, the idea of using innocent-looking vessels to kill enemy ships is nothing new. During World War I, the British deployed Q ships—essentially merchant vessels that concealed heavy guns behind collapsible deck structures—in order to lull German U-boats to the surface before dropping the disguise and opening fire. (In those days, U-boats would conserve their torpedoes through extortion; they would surface, threaten to torpedo a defenseless merchant ship, force the crew to abandon, and then sink it with a deck gun or, after boarding the merchant ship, opening its sea cocks. What the U-boat didn't expect was a merchant ship that fired back.)

It wasn't hard to imagine the crew of this Iraqi boat suddenly stripping off a canvas tarp on deck to reveal a chemical-tipped Silkworm missile aimed at us. Suicidal, yes, but we were sailing on the Sea of Suicide, bordered by the Lands of Suicide, places whose religious constitutions had preambles written by Osama bin Laden, indicting the West for being weak because we love life too much to risk losing it. This twisted strain of Islam took Prophet Muhammad's acceptance of the divinity of the Torah and the Gospels but forgot about Deuteronomy 30:19: "I [God] have set before thee life and death, the blessing and the curse; therefore choose life, that thou mayest live, thou and thy seed."

One day, Saddam Hussein's discount Stalinism, Osama bin Laden's jihadists, Saudi Arabia's fanatical Wahhabis, and the rest of these ambitious killers or lights-unto-killers will finally strike the world as insane as Hitler's cry for Lebensraum strikes us today.

Until then, I suppose lanky sailors will just have to float off their shores with their eyes open and F-18s at the ready.

1900
The RAS

Tonight it's cigar time on the signal bridge with Dr. Elster, Pastor Roman, and Dr. Chris Bellard, the ship's Clark Gable-like senior flight surgeon. The horizon is clear, and the gloaming at sea is sublime. The pale blue sky deepens by a mysterious gathering mist into a rich, dark blue that bends heaven itself into a star-bejeweled dome. No jets fly, and except for the sounds of meandering conversation and the low, reassuring vibration of the ship's engines, an unexpected peace has settled on this bridge.

For a time, my back was to the horizon, my head tilted up, eyes searching for the zenith. Then I turned around, and everything changed. While I was silently waxing poetic on the celestial wonders, the USS *Niagara Falls*, a 581-foot tender, had silently pulled alongside the *Kitty Hawk* and was now sailing on a course precisely parallel to our own, and no more (or less) than 150 feet away. In another moment, reports of rifles were heard, although not discharged in anger. I couldn't see them, but from the hangar bay of the *Kitty Hawk*, M-14 rifles had fired rubber-tipped projectiles attached to a cable. These landed on the *Niagara Falls* and, in part, would prove by their tautness that the two ships were indeed maintaining a parallel course. Were these two vessels to collide, it could result in a major disaster.

What I was witnessing was a replenishment at sea, shortened military-style to RAS but pronounced RAZZ. Like so many military acronyms, it explains everything and describes nothing. The words denote the function adequately enough; for the *Kitty Hawk* to remain at sea, it must be resupplied at sea. This means taking in everything from food to fuel oil, bombs to bandages, and the hundred thousand other items required to support the needs of more than five thousand sailors. But how this is done is a marvel of seamanship. As I observe these operations, somebody mentions that for all the obvious reasons, a RAS at night is especially hazardous. Indeed, the claim is also made that in addition to the U.S. Navy, only the British and Russian navies can perform a nighttime RAS.

Dr. Elster taps my shoulder and points to the bridge just above ours. Standing at temporary attention is a sailor with handheld signal lights; in a moment she (from the cranial, vest, and uniform, I believe she is a she) moves her arms in a series of highly disciplined and repetitive motions that signal to her counterpart on the *Niagara Falls* to go or not to go, to stop or to start the re-supply. What strikes the landlubber is that today's electronic communications notwithstanding, the reliability and instantaneousness of handheld signal communications make them just as useful as they were for Napoleon, Nelson, Grant, and Lee.

There are two types of RAS. The first is the CONREP (connected replenishment), the means by which fuel oil, among other things, is transferred from the tending vessel to the receiving ship. The cables that are shot across with the M-14 rifles are used to guide hoses into the receiving ship, which are then hooked to the fuel tanks. Through these hoses flows the oil that the *Kitty Hawk* (unlike a nuclear-powered carrier) needs for engine fuel. What I am witnessing tonight, however, is the second type of RAS, the VERTREP (vertical replenishment). Here helicopters transport cargo from the tender to the receiving ship. Like all carrier flight operations, it's hazardous and weather-sensitive, and it perks the adrenaline of players and witnesses alike.

The RAS is distinguished from the other complex naval operations I've witnessed in a way that makes it doubly impressive, compared with anything I've yet seen. Unlike the high-tech whirligigs that dazzle, blink, and bomb, the RAS seems to rely on uniquely human skills: an eye for navigation, a sense of the wind and water, a quick judgment following a look-see on the deck before flashing the green light for a helicopter transfer. The RAS relies on few technology fail-safes that might avert, abort, or evade its various hazards. It all comes down to a handful of sailors on each ship who look, listen, think, and then act. There is something elemental about the RAS that brings to mind the world of Richard Henry Dana Jr., when the captain's judgment about weather, ship's weight, and wind might cause him to reef the topgallants and furl the spankers, and that could make all the difference.

The helicopter landed on the bow decks of the *Niagara Falls*, lifted its pre-positioned cargo, and then ascended. But it remained hovering above and between the two ships, as if suspended on a thread from the sky, awaiting the green light to deliver the goods on the *Kitty Hawk*'s deck. There was nothing foregone about any of this, for each move in the process required some human being's assent.

"There's quite a crowd up here tonight," Dr. Elster observes.

"I'll give you one guess why," Dr. Bellard answers, pointing to what's being loaded into the cargo boxes on the deck of the tender.

I squint and followed his finger toward the *Niagara Falls*. For the first time, I notice that the deck of the *Niagara Falls* is covered with stacks of bombs and missiles of every description.

And from the darkness behind me, an unfamiliar voice mutters, "Showtime, soon."

Bands of Brother and Sisters

March 19
1100
SEAL Berth

LAST NIGHT I FELL ASLEEP sometime between 4:00 and 6:00 A.M.; most days I wake up at 9:00 or 10:00 or 11:00. Today it is 11:00. Hu from Xinhua taps me on the shoulder. "Uh, admiral soon. You go?" he asks. The admiral is Vice Admiral Timothy Keating, commander of Fifth Fleet. He will address the crew on the hangar deck, the only indoor space large enough to accommodate the several thousand crew members expected to attend.

1230
Hangar Deck

Hangar bay door #2 is a massive oval open to the sea on the ship's starboard side. Through this portal, aircraft are lowered from the flight deck on a piece of that deck that doubles as an elevator. The hangar deck serves as a floating garage. After repair, planes return to the flight deck on the same elevator. By day, the inside of the hangar deck is always darker than the ocean and its horizon. The effect is to silhouette anything that moves or stands on the hangar deck in front of the bay. Although today's sea is an indifferent gray, the sky, while overcast, is very bright. It sharpens all silhouettes, and the effect is visually dramatic.

Most of my colleagues arrived at hangar bay door #2 earlier, to scarf up a good seat near the speaker's podium. This is essential for both the photo-journalists and the foreign reporters whose grasp of English is poor. But my place is in the back with the crew. War is near, and we are told that the admiral wants to deliver a pep talk to the ship.

Calling these speeches "pep talks" cheapens them, since this genre has long been accepted into the canons of Western literature or classic military historiography. William Shakespeare's Henry V's address to his men on the eve of battle probably epitomized a thousand unrecorded speeches before and since, articulating the warrior's creed in words that might sound ridiculous in any situation other than the one for which they are intended:

> This day is called the feast of Crispian:
> He that outlives this day, and comes safe home,
> Will stand a tip-toe when this day is nam'd.
> And rouse him at the name of Crispian.
>
> . . . .
>
> We few, we happy few, we band of brothers;
> For he to-day that sheds his blood with me
> Shall be my brother.

Eloquence is not always conveyed by the spoken word. The situation in which men on the verge of battle find themselves can charge ordinary words or deeds with electricity that is unforgettable to those present and possibly later generations. Here's Lord Nelson from his flagship as the English fleet prepares to break the French line at the Battle of Trafalgar. He verbalizes nothing but sends this message by raising signal flags, letter by letter, as every eye in the British fleet is upon him: "E-N-G-L-A-N-D E-X-P-E-C-T-S T-H-A-T E-V-E-R-Y M-A-N W-I-L-L D-O H-I-S D-U-T-Y." Sometimes even this much is unnecessary. After slugging it out at Wilderness against Robert E. Lee's vicious flanking attacks, most of the Union Army expected, once again, to return north of the Rapidan. But Grant had other ideas. He ordered the Army of the Potomac south, and on the night of May 7, 1864, when soldiers saw their commander riding in that direction on the Brock Road, men instantly understood that they weren't retreating this time and that they were going to finish the damn business whatever it cost, and they cheered Grant as he rode by, even though the noise attracted rebel fire. Grant never had to say a word.

A year or two earlier, the crowd on this morning's hangar deck might have been found at a high school basketball game. They are the crew, and they are young, many in their late teens. They mill about in nervous excitement, high-fiving shipmates, trading scuttlebutt, chewing gum, and griping. Some are probably nervous about what the admiral will have to say on the brink of war; the few I speak with are happy for the certainty that the war will now happen, which, for a crew that has been at sea for far too long (just ask any one of them!) means that they are a step closer to port and home. But I think the main reason for their excitement is that they are part of a large crowd with their peers. Such gatherings usually occur at ball games and rock concerts, pleasurable occasions.

"Attention on deck!" Lounging sailors with young, plastic bodies suddenly snap to attention; machinery is switched off and tools put down. An unaccustomed silence fills this huge space. In the distance stands a lone figure behind the podium. It is Admiral Keating, and he is about to record his contribution to the ancient anthology.

He first makes the usual concessions to our egalitarian times. This ship is like home to him, he declares, and he proudly touts the *Kitty Hawk* cap that at least three out of five of his audience (including me) are wearing. He compliments the captain and the crew, reiterates his confidence in CENT-COM, and is interrupted by cheers and applause when he is especially effusive. I resign myself to something banal but don't blame the admiral. I think to myself that great words are sucked out of speakers by the erudition of the audience, and while I have deep respect for this audience, there are few enough classics majors at Harvard, let alone in the Navy.

Then suddenly my snobbery comes up short, because when Admiral Keating's speech begins in earnest, it is clear that while standards of eloquence may evolve, the hearts of chivalrous warriors do not. The high points:

> This is a war for the liberation of the Iraqi people. Every one of you will have played a pivotal role in what happened here. Your names will be written in gold in the pages of history. As you will have played a major role in the liberation of the Iraqi people, in future years you will have every right to recall with pride what you have done for that people, to have allowed an entire country to enjoy the fruits of liberty that we enjoy today. You will know in your hearts that you have made a difference. You will help welcome the Iraqi people back to the league of nations. So thank you for what you have done. Thank you for what you are about to do. And as you do it, remember that millions of Americans and hundreds of millions around the globe support what you are doing.

This was good stuff. Of course, the admiral is an American addressing other Americans, so his closing, if less eloquent than his main thrust, was culturally exact: "The folks back home worry about you. So call your parents and let them know that you're OK."

I'm a parent, and speaking as such, I appreciated this advice. But the admiral wasn't quite finished, because no matter how young these kids might look to him, he knew that they will soon bear an adult's duties and perhaps something more than even this word denotes. So in closing, Mom and Dad were moved back from the foreground, and their place taken by other authorities. Gazing over this vast and trusting assemblage, he raised his hands and said:

God bless the ship *Kitty Hawk!*
God bless the United States Navy!
God bless the United States of America!

Admiral Keating is my kind of guy.

1900
Wardroom II

I'm watching Fox News with the usual suspects. I'm drinking coffee now the way I used to drink Coca-Cola in the days before my blood sugar sky-rocketed. But I'm in good company. Everybody on this ship who can stand coffee drinks as much of it as I do. Civil War veteran John D. Billings titled his famous reminiscence of the war *Hardtack and Coffee*. "Whatever words of condemnation or criticism may have been bestowed on other government rations," Billings recalled twenty years after leaving the Army of the Potomac, "there was but one opinion of the coffee which was served out, and that was unqualified approval." It was, he noted later, "a Godsend." Well, nothing has changed.

As I gulp down my nth cup of the day, Fox News is broadcasting a story from the USS *Abraham Lincoln*, another of our aircraft carriers somewhere in the Gulf. Lo and behold, who should appear on camera but Admiral Keating! He's addressing the *Lincoln*'s sailors on their hangar deck, and he's wearing a USS *Abe Lincoln* cap! Moreover, the sound bite from his speech matches, almost word for word, a similar 10-second stretch from his *Kitty*

Hawk address. We don't have a Fox reporter embedded on this ship, so I suppose the tree fell here without making a sound, at least on Fox. However, no one in wardroom II, all of whom were present at the admiral's speech, cares very much. When I wonder aloud if what the admiral just said sounded familiar, an old salt replies, "Screw the *Lincoln*."

Probably nobody cares because it's a detail that's relevant only to the self-absorbed. You have to think you're important enough to merit a speech that, like a bespoke suit, is custom-tailored for you. The wardroom is full of pilots and flight deck officers, people who within days or maybe even hours, will be sitting on the point of the spear. In John Huston's 1956 film of Stephen Crane's *Red Badge of Courage,* General Winterburn, the Union commander, visits his battle line on the morning of the big fight and has the same conversation with each company. "What ya' havin' for supper, tonight, men?" he asked. "Hardtack and beans," they would reply." "Mind if I join ya' fer supper?" Winterburn would ask. "Why, we'd be honored, Sir" was the invariable reply. Within two minutes, he had committed to have the same dinner with half a dozen different companies. Given the mise-en-scène, these companies were close enough on set to have heard each conversation, but they didn't care. All that mattered was that the general cared enough to ask.

2030
Media Room

We have another GQ drill scheduled for 2100. As with the first drill, the media is asked to assemble at their GQ station (today's counterpart for the old World War II movie "battle station") a half hour before the alarm is sounded. The reason is the same as it was before: GQs are taken seriously, and nobody trusts that a bunch of journalists, whose command of the English language is either too rich or too poor, will be able to arrive at the media room within four minutes of the alarm.

Tonight's GQ has a very specific purpose: to review and review again the procedures for protecting ourselves against a chemical or biological attack. This means learning to don the chembio protective suits. The gas mask is put on first and must be done within eight seconds. As Lieutenant De Walt counts off with his fingers, the rest of us take turns with the mask. Some do it right (I do); others become entangled in the head straps (for some reason, the Japanese reporters). Then Brook demonstrates the rest of the suit: fish shoes, charcoal-lined pants and jacket, cloth gloves first, then the rubber gloves over those. I've been through this training but am glad (if unsettled) to get it again.

What is new this time is the video. On closed-circuit televisions through-out the ship, Flight Surgeon Chris Bellard is narrating a twenty-minute show (which will be repeated six times during the next two hours) that depicts what is likely to *really* happen during one of these attacks. First, we're shown the medical packets that are issued with our protective suits. They contain three auto-injectors of atropine, three of CANA, and one of diazepam. The length and width of a Churchill-size cigar, these injectors are to be jammed through the charcoal-lined pants into our thighs in the event of exposure. That thought alone unsettles Leila from AFP. She turns to me and says, "If we are gassed, just let me die. I can't stick myself with one of those." I thought she was joking, but before I could dispatch some bon mot, another reporter told her, "Don't worry, I'll be happy to stick you." Freudian sub-text notwithstanding, Leila was genuinely upset.

And why shouldn't she be? At that moment, over five thousand already practiced guys and gals were practicing in their suits once again. After tonight, the chembio alert would be raised one notch, which required that gas masks would have to be carried at all times. Also, hatches were converted to Zebra status, which meant that the main hatches between decks were closed, and a smaller hatch, about the size of a manhole cover (which sits atop the main hatch) would be open. What this meant for certain over-weight, middle-aged guys trying to enter and exit these spaces was some-thing like attempting chin-ups after a hiatus of twenty-five years.

But Cdr. Bellard's real concern was the individuals' response to a chemi-cal attack. Although "bio" was ritually mentioned along with "chem," the hard truth is that, given the incubation periods for disease, it is unlikely that exposure to bacteria or viruses would immediately prevent anyone from doing their job. Not so with exposure to chemicals. The effect of nerve gas— and the gas that Bellard seems focused on is VX—is immediate. Just how immediate is the subject of the scariest part of the video.

In the event of an attack, over five thousand people would don suits. Aside from problems of mobility, vision, and hydration (not to mention bowel function), the first issue on everybody's plate would likely be anxiety—the potential instant creation of a huge class of "worried well." Do I have the suit on properly? Was I exposed before putting on the suit? Does the suit even work? With nerve agent speeding through the p-ways of the ship, few might be able to answer these questions with certainty. So Bellard is concerned that some might confuse the symptoms of panic anxiety with those of exposure to chemicals. And those souls might well begin stabbing themselves with the antidote drugs, which, Bellard emphasizes, carry serious, sometimes lethal, side effects. *Antidote* is actually the wrong word. For example, atropine works not by negating the nerve agent but by increasing heart rate and respiration in the hope of "sweating it out." Diazepam is another name for Valium, and all it does is mitigate convulsions.

So Bellard shows us what exposure to nerve gas looks like. The doctor narrates as a corpsman pretends to be stricken. As Bellard describes the nausea, sweats, and pinpoint pupils, the corpsman collapses to the ground and goes into convulsions. His body's trunk is rigid while his arms and legs convulse. While this is being shown, the chatty camaraderie of the media room ceases. All look on in silence.

I think of the last time that Americans were gassed in wartime, during the Great War, but the only man who comes to mind is the English poet Wilfred Owen. A year before he was killed by German machine-gun fire while leading his men across the Sombre Canal, he wrote "Dulce et Decorum Est," perhaps the greatest poem of that war and probably the only poem ever to memorialize poison gas. Later, I record lines from it:

> Gas! GAS! Quick, boys!—An ecstasy of fumbling,
> Fitting the clumsy helmets just in time;
> But someone still was yelling out and stumbling
> And flound'ring like a man in fire or lime . . .
> Dim, through the misty panes and thick green light,
> As under a green sea, I saw him drowning.
> In all my dreams, before my helpless sight,
> He plunges at me, guttering, choking, drowning.
>
> If in some smothering dreams you too could pace
> Behind the wagon that we flung him in,
> And watch the white eyes writhing in his face,
> His hanging face, like a devil's sick of sin;
> If you could hear, at every jolt, the blood
> Come gargling from the froth-corrupted lungs,

> Obscene as cancer, bitter as the cud
> Of vile, incurable sores on innocent tongues,—
> My friend, you would not tell with such high zest
> To children ardent for some desperate glory,
> The old Lie: *Dulce et decorum est*
> *Pro patria mori.*

Owen isn't mocking causes here, just the lie that death in combat is some-how sweet. But I'll be damned if I need Wilfred Owen to carry this argu-ment.

For the first time since I boarded this ship, I feel afraid.

March 20
0300
Khaki Smoking Sponson

I go to the khaki smoking sponson because it is much less crowded, and the officers tend to avoid the media. Right now, that's fine with me. I want to be alone. I'm frightened about the war and have to deal with it.

But I am distracted by the magnificent evening. The water is calm and the moon is up and bright, though low on the horizon, and it beckons the eye with its glistening silver pathway on the sea. There is a slight but pleas-antly cool breeze that lingers on my cheek and slips away, only to return a moment later. I remember that Pesach is next month, and afterward, between it and *Shavuos*, the *Pirke Avos* is read on *shabbos* afternoons. I have followed this tradition for years, not just because it is a tradition but also for the sheer pleasure of the reading. The next instant, I understand that these thoughts are in fact linked. They have brought me to the words of Rabbi Akavia ben Mahalalel:

> Consider three things and you will not come into the grip of sin: Know whence you came, whither you go, and before Whom you will give judgment and reckoning. "Whence you came?" from a putrid drop; "whither you go?" to a place of dust, worms and maggots; "and before Whom you will give judg-ment and reckoning?" before the King Who reigns over Kings, the Holy One, Blessed is He.

Whither I go. Fear of dying in a war is new to me. Like all fear, it's a physical sensation—a deep, smoldering anxiety arising from my bowels, an almost palpable thing that has the gravity of a black hole from which not even the normally dependable "light" of rationalization can escape. It is the fear of death, but not the civilian's death—no sudden coronaries or prolonged lingering from a ruthless disease. That kind of mortality is inevitable, a "standard" experience as the world of one's grandparents and later one's parents passes; most important, civilian death is perpetually distant, a chimera, floating barely visible in the hazy seas of the Great Deniable Future. It's the normal fear of death that can be suppressed by the distraction of a morning's newspaper headline.

But the fear of dying in a war is different. It's not just the application of Dr. Johnson's observation that "when a man knows he is to be hanged in a fortnight, it concentrates his mind wonderfully." That is an element that war shares with the terminally ill. There is a feature unique to war. Both the condemned of Dr. Johnson's wit and the terminally ill have no choice. The condemned has been convicted of something and will die in two weeks, time and manner certain and appeals exhausted. The jury that convicted him and the judge who sentenced him all had faces, and the process that delivered him to the gallows, just or unjust, was deliberate. Even the hangman, while presumably masked, hooded, or perhaps out of sight, will still be an identifiable man, a man nearby, a single man who will cause a single death. But gas is dumb and kills anyone who happens to breathe its air. It doesn't distinguish between combatants and noncombatants, widows and orphans, old and young. It only distinguishes between oxygen-breathers and inanimate objects, and it kills the former.

As I lean on the rope rail and stare at the ships' undulating wake, another thought occurs, one that is perhaps the core of this fear, a seductive regret that is probably shared by many on board the *Kitty Hawk*, in Kuwait, and among those playing hide-and-seek in the deserts of western Iraq: *I don't have to be here, doing what I'm doing and taking these risks.* Nope, everybody's a volunteer, from the Special Forces operative lurking near an Iraqi Scud launcher to media dingbats like me.

And getting out is easy. For me, I just tell Mike Brown that something's come up ashore and I need a COD out of here, pronto. For sailors, it's a bit more complicated, but still very doable. Scuttlebutt I've heard illustrates one extreme: In the past year, a sailor jumped overboard in a self-advertisement for being a nut case and was promptly shipped out. Dr. Jennifer Johnson, the *Kitty Hawk*'s psychologist, says that some sailors just walk into her office and announce that they're homosexuals, knowing full well that she's required to disclose it to the Navy. That's their ticket ashore. In a high-tech volunteer military, morale and motivation is everything. If you don't want to be there, they don't want you there.

My fear gives way to anger. Screw it. I'm not leaving until my assignment is over. And virtually no sailors will leave either. Living with this fear, eating it, swallowing it, and trying to keep it down is *the* fact of life, and this suppression may constitute a species of courage—albeit a very low-grade variety. In *The Mystery of Courage*, William Ian Miller discusses the history of the idea of courage. One species of courage that has attracted thinkers from St. Thomas Aquinas to Vietnam War vet author Tim O'Brien is the fortitude required merely for enduring. It may not be the highest form of courage but is, as O'Brien terms it, "doing well on average." Perhaps this begs the question (why do well?), but it seems to describe anxiety management well enough. You do what you can. (So as not to beg the question in my own case, let me say that I wish to do well on average in part because I don't wish to appear the coward to my wife and children, in part to retain whatever personal and professional respect I have earned from my colleagues and shipmates, and to retain my own self-respect. This, I decide, is the true face of peer pressure.)

Ah, but "whither I go?" If the righteous and wicked alike end up in a place of "dust, worms and maggots," why care about doing well on average, or doing well ever? Because for people like me, it is the last question in R. ben Mahalalel's trilogy of questions that determines whether I shall stay or go, do well or badly, feel remorse or feel nothing for acting badly: "Before Whom you will give judgment and reckoning? Before the King Who reigns over Kings, the Holy One, Blessed is He."

And like countless generations of human beings before me, this thought settles the matter, if not my stomach. I am afraid, I will continue to be afraid, I might get sick to my stomach, I might even beshit myself, but in fearing death alone, my apprehensions are misplaced, premature as it were, because, as David wrote in Psalm 111: "*Raisheet chochmo y'rat Hashem*"; "The beginning of wisdom is fear of the Lord." I may puke my guts out, but I will accept the nausea, the discomfort, and the raw, gut-twisting fear—much as I witnessed my dying mother do—and remain to finish my assignment, just as she did as her hour approached.

Suddenly, I'm distracted by the loud whispers of two officers who are pointing toward the water at the place where the ship's wake begins. Amazing! A pair of dolphins, their smooth skins shimmering silver-gray in the moonlight, arc gracefully above the water before diving again and then rise to repeat this undulation with a felicitous and assuring regularity. The whispers subside; for a moment, the mind is filled only with dolphins and not the war or poison gas or the looming, hydra-headed Death that lurks in the deserts just beyond the western shore. Is it an augury of some kind? Of course not, but it's damn relaxing to watch.

My supply of cigars is dwindling fast, but this sight is worth having one more.

0430
SEAL Berth

The president's deadline expired thirty minutes ago. A few reporters, including me, remained awake to see what would happen at 0401. Nothing did happen, so I've retired to my rack.

0600
SEAL Berth

Hu nudges me awake and tells me that President Bush will be speaking in fifteen minutes. I get up and hustle down the p-way to the wardroom II TV, hoping that reception is good. It is. The room is packed with officers, and no one is saying a word. The faces of these men and women reveal some deep reflection, as if reviewing checklists, thinking of dear ones at home, or wondering what the next day (or hour or few minutes) will bring. I must remember that while nearly everyone in this room votes for the president of the United States, only those wearing a uniform work for him. What he says matters to us all, but it matters most of all to them.

The president, like Admiral Keating, made no attempt to outcoin William Shakespeare in prebattle phrasemaking. The president said that he hadn't asked for 9/11, but it was visited upon us by our enemies. There was something genuinely sad in his remarks. As the decades pass, and historians unfold the events leading to this conflict, it may well be that this administration wanted this war, but that in no way lessens the sadness of the man who ordered it and who will have the burden of living with the dying that will ensue.

Bush's sadness seems mirrored in the faces of those in this room. After the speech, everyone leaves quietly. The officers silently shrug or nod sadly to one another; a few walk out with a will, but the mood, while determined, is joyless. Now that war is come, it is clear that the ambivalence about this war that many of these men and women privately expressed to me was genuine. These sailors will do their job and do it well, but they would just as soon be steaming for home.

I have returned to my rack. Up the ladder and outside our hatch are rows of indifferently stacked gray Phoenix missiles. As I pass them, I, too, feel ambivalent about this war.

"And the war came."

And the war came.

> —Abraham Lincoln, Second Inaugural
> Address
> MARCH 4, 1865

0800
Media Room

T*HE WAR SHOWS UP.* We are summoned to the media room to receive further details about an action already reported on the cable networks. Early this morning, somebody dropped a dime on the whereabouts of Saddam and his two delightful sons, Uday and Qusay, and the Navy politely responded with a slew of Tomahawk cruise missiles. There are two names for this sort of thing: (1) assassination and (2) a new name (to me at any rate), decapitation. I suppose *decapitation* is the term preferred by the assassins; *assassination* is usually preferred by the dead person's family. This morning, from the White House all the way to Lieutenant De Walt, *decapitation* is the preferred term. Either way, I hope they killed all three snakes.

Communications are dead except for E-mail, so I send Ellen Ratner the following dispatch, hoping that she can use it. I've divided it into straight news and analysis, although it's not meant to be read verbatim on air. Since I don't know what she knows, I can't be sure if it contains anything useful.

To: Ellen Ratner
From: Richard F. Miller
Subject: News

ELLEN: THE NEWS

The USS *Cowpens*, a member of the *Kitty Hawk*'s battle group, was among 4 other destroyers and two submarines launching the forty-plus Tomahawk cruise missiles this morning. The *Cowpens* launched ten of the missiles at two military targets in and around Baghdad. The *Cowpens* received word to launch only thirty minutes ahead of time and had to perform a very rapid missile targeting sequence.

ELLEN: THE TAKE ON NEWS

This was part of the action to "take out Saddam/military brass/who-knows-who-it-hasn't-been-disclosed-yet." That this was a deviation from the so-called war plan is clear from the thirty minutes heads-up received by the *Cowpens*. It's safe to assume that the *Cowpens*' other targets of the larger war plan have been in their possession and a part of their targeting models for days if not weeks. Analysis: Shows that the war planners are going to run this thing in an "entrepreneurial" style—the plan will shift as opportunity and intelligence information dictates. Keywords: Has Rummy written all over it. Flexibility, turn on a dime, and use of "that-was-then-this-is-now" type thinking. Thrust, parry, thrust. A sword fight, not a prescripted play.

End

March 21
Forenoon
Media Room

This morning, all reporters are gathered here for the ultimate gesture of trust to be shown in the media by this or any other government. We are to witness a premission pilot briefing. In other words, we're going to sit in and learn as the pilots themselves learn where they're going, how they'll get there, what targets they'll be hitting, what kind of ordnance they'll be delivering, and other details, including attack altitudes, route to target, route from the target, take-off time, and who knows what else.

Personally, I can't believe the Navy is really going to let this happen. I take Lt. Brook De Walt aside.

"What are you guys, nuts?" I ask him. "I ought to write my Congressman and complain about the security on this ship." I was being sarcastic—sort of.

Lieutenant Kretzer, De Walt's colleague, was standing next to him when I made this comment, and she gave me a sympathetic look. "I don't make the rules," she sighed. But Lieutenant De Walt had a different take.

"Look, it's a gamble, I'll admit," he said, "but as long as everybody follows those rules, it's not too much of a leap of faith." He then looked at me sternly. "Just remember," he added, "once you know what you're going to know, you will have the lives of those pilots in your hands. So don't report a thing until we give you the green light."

Everyone was now in the room, and Lieutenant De Walt asked that the door be closed. Just to be sure, he reviewed the rules that we must follow in order to attend a briefing.

1. No photography during the briefing.
2. No questions during or after the briefing.
3. All stories about any aspect of the briefing, including that a briefing had taken place at all, were embargoed until the PAO gave the green light.

In short, we were to silently enter the briefing room, silently remain in the background, and silently leave.

"No communication means exactly that," Lieutenant De Walt warned us. "So let me spell it out: no E-mail, no telephone, no satellite telephone, and no broadcasts of any kind. If we catch you out on the fantail trying to make a sat phone call or something, you can be sure there'll be consequences."

He was emphatic, sincere, and genuinely concerned that somebody would do something stupid. But he didn't scare me, because there wasn't anything he or the Navy could do that would be worse than the guilt and shame I'd have to carry in my heart for the rest of life, were I to jeopardize the lives of any of these kids.

One Half Hour Later
Briefing Room, Fighter Squadron 154

Eight of us are escorted down the p-way to the door of the briefing room of Fighter Squadron 154, known as the Black Knights. While Lt. De Walt slips inside to double check our welcome, I look at the door's panel, which bears the unit's emblem. It's a circle, within which stands the figure of a fully armored knight, holding a shield (defense) in his right hand and a sword (offense) in his left. (There is an interesting symmetry between this emblem and the eagle featured in the Great Seal of the United States, which holds the olive branch of peace in his right talon and the arrows of war in his left talon.) Behind the knight's head are horizontal, pencil-thin, parallel contrails of four jets flying to his right; behind his knees are similar contrails of four jets flying to his left.

The Black Knights are one of nine squadrons of aircraft in Carrier Group Five (CVW-5), the *Kitty Hawk*'s air wing. Each squadron has a separate function and identity. Four of these squadrons, including the Grumman F-14A Tomcats flown by the Black Knights, are fighter jet units. These are the Royal Maces (Strike Fighter Squadron 27), the Golden Dragons (Strike Fighter Squadron 192), and the Dambusters (Strike Fighter Squadron 195). The last three fly the F/A-18C Hornet, which is a newer and smaller jet than the F-14, although tasked with the same mission.

The other squadrons of CVW-5 are the Red Tails (Sea Control Squadron 21), which fly the S-3B Viking and provide airborne tracking and force protection for the carrier battle group; the Gauntlets (Electronic Attack Squadron 136), which fly the EA-6B Prowlers and provide electronic countermeasures; the Liberty Bells (Carrier Airborne Early Warning Squadron 115), which fly the E-2C Hawkeyes (Captain Parker's plane); the Chargers (Helicopter Anti-Submarine Squadron 14), which fly Sikorsky helicopters and conduct anti-submarine warfare and both combat and noncombat search and rescue; and the CODs (Fleet Logistics Support Squadron 30 Det FIVE), which brought me to the *Kitty Hawk* and is the major air transport link between the shore and the ship at sea.

From a management perspective, CVW-5 is entirely self-contained. The wing includes its own doctors, a chaplain, mechanics, and administrators. This means that when CVW-5 travels, it's not only green-suited flyboys and girls that move but also the support specialists. What distinguishes this particular wing is that, like the *Kitty Hawk*, it is the only permanently forward-deployed air wing in the Navy and is based in Atsugi, Japan.

CVW-5 also has a past. The sleek designs and hyperweaponry of its aircraft tend to obscure its long history and low-tech origins. When the fathers and grandfathers of today's baby boomers were young men, the predecessor to CVW-5 was established in 1938 as the air wing of the original aircraft carrier, USS *Yorktown*. It flew from the *Yorktown* at Coral Sea until that carrier was sunk at the Battle of Midway. Afterward, it redeployed onto the new USS *Yorktown*. During World War II, it flew the island-hopping strategy in the Pacific, flying missions over Truk, the Gilberts, the Marshalls, and the Marianas. But in the final months of the war, CVW-5 was virtually wiped out when its carrier was severely damaged during a Japanese attack and most of its aircraft were destroyed.

Following the war, CVW-5 was reconstituted, and the wing was on the cutting edge of the jet age. It was the first to land jets on carriers and the first to enter the Korean War, during which, according to one history, a plane belonging to it "recorded the first air-to-air jet kill in U.S. Naval history." They were also present at one of the most important events of the Vietnam War. Planes from CVW-5 contributed to the defense of the USS *Maddox* against North Vietnam PT boats, the incident President Lyndon B. Johnson used to justify the Gulf of Tonkin Resolution. During the entire Vietnam era, the air wing completed eight combat cruises in the Gulf of Tonkin, and its sorties probably numbered in the tens of thousands.

The itinerary of CVW-5 changed along with American strategic interests. In 1973, the wing moved to Japan, thereby becoming the first air group permanently deployed abroad. During the next twenty years, it accompanied its assigned aircraft carrier, the USS *Midway* in order to, in the words of one historian, "counter the communist Soviet threat in those areas." These included service throughout the Western Pacific, South China Sea, Indian Ocean, and Northern Pacific. In 1984, the wing patrolled the skies over the Straits of Hormuz for 111 consecutive days to, quoting the same historian, "guarantee the continued flow of vital oil to our allies in Japan and Western Europe." Six years later, CVW-5 had returned on the *Midway* for Desert Shield and Desert Storm. The air operations of the latter were commenced by an A-6E Intruder belonging to the wing. In the forty-three-day action that ensued, CVW-5 flew 3,339 sorties while unloading over 4 million pounds of explosives.

By April 1992, the wing was back in the Persian Gulf, tasked with enforcing the southern no-fly zone over Iraq. That year, thousands of flights were logged in support of Operation Southern Watch. In 1998, the *Kitty Hawk* replaced the USS *Independence* as the country's only permanently deployed forward aircraft carrier, and as part of that transition, CVW-5 was assigned to the *Kitty Hawk*. In 1999, the wing and the *Kitty Hawk* were back in the Persian Gulf enforcing the No-Fly Zone; that gig lasted 116 consecutive days, with the wing flying 8,800 sorties; of these sorties, 1,300 were combat, and more than 110,000 pounds of explosives were delivered.

As Captain Parker had observed, when the president of the United States dials 911, the telephone rings on the *Kitty Hawk*, which, of course, has an extension line in the pilot briefing rooms of CVW-5. A mere nineteen days after the destruction of the World Trade Center, the *Kitty Hawk* and its air wing were en route to the Indian Ocean, there to serve as the country's steel island in support of Operation Enduring Freedom (OEF). The *Kitty Hawk*'s principal function was to serve, in the Navy's terminology, as an "afloat staging base"; during OEF, the carrier housed Delta Forces, Navy SEALS, CIA people, and other assorted black baggers, all of whom were en route to or from Afghanistan. Originally, CVW-5's role was purely defensive and limited to force protection of the carrier battle group; but reading between the lines of the history, some combat-entrepreneur managed to persuade the Pentagon that if there wasn't any "gold in them thar' hills" of Afghanistan, there were lots of Al Qaeda and their Taliban bootlickers, more than enough to allow CVW-5 a piece of the action. As a result, CVW-5 did manage to fly 600 Afghan War sorties, including over 100 combat missions.

As a historian, I often wonder what the point of unit histories like these are: that is, outside of those who study them, what impact do long-ago events have on the present day-to-day reality as lived by a given crop of warriors? The answer lies in how the history serves to enhance the small-unit cohesion of these squadrons and how the immediate experience of the past is transmitted through a small-scale oral tradition that, in an odd way, places in today's briefing room the experience of the first pilot to land on the USS *Yorktown* in 1938. During each of the sixty-five years that CVW-5 has existed, a new generation of pilot, mechanic, or administrator joins up as an older generation retires, transfers, or dies out. Within twenty years of its establishment, CVW-5 contained every element of a living generation writ small, comprised of those who were young, middle-aged, and old, as defined by experience. The experience of the early days, the last war, the last battle, and the last sortie is communicated to the newcomers, forming an unbroken chain of more than six decades of pooled human experience that comes to a perpetually renewing focal point in the present, which today is in this room. In that sense, the first pilot who landed on the *Yorktown* in 1938 is represented here, as is the last Black Knight who radioed in weather conditions, reported mechanical difficulties, or made an observation about which route to take to the target.

When Lt. De Walt emerges from the room, he puts his index finger to his lips in a gesture of silence, and we enter.

"Briefing room" doesn't come close to describing what this place is. The dim light, the double rows of movie theater-type seats facing each other, the walls lined with maps, personalized coffee cups, family photos, weather charts, bulletin boards, and most importantly, the clutch of green-suited pilots seated around the center give this room a templelike ambience or, more accurately, a synagogue of war. The huddled pilots look intently at the maps, charts, and prose in their notebooks. They could just as easily be a study group; their common texts, their Talmud; and the senior pilot who leads this briefing, the senior rabbi, taking them as if through difficult passages, his learned exegesis interrupted occasionally by questions asked of him or by him. There is the same focus, the same quiet intensity that marks any close endeavor motivated by religious passions or, in this case, survival and a will to win.

More details of this room sink in with each passing moment. Eight pilots in two rows face one another; a large banner declaring "We Miss You" is tacked to a bulletin board on which are photographs of families smiling out from backgrounds of suburban homes, woods, and green lawns. More wall space is covered with boards that seem to schedule, chart, or record practically everything involved in flying a jet fighter. Another wall is covered with small hooks on which are hung the pilots' personalized coffee cups.

The pilot leading this briefing is Lt. Cdr. Victor ("Dirk") Bindi. A thirty-something man with fine features and a thin mustache, Cdr. Bindi is walking these pilots through the business of getting to the target. Which route to take? In his discussion, the commander notes that the shortest distance between two points is not always the best; there's the latest intelligence on enemy anti-aircraft fire and missiles to consider. But the safest route is not always possible—there's the matter of flying time and fuel savings. As Bindi talks, I notice that in a corner of the room a TV is constantly scrolling reports on "Intel Operations." I can't see much (an old eyeglass prescription!), but it appears to consist of the very matters Bindi is now discussing, the whereabouts of Iraqi anti-aircraft artillery and missiles and so forth. But I can't be sure of even this much, as too many of the words are code names and jargon. The only thing I can see is that some of these places and numbers are described as "minimum risk routes."

Two targets are mentioned—but not described. That part of the discussion preceded our arrival. In case these pilots have trouble, Cdr. Bindi notes the location of two emergency landing strips in Kuwait. But he doesn't give any fancy electronic coordinates. Instead, he describes what they'll look like from the air, and I'm struck with how, should any of these planes' avionics be shot away, it will all come down to the same flying skills that Charles Lindbergh used between Long Island and France in 1927. ("You'll know the Al Jabra airfield," Bindi explains, "because at 12,000 feet, the runway breaks out beautifully against the sand.")

Bindi next goes into detail about the safe areas. These are preselected respites in the sky where pilots can fly holding patterns out of range from known anti-aircraft defenses. They're also useful as a gathering point in case the attack squadron is scattered or planes are otherwise separated.

This is not a lecture. As he completes his discussion of each section (route, fuel, etc.), Cdr. Bindi pauses. He might ask a question, and he always invites questions. What's interesting to me is how these Q&As actually result in subtle changes to the mission. Somebody may have better ideas about altitude or route, for example. It's quite different from the scenes in *Thirty Seconds over Tokyo*, the movie about Jimmy Doolittle's April 1942 air raid on the Japanese capital. In the film, the character of Doolittle was played in deadly earnest by Spencer Tracy, and the briefings were not only brief but also something of a deus ex machina in which somebody yelled, "Attention!" and Tracy appeared on a stage to emphasize the risks, pump morale, ask for questions, not get any, and then depart.

The critical question of attack altitudes is discussed next. Several planes will attack simultaneously, and the target will be approached from different altitudes. Three attack altitudes are assigned: 6,000, 7,000, and 8,000 feet.[1]

---

1. I have changed the attack altitudes as well as their relation to each other.

What Bindi emphasizes more than anything else is speed. "You must maximize your attack advantages," Cdr. Bindi stresses. "I want you to push your speed fast, and then push your jets faster." Next, taking a pencil and scratch pad, he sketches a diagram showing the relationships among routes, targets, national borders (there are three in the area: Kuwait, Iraq, and Iran), and the so-called safe areas. Borders are of obvious importance, because Iran—whose own regime is only slightly less toxic than Iraq's—is just minutes away by Tomcat.

The speed and ordnance of the F-14 will permit no margin for error, especially in the sharply political world of Middle Eastern warfare. The F-14 Tomcat flies at Mach 2+—or faster than twice the speed of sound. Its ordnance naturally follows its three primary missions: air-to-air defense (for these purposes, it is equipped with an M-61 gun and can carry the Sidewinder, Phoenix, and Sparrow missiles), fleet defense, and precision ground bombing. For this it has a LANTIRN targeting system for laser-guided weapons and night-vision technology, which enhances its existing capabilities for all-weather attacks. And not coincidentally, just this month, one of the F-14 series (D series) was enabled to carry the JDAM, bringing this fighter, first deployed thirty-three years ago, current in weapons technology. Each of these weapons deploys and kills in a matter of seconds, which guarantees that pilots and their radar intercept officers (RIOs) in the second seat are perpetually at risk for sinning in haste but repenting in leisure.

In the kangaroo (but unavoidable) court of public opinion, the military is now being held to the same standards to which plaintiffs' lawyers routinely hold automobile, drug, and tobacco companies. In other words, no cost, whatever the benefit, is acceptable. Part of Cdr. Bindi's briefing reviews the RIO's deployment instructions regarding the laser-guided weapons. "You RIOs," he cautions, "make sure you call for a laser on target at least 15 seconds before you drop. It's the only way to make sure that you're going to hit what you want to hit."

The briefing is winding down, but Cdr. Bindi is winding up.

"Does anyone see a flaw in this plan?" he asks and gives the group a moment to reconsider. No one does. He looks around and nods slowly.

"OK, then," he says. "I want everyone to keep three things in mind."

The tone has been quiet and professional throughout, but this moment has a natural, unavoidable drama, and Bindi pauses as his colleagues brace for the wrap-up.

* The faster an aircraft flys, the quicker its fuel is exhausted. The greater the rate of fuel consumption the fewer miles the aircraft can fly.

"I want the wind at our backs," he says slowly. "I want position on the target. And most importantly," he declares, "I want you to come in stupid fast over it. Put a lot of smack on."

Lieutenant De Walt signals that it's time for us to leave. Once out, I head down to the enlisted sponson for a cigar. The p-ways are buzzing and seem more crowded than usual; the step is livelier, noise levels on the hangar deck are higher, the conversations are flightier, people are busier, and the line for the smoking sponson is longer than ever—but the turnover is faster. It seems that fewer cigarettes are being puffed faster, and the entrance connecting the hangar deck and the sponson is like a revolving door.

But unlike these sailors, for the moment I have nothing to do. All stories are embargoed, and I wouldn't even think of logging on to E-mail, even only to check incoming messages.

So as I stare at the bright horizon, ears wadded against the roar of jet engines from the flight deck above, little bits of the pilots' briefing, things that on first hearing I didn't completely grasp or was too distracted to comprehend, are coming back now, only reassembled by the mysterious power of retrospect. I'm suddenly engulfed by a wave of feeling stupid, because for the first time today, I understand exactly what I had been listening to in the briefing room.

Cdr. Bindi wasn't planning some routine Operation Southern Watch patrol. He was talking about flying ground support for troops moving from Kuwait into Iraq—that is, troops that were about to move today, any minute now, if not already. And the Black Knights would be there in the sky, guardian angels to our soldiers and the *Molochmovitz* (angel of death) to many Iraqis.

I knew that for many Iraqi soldiers, this was to be the final act of a latter-day Pesach, and before this night was through, the air would be filled with the cries of the dying. The prospect of this fills me with an unexpected sadness, pausing my aggression for the enemy. There is a story from the Talmud, Trachtate Bavli, which has been told at Pesach seders for thousands of years: "Our rabbis taught: When the Egyptian armies were drowning in the sea, the Heavenly Hosts broke out in songs of jubilation. God silenced them and said, 'My creatures are perishing, and you sing praises?'"

For every other Iraqi, I could only pray that they would, for the first time in thirty years, soon find themselves walking on dry land between the waters of a parted sea.

Showtime

2040
Media Room

I'M STANDING IN THE media room of the USS *Kitty Hawk*, along with every other journalist embedded on this ship. Normally, this room is used to stage broadcasts on the ship's closed-circuit TV system, but tonight the television camera is shunted to the side. The studio lights are burning, which, together with the heat of this excited crowd, completely negates the air-conditioning. Like every other space on board, the media room is small. It can comfortably accommodate five or maybe ten people. But right now, the journalists number at least twenty and are joined by five officers. Mounted on the wall behind us is a small television carrying Fox News. No one is sure whether to turn the volume up or to turn the television off. Is the news there or is the news here, in this very room?

I look around this room. My colleagues are as motley as the *Kitty Hawk*'s crew. There are four Japanese journalists representing some of the largest newspapers from that country, a South Korean television crew; two Americans from Reuters, a British crew from Sky Television, a Chinese reporter from Xinthua, an American photojournalist from Gannett, a reporter from C-SPAN, another from *Stars and Stripes*, a photojournalist from Agence France-Presse, another with the Department of Defense, and two writers from AP. Their experience is likewise diverse. They are men and women, old and multicolored. One is a Navy veteran, several have reported extensively on the Japanese Defense Forces, another has covered the West Bank and

Gaza, another lives in Amman, another is from Australia, and the Brits from Sky have been everywhere and seen everything. But judging from the excitement tonight, it is almost as if we were all covering our first story.

Behind the studio desk stands Rear Admiral Matthew G. Moffitt. Permanently stationed on the USS *Kitty Hawk*, he is a bespectacled, bookish-looking man with receding hair, who, were he garbed in tweed, could easily be imagined hurrying through Harvard Yard, late for a class. Next to him stands CAG leader Pat Driscoll. There is nothing bookish about him. Dressed in his green flight suit, he is what should be called "aviator handsome." His hair is military short, and his eyes convey a warrior's intensity, his gaze penetrating wherever directed. But it is a controlled intensity. What he is like off-duty, at home, relaxing with his family, cannot be imagined, at least not tonight. For tonight he wears his war face.

These two men are introduced by Lt. Cdr. Michael Brown, head of PAO for the admiral. PAO means public affairs office. To civilians, the abbreviations, short talk, the numbers and letters and nicknames of military-speak seem like an affectation. It isn't. It's simply efficient, saves time, and prevents redundancy. I've been on the boat for almost two weeks and have begun not only to speak this special language but also actually to *think* in it.

Cdr. Brown is tall and unusually clean-cut, even for a military man. But tonight, Brown, usually Johnny Carson cool, is visibly nervous. Not unsettled, just excited. He introduces the admiral, and somebody mutes the TV volume.

"One hour ago," Moffitt solemnly begins, "320 T-LAMs were launched toward Baghdad and vicinity. We expect the first of these to strike their targets at exactly 2100 local time." I glance at my watch. It's now 2045. I look to the television set, which displays a live shot of Baghdad's still-peaceful skyline. Well, it's not burning yet. But because of what the admiral just said, I can now provide a future caption for an event that hasn't yet happened. The city of Baghdad—or at least carefully selected buildings—have just joined the steadily lengthening column of dead men walking.

Brown introduces Captain Driscoll. No doubt reflecting my own inexperience as a journalist, I am paying more attention to the night sky over Baghdad on the television screen. However, not all of Captain Driscoll's words are wasted on me. "This strike will be three times the magnitude of Desert Storm I," he says. "Virtually 100 percent of the ordnance will be precision guided." *Three times the magnitude*. What does this mean? It has been only two weeks since I saw my first 2,000-pound bomb, JDAM, Phoenix, Side-winder, and Harm missile; only two weeks since I began to eat, walk, talk, and take "Hi, Mom!" pictures with the G-3 Mag Rats of the *Kitty Hawk* in the presence of these awesome engines of destruction, as the Civil War generation might have called them. How much damage can they do? How much noise do they make? How much energy is released at detonation?

I look again at my watch. It is now 2059. My wife gave me a new Hamilton khaki mechanical for Chanukah. It's amazingly accurate. In fact, if I wanted to endorse this product and offer to make a commercial that the company would never approve, I might write them a letter and state that when my watch showed 9:00 P.M. exactly—*exactly*—the T-LAMs began striking Baghdad. And that's just what happened. Although the TV screen is small, what it depicts has transformed this tiny Media Room into a giant operating room amphitheater, in which we, the detached observers, note that the patient is in crisis down there, is being cut open by grotesque instruments, and all the while, we're secretly glad that it's not us, glad that we don't live there, glad that we're not Iraqi. Although the ceiling has begun to reverberate with the bowling alley–like sound of the catapult, the crowded room suddenly seems hollow. Military and media alike are silent, transfixed by the flashes on the television screen. Everyone in the room, whether for the war or against the war, whether knowledgeable about weapons or unable to remember their names, whether they wear an admiral's star and anchor or a t-shirt from Abercrombie & Fitch, whoever they are and wherever they're from—all are at one now, as they watch death dealt slowly. And all adopt the humble, fearful respect usually reserved for the hospice or the charnel house. The God of history may decree that this war will prove for good or evil. But all we know at this moment is our witness to a thousand funerals.

The bombs and missiles are now falling in such rapid succession that they feed the constant yellow and reddish glow framing the Baghdad skyline. The *Kitty Hawk*'s fighters are set to take off at 2115, and I have been invited to watch them launch. I accept but find it difficult to pull away from the television. At the Battle of Fredericksburg,*Confederate Gen. Robert E. Lee reportedly said, "It is well that war is so terrible, or we should grow too fond of it." I must be careful not to confuse the live shots of what is now happening to Baghdad with the horrors of war itself; otherwise, limited to precision strikes that claim to do what heretofore only God himself did when

* one of Lee's most impressive victories.

he sifted the righteous from the wicked before destroying the cities of Sodom and Gomorrah, if modern war could do all that, then, indeed, I should grow too fond of it. But I am past fifty years of age, and as a military historian, I know better. For no matter what the claims, every war that ever was, just or unjust, could stand for the proposition that men, when they try, imitate God very poorly.

The television shows the impotence of Iraqi AAA as it spurts upward toward an invisible and bloodless enemy. Tiny spots of light arc toward azimuth, the tracer rounds blindly seeking our winged needles in the sky, hoping that the clouds of exploding metal shards will bring them down. The admiral explains that only one of every seven AAA rounds is a tracer, the shells that leave a streak of white light to mark their path. Thus what we see is but a fraction of the actual resistance. But what we see is also only a fraction of the actual offensive. Not visible to us are the EA6B Prowlers, flying somewhere offscreen, jamming Iraqi radar. And without radar, the Iraqis haven't got a clue what's up in the sky or where it's going.

The networks have been showing the Baghdad skyline all day (or night, as is the case here). Every hour that passed brought the world another hour closer to the attack. As tens of targets are now sending flames shooting into the Iraqi sky, I remember when U.S. Special Forces landed on a beach near Mogadishu in 1992 and were stunned not by enemy resistance but at the television cameras broadcasting their arrival. Tonight is a new milestone in the modern, deadly, but fascinating ritual, warfare by appointment.

My trance is broken by Lt. Brook De Walt. "Don't worry," he says, hand on my shoulder. "This will be a while." Suddenly, the ceiling shakes with a familiar sound, filling the media room with its rutting. It's the *Kitty Hawk*'s steam-powered catapult. It has just launched the first fighter jet in its contribution to Shock and Awe. These planes will follow the missiles into the night. And I will now follow the planes.

Moving up the "stack"—the series of increasingly narrow levels above the flight deck—is like scaling the inside of an upside-down funnel. The ladders that link the decks on an aircraft carrier are not set at the usual 30- or 40-degree angle of the stairwell at home. Seventy degrees is more like it. And moving up these decks at night is no Icarus's flight either, for as one ascends, it becomes darker. At last, the only light shining is the familiar dull red bulb of the smoking sponson.

Before making this climb, I make the required stop at the PAO. No one is allowed anywhere near the flight deck without first donning a cranial and a vest. Confronting jet blasts, the cranial means the difference between a lifetime of normal hearing and eardrums killed in action. Just how loud a screeching F-18 Hornet is can be surmised by the additional requirement that underneath the cranial, one must also wear foam earplugs. And the vest is to vests what the cranial is to ordinary football helmets. The required vest is actually a gas-inflated life preserver (with a tube used for manual inflation in case the CO_2 fails), a dye marker for identification in the water, a light that automatically illuminates on water contact, and a whistle. All of this is necessary because somewhere between a pitching flight deck and man-killing jet blasts during windup, launching, or recovery, there is a possibility of simply being blown overboard. (Or worse. Lt. De Walt tells the tale, which he insists is no Navy legend, of a sailor who was *sucked into* a jet engine. The man miraculously survived.)

2120
Signal Bridge

I step out the hatch and onto the signal bridge. The bath of red light inside did little to condition my eyes for what I see on the outside, or rather what I don't see, which is anything at all. I stand motionless, head sealed and thorax tightly bound. My eyes will adapt slowly, but in the meantime, hemmed in by steel walls, surrounded by unfamiliar hatchways and, of course, the Persian Gulf somewhere below, I dare not move before I am ready. In any other circumstance, the silence resulting from the cranial would seem like the quiet of death itself. But in these circumstances, one senses life by a rapidly developed "seventh" sense—the feeling of whole-body vibration that moves upward through the feet and legs and lingers in the genitals before filling the chest, neck, and head. It is the energy of jets launching.

   Out of darkness, hands are suddenly placed on my shoulders. I don't know whose they are—I will never know—but I've been on ship long enough to accept their guidance without feeling invaded or reproved. The hands steer me around a corner and toward an outdoor ladder, then motion me to ascend. By the time I do, I'm welcomed by the familiar face of Lt. Richard Reyes, who is also wearing cranial and vest. We don't speak, of course, but at a social distance acceptable only near the flight deck of an aircraft carrier, I peer into his face, and he gestures me forward. In a moment, I'm standing next to Oshima and Hiroshi on the signal bridge. Perhaps twenty-five feet below me is the flight deck. A fighter jet has just left; another taxis into position for the launch. It is an F-14 Tomcat, probably belonging to the squadron whose briefing we had been allowed to monitor earlier that afternoon.

Oshima and Hiroshi are reporters for two large Japanese newspapers. Their embedment with the USS *Kitty Hawk* is much more logical than my own. The *Kitty Hawk* is based in Japan. Many of the crew have Japanese wives and families. And what the *Kitty Hawk* does over here is very big news over there, much bigger than in, say, Concord, Massachusetts, whose links to this boat are far more tenuous. Standing between these two men, whom I like and admire, I nonetheless remember a scene from the 1970 movie *Tora, Tora, Tora*. It offers two "real-time" narratives of the December 7, 1941, attack on Pearl Harbor. One depicts the Japanese view as the attack is planned and executed; the other is the American view, depicting the difficulties the United States had in assimilating intelligence about the forthcoming attack—how information snaked through a bureaucracy that was unprepared to imagine not only the war that was coming but also the fact that it was about to arrive from the decks of Japanese aircraft carriers. Looking on the flight deck, I recall the scene where crew members of the Japanese carrier stood in line and cheered as each plane was launched toward Hawaii.

There is none of that tonight. No cheers or anything else could possibly be heard above the whines and blasts of the fighter jet engines. But even assuming that those sounds could be muted, it's unlikely that any cheers would be offered. Unlike lumbering passenger jets, whose ungainliness on the ground belies their sleekness in the sky, the F/A-18 Hornets and F-14 Tomcats look on the ground what they are in flight—compact, deadly razors, whose cutting edges are the weapons they carry beneath their wings. They are a drab gray color, with former markings, squadron logos, and pilots' names barely concealed under thin coats of paint. They are the business end of U.S. foreign policy; in spite of their futuristic shape, there is no elegance about them, nothing in their appearance that summons the martial glory of wars past. There is too much hazardous energy being released on the flight deck to permit anything other than a laserlike focus on the mission.

Jet fighters are referred to as "platforms" for "delivering" weapons systems. No more point and shoot. Now one flies proximate to the target and releases "packages." Satellites hundreds of miles above or Special Forces on the ground below electronically "painting" targets do the rest. Several days earlier, one of the *Kitty Hawk's* fighter pilots told me that at bottom, his job was to fly near the target while the specialist in the second seat programmed the weapons and then released them. "Dropped" is no longer accurate, because most precision-guided munitions now do some flying on their own. The work is dangerous; machines can be unreliable, and enemy anti-aircraft defenses are real, if not quite the factor they were in World War II.

Flight deck jobs are too important, checklists too long, and technology too demanding to permit anything more than obsessive professionalism. Herman Melville caught something of this for the first time in "A Utilitarian View of the Monitor's Fight," a poem that described the battle in Hampton Roads between the *Monitor* and the *Merrimac*:

> Yet this was battle, and intense—
> Beyond the strife of fleets heroic;
> Deadlier, closer, calm 'mid storm;
> No passion; all went on by crank,
> Pivot, and screw,
> And calculations of caloric.
>
> .   .   .   .
>
> War shall yet be, and to the end;
> But war-paint shows the streaks of weather;
> War yet shall be, but warriors
> Are now but operatives; War's made
> Less grand than Peace,
> And a singe runs through lace and feather.

On the flight deck below, the jet fighters line up, each to take the same circuitous route to the runway. For the moment, the planes strike me as birdlike. As they taxi, their wings unfold and lock at full length. Scurrying underneath are the color-coded crews, baby chick–like but minutely choreographed in a ballet of checklists. They scrutinize wheels and wheel wells, ordnance, control surfaces, lights, antennas, and, most important, the connection between the nose wheel and the catapult. Quickly, two minutes perhaps, the crew's work is done, and their numbers are reduced to one. That one is now prone and performing a final check on the catapult connection; then he suddenly darts ten yards to the right of the plane to rejoin his crew standing in line. On every carrier, this sailor is known as the "shooter."

There is a tireless emotional rhythm to all of this. From the moment a jet first taxis into position, anticipation builds—an excitement, fed also by the roaring noise, the blowing wind, the pitching deck, the ocean just a few yards away, the flight crew hustling in the semi-darkness—until the repository of all emotion—mine, the Japanese journalists standing next to me, the pilot's, the crew's, perhaps even that of Capt. Parker and Adm. Moffit watching unseen on the bridge—resides with the shooter. With him is now vested the power to relieve, delay, release, frustrate, or satisfy the desire of every onlooker: Launch! Make it "good to go"! I want it, my journalist colleagues want it, the Navy wants it, and President Bush wants it. Even a pacifist on board ship would want it.

Now everything spikes. The jet blasts reach a crescendo; the shooter has rejoined the line, his clothes flapping in the breeze, body rigid, outstretched hands now holding the expectations of hundreds, thousands, millions. Just aft of the jet's twin exhausts is the jet blast deflector (JBD), a raised panel that doubles as a piece of the runway. Now it is elevated to a 60-degree angle, and as the engine noise increases beyond anything thought sustainable by a contraption of metal and wires, the lengthening red-hot exhaust plume strikes the JBD and is deflected upward at 90 degrees. This is energy so powerful that it actually seems converted into something solid or liquid, something like lava or a piece of a star.

Then we witness the convergence of powers. The shooter drops prone with hands pointed toward the sea, the catapult fires, the pilot guns the thrust, and the jet is snapped into the sky, twin exhausts resembling a double meteor ascending. But the eye is permitted only a moment's wonder: No sooner has this jet gone than another is in its place. The fascinating ritual repeats and will keep on repeating until 0400, March 22.

2230
Smoking Sponson

I have one cigar left, and it's time to smoke it. The line for the smoking sponson, which has been lengthening in recent days, is now the longest since I arrived on the *Kitty Hawk*.

"Gotta light?" a soft voice inquires from the darkness. When I flick my lighter, I can see that this smoker is a young woman in her early twenties.

"How ya' doing tonight?" I ask.

"So-so," she replies between drags.

"Been too long at sea?"

"No," she replies. She pauses, probably deciding how much, if at all, to talk. Since I am probably old enough to be her father, not connected with the Navy, and likely to know nobody she does, she decides to take the plunge.

"I didn't bargain for any of this." Her tone was in deadly earnest.

"The war?" I ask.

"I enlisted in 2000, before any of this started. I don't mind the war, though. But the gas, that's different."

I, of course, did bargain for this. Yet there wasn't anything she felt now—no fear of a horrible death by VX or sarin, no anxiety, no foreboding—that I also didn't feel. When she mentioned her year of enlistment, 2000, I recalled a different world. That was the year I decided to make my Civil War history-writing avocation my vocation. The same year the NASD Composite peaked after a six-year bubble, the year the company I had been involved with for over a decade was sold to a European conglomerate for a good price. Clinton was president, and the destruction of the World Trade Towers was still the homicidal fantasy of a handful of pious young men who, their conceits notwithstanding, may have been instruments but could not be genuine advocates of the God for whom they claimed to speak.

I told her about the press conference with Capt. Parker and how he had explained why a chemical attack was unlikely. Even if one should be attempted, the *Kitty Hawk*'s sealing procedures and its mobility almost guaranteed that such an attack would fail. At the conclusion of this speech, I damned myself for my narcissism. I could tell that my new feeling of comfort contrasted sharply with the skeptical look on her face. I hadn't made a damn bit of difference except to persuade myself.

"Thanks," she said, flicked her butt overboard, and walked away. She might have added, "for nothing."

March 22
0200
Media Room

Now the denouement arrives. One of the "unities" nineteenth-century literary critics thought necessary for a well-told story—a neat, carefully weighed-out conclusion to the plot with all tensions resolved and these respectably—comes with a telephone call to the computer room. At 0200 Lt. De Walt rings to tell us that one of the pilots we had seen at the mission briefing earlier that afternoon has returned from over Iraq, has been debriefed, and is now willing to appear at a press conference scheduled in ten minutes.

0230
Media Room

Man!

Standing before us was Lt. j.g. Jeb Colt. He is a twenty-six-year-old boy from Fairfax, Virginia, with a faint touch of the Old Dominion in his voice and an FFV first name that immediately rang bells with this old Civil Warrior. "Any relation to James Ewell Brown Stuart?" I asked him much later, referring to the legendary Confederate cavalry commander. Colt smiled and looked surprised. "Well, no," he replied a bit embarrassedly, "but my father is kind of a Civil War buff, and, well. . . ." With a dog named Sherman, another named Beauregard, and a third named Lee, I understood completely.

Lt. Colt is a graduate of the Naval Academy and flies second seat in an F-14 Tomcat. In World War II movies like *Thirty Seconds over Tokyo*, the offensive mission of today's second seat was portrayed by the bombardier. He was usually depicted hunched over a Norden bombsight as the plane passed over the target before dropping its bombs with a combination of (according to these movies) science, art, and, of course, great instincts informed by a just cause. The sense that there was any precision to this was always implied in the script (the top-secret Norden must never be allowed to fall into enemy hands) and also visually, by the image of the bombardier peering into his bombsight as if it were a microscope. But in truth it was little different than a Boston Red Sox pitcher throwing a fastball into a New York Yankee batter's strike box: skill, a good eye, lots of practice, and, of course, luck, favored by a just cause.

If a movie were made today of a bomber crew, it would feature just two actors: the pilot and Lt. Colt. The pilot still flies the plane, but virtually every other function—that of the navigator, the bombardier, and the tail, waist, and rear gunners—are assumed by the lieutenant. Aided by nose radar, satellites, and inputs coming from other aircraft (whose function is solely to advise fighter-bombers), Lt. Colt navigates; these same technologies (aided by a few others relating to infrared and laser) make him something like a bombardier insofar as he releases the weapons, although actual guidance to target is handled by computer chips and servos. He is also the defender of his plane. Besides monitoring the approach of friendly and not-so-friendly aircraft and the blinking eyelids of hostile ground radar, Lt. Colt manages the electronic counter measures, the various darts and dodges of the plane or its decoys designed to convince other computer chips and servos that his plane is where it isn't. During Operation Southern Watch, the surest way for an Iraqi radar operator to commit suicide was to lock on his radar to a passing U.S. or British fighter jet. Second-seat officers like Lt. Colt would answer such emanations of enemy radar signals with a precision guided missile, usually destroying the site along with its hapless occupants.

At the moment, a very tired Lt. Jeb Colt is facing a pack of media with deadlines, competitors, and pushy editors in a news-rich environment. After flying for three hours, he looked exhausted.

Lots of reporters want to know lots of things about targets, bomb drops, speculation about battle damage, and Iraqi defenses. But I wanted to get inside his head, looking for a story that wasn't news, although of academic interest to me. So after the bomb-go-bang-bang questions were finished, I piped up.

"How do you feel?" I blurted out.

"You mean in combat?" I nodded, but I was being disingenuous. I never specified a subject because I didn't have one in mind.

"It's like a rush of adrenaline," he said, becoming livelier. His drawn expression seemed to tighten. Then I unloaded a precision question of my own.

"Did you at any time feel like God was your copilot?" I thought I heard snickers from my fellow reporters, but I don't think the lieutenant did. His adrenaline seemed to stop, and his face assumed a more contemplative cast. He paused for what seemed like a long time.

I blundered into the question, driven by my own theological concerns. It was only later that I realized how inapt the metaphor, purloined from the title of an old movie, was. God isn't flying the plane; the pilot is. God isn't the copilot on the morality of the mission, and my question was indifferent to the issue of whether God is "on our side." God is on everyone's side—and nobody's. All will have to answer for the part they play. The pilot, his commander, the admiral, the president, and the country have all made their choice. The mission may be suicidal, the war a mistake, the ordnance accidentally dropped on a schoolhouse—but God is still there. He doesn't take a hike just because the business is supposedly Caesar's and not the Lord's. King David said, "The earth is the Lord's and the fullness thereof"—all of it, including bombing runs. What I was asking wasn't whether God was with Lt. Colt—my belief tells me that he most certainly was—but, rather, whether Lieutenant Colt believed that God was.

The young officer was looking right at me. It was then that I noticed something I hadn't earlier. He seemed much older than when I first saw him that afternoon.

"You know, this mission was my first time in combat," he said softly. "Was God my copilot?" He paused again, remembering something. "Most definitely. God *was* my copilot."

As he walked out of the room to a well-earned rest, he looked over his shoulder and nodded at me—a minute gesture to the long thread that now connected this twenty-six-year-old Christian with a fifty-one-year-old Jew.

Shocked and Awed

March 23
1600
Diplomat Hotel

*W*ITH THE END of Shock and Awe, my assignment ended. I'm now back in Bahrain at the Diplomat Hotel. Now the war story will move with the ground troops, and Ellen has Garreth and Choline with the Army and the Marines. May God keep them and our soldiers safe.

Lt. De Walt promised me a COD yesterday at 1300, but he was better than his word. At 1030 the SEAL berth telephone rang, and Brook told me to present myself at the PAO's office in 30 minutes, because the COD was leaving early. Fortunately, most of my colleagues were still in the SEAL berth, so I had the opportunity to say good-bye. I will miss them—Faram's and Hanna's talent with a camera, and the friendship of Hu and the Japanese press corps. James Furlong is too damn British to be effusive, but I've enjoyed listening to him and learned something about television news and his nomadic life in particular. Bequeathed my storage locker to Jimmy Wolf from Reuters, and—

But I couldn't escape quite clean. Just as I was about to trudge up the ladder, Bill Reilly from C-SPAN asked me to do an interview. He's a genuinely nice man, and I'll be damned if, sad to leave as I am, I would refuse him anything. So he questions me on camera about my experience embedding and I play the wiseass, albeit an honest one. It's the media talking about the media. How original. In fairness to Bill, I suppose that one definition of Hell is being responsible for filling the boob tube with stuff 24/7.

The COD ride out didn't jar me as badly as the one in. Deceleration on landing meant that the tissues encasing your GI and cerebrospinal fluids stop, although the fluids keep traveling. By contrast, the rapid acceleration from being launched from a catapult means that everything moves in tandem, just as they do on a leisurely walk down a country lane, only on take-off, they move at 150 miles an hour. My heart stopped, my blood froze, and I may have experienced something like the death moment (sans the legendary white light), but it lasted only a moment. Soon we were airborne, and the only thing left to worry about were enemy missiles, friendly fire, hostile aircraft, and midair collisions. Jay, the newspaperman from Taiwan, traveled with me. He's on his way to CENTCOM headquarters in Qatar or possibly Camp Doha in Kuwait.

What a difference two weeks make! The aviation facility was much more crowded with soldiers and sailors and airplanes and helicopters, some, we're told, having just returned from battle. We're met at the airport by an officer from CPIC wearing his civvies.

"How's it been over here during the last couple of weeks?" I asked.

"Well, not too bad. We've had a few demonstrations down at the embassy, but nothing too terrible," he replied.

"Any shooting?" I asked.

"No, not really," he said matter-of-factly. "Students, rocks, tear gas, cops, the usual."

We were checked through Bahraini customs and then proceeded to the exit gate. Two weeks ago, there were only two heavily armed guards; now there were six. Several had double clips on their M-16s, reversed and bound with duct tape. This was the official emblem of no bullshit. It meant that if they went to live fire, they'd waste no time rummaging around for reloads. And these guys sure looked ready for live fire.

"Do you think it's safe to go down the souk?" I asked our escort.

"Well, I wouldn't say that it's not safe, but I—"

I didn't bother listening to the rest of his reply before I realized what a stupid question it was. Of course, it's safe—if you don't get your head blown off. And if you do get your head blown off, well, I guess it wasn't safe after all.

It's not safe.

1800
Diplomat Hotel

The Kingdom of Bahrain doesn't think it's very safe. On our way to the hotel, every official-looking building had soldiers walking around with submachine guns. This is one change from two weeks ago. Another change is that the Diplomat Hotel looks even more deserted than two weeks ago. Or maybe everyone is just hiding in their rooms.

The first thing I did after checking in was buy more cigars and order mint tea with hummus and tabouli, which really ought to be considered nectar and ambrosia for diabetics. Then I called Cousin Ellen.

"Oh, Cousin Richard," she gushed, "you're back, you're back, I'm so happy that—"

"LZ," I interrupted, "please cut the bullshit. How many stations do you want me to do?"

She never missed a beat. If I didn't mind, she said, there were radio stations in Washington, D.C.; London, England; somewhere in California; Long Island, New York; somewhere in the State of Washington; Vermont; and New Hampshire. They were all seeking jaw from someone who had *been there* or, better yet, was still *over there*, as in "And now, as a special feature of this broadcast, *we're* going to cut away to *our* correspondent in the Persian Gulf, Mr. Richard Miller." And, oh, by the way, could I file more prerecorded reports? And, oh, by the way, would I mind staying in Bahrain or going to Kuwait and staying for another week or two? And, oh, by the way, she had a request from a producer friend of hers; would I mind embedding with the Army in Turkey?

c. 1900
Café off the Main Lobby, Diplomat Hotel

Ellen almost had me, but not for her reasons. I was sitting alone in the café this evening, feeling a bit like Howard Hughes. I was the only diner in this cavernous yet bright and cheery room, with an entire staff of accommodating and tuxedoed waiters with little to do but look after my welfare.

The truth was that I hadn't slept right in three weeks and had probably averaged three hours a night for the last two weeks. I was crazed with exhaustion, like a man dying of thirst who sees a mirage and suddenly musters energy that he doesn't have for one final rush toward the water. I felt manic, like I could do another week, another month, or another year out here. I was 21 again, all piss and vinegar. It felt great.

Then there was the sound of the explosion. The huge picture windows of the café bowed and shook to almost bursting, and the waiters hit the deck.

"Are you all right, Sir?" the maitre d' asked, as he got up and rushed over to my table. It suddenly dawned on me that there was a problem.

"What was that?" I asked.

"It was bomb, I think," he replied, a bit out of breath. "This is a very crazy place," he added, "and you never know what's going to happen next. May it be for peace, inshallah."[1]

"Inshallah," I answered, nodding my head. I slumped in my chair, suddenly feeling very tired. The weight of my years, which had been levitated by no more than a wish, now settled upon me and resumed its burden on my spirit.

It was time to go home.

---

1. It was indeed a bomb. In the midst of a peaceful protest nearby, somebody bound together and then detonated six propane gas cylinders. No one was hurt in the explosion.

Any conflict that is for the sake of Heaven will have a con-
structive outcome; but one that is not for the sake of Heaven
will not have a constructive outcome.

—PIRKE AVOS

Index

Finlander, Capt., 156
First Bull Run, 11
Fitzgerald, F. Scott, 45
Fleischer, Ari, 161
Flight Deck, *U.S.S. Kitty Hawk*,
    description, 67; nighttime flight
    operations, 67; crew, 67–68
Force protection, description, 76,
    131–132
Forecastle, description, 171–172
Fort Sumter, 105
Forty-fifth Massachusetts Volunteer
    Infantry, 174
Forty-ninth Massachusetts Volunteer
    Infantry, 174
Fourth Hussars, 82
Foxe, John, 102
Fox News, 1, 64, 76, 135, 193, 212
France, 160, 209
Frank, Anne, 28
Frank, Otto, 28
Franks, Gen. Tommy, 11
Fredericksburg, battle of, 215
French, 64
French Foreign Legion, 112
Freudian, 149
Friday, Sgt. Joe, 48, 140
From Here to Eternity, (film), 131
Front Page, The, (film), 143
Full Metal Jacket, (film), 56
Furlong, James, 89–90; 224

Gandhi, 127
Gannet, 89, 212
Gardiner, Chauncey, 162
Gas, poison, 126
Gatling gun, 181
Gaza, 89, 144, 181, 213
Gecho, Gordon, 157
Geneva Convention, 4, 37
Genoese, 21
Georgetown, 12, 14
Georgia, (United States), 15, 29
German army, 29
Germany, 28, 160
Gilbert Islands, 206
Glory, (film), 55–56
"God Has Smiled on Me," 173
Gone with the Wind, (film), 56

Good Will Hunting, (film), 73
Gorbchav, Leila, 195
Gordius's Knot, 30
Gospel, 57
Gospel singers, 172
GQ (General Quarters) Station, 194
Grant, Gen. Ulysses S., 19, 47, 188,
    191
Grasshopper, 26
Gray, J. Glenn, 3
*Great Devonian Controversy: The Shap-
    ing of Scientific Knowledge among
    Gentlemanly Specialists, The* 48
Great Seal of the United States, 205
Grenada, invasion of, 159
G-3 Mag Rats, 214
Gulf of Tonkin, 206
Gulf of Tonkin Resolution, 206
Gulf War of 1991, 30; Round 1,
    Round 2, 45; 64; evacuation due to
    dental emergencies,
92; 160

Ha'aretz, 144
Halabja, 30
Hamilton watch, 214
Hampton Roads, Virginia, 218
Hangar bay door #2, 190–191
Hangar deck, *U.S.S. Kitty Hawk*,
    description, 62; 74; dangers, 74–75
Hanks, Tom, 56
Hanley, Lt., 34
Hanna, Paul, 88, 224
Hannity and Colmes, 76
Hannity, Sean, 76
Hardtack and Coffee, 193
Harm missiles, 214
Harvard, 6, 58, 192
Harvard Business School, 127
Harvard, Science Center, 95
Harvard Square, 185
Harvard Yard, 163, 213
Hawaii, 15, 218
Hebrew, 144
Helicopter Anti-Submarine Squadron
    14, (Chargers), 205
Helmer, Kendra, 162
Henj, Cap. Thomas A., relieved, 120;
    160, 165

About the Author

Richard F. Miller is a retired investment banker, a historian of the American Civil War, and a correspondent to Talk Radio News Service. He is a coauthor of *The Civil War: The Nantucket Experience* and the author of *Harvard's Civil War: The History of the Twentieth Massachusetts Volunteer Infantry*. He is a graduate of Harvard College and Case Western Reserve University School of Law. Miller is a fellow of the Massachusetts Historical Society who lives in Concord, Massachusetts.